The Manager's Lifelong Money Book

A Complete Guide to Personal Financial Planning for Business People

David M. Brownstone
and Jacques Sartisky

American Management Association

Library of Congress Cataloging-in-Publication Data

Brownstone, David M.
    The manager's lifelong money book.

    Includes index.
      1. Executives — Finance, Personal. 2. Businessmen —
Finance, Personal. I. Sartisky, Jacques. II. Title.
HD38.2.B76 1986   332.024'658   85-26819
ISBN 0-8144-5817-3

Printing number

10 9 8 7 6 5 4 3 2 1

Preface

As we see it, sound lifelong financial planning is not nearly as important as love, hope, and some of the other major intangibles through which we find it possible to define ourselves in an uncertain world. On the other hand, such planning is indispensable, for without it everything else comes into question and all personal goals are endangered. Learning to handle the financial side of life exceedingly well can provide the kind of material basis from which a great measure of personal freedom can flow; worrying about money all your life can — and usually does — limit freedom and build a sense of personal failure, no matter how well your career goes.

In this book, we focus on how managers and other business people can help make the financial side of life come out very well indeed, by planning and executing properly all their lives, while avoiding some of the key mistakes that can all too easily occur in the new financial marketplace.

For their considerable contributions as the work has developed, we thank Irene M. Franck, whose skills and insights have helped create the work; Ruth Siegel, for her continued warm support; Michael Albano, CLU, and Leona James, both of Pensions For Business, Inc.; Robert Madow, of PFB Pension Plan Corporation; Fred Steiber of Kurz-Liebow & Company, Inc.; Gene R. Hawes, for his always cogent comments; Mary Racette and Shirley Fenn, who very effectively copyread and typed the work; and last but far from least, our editor, Peter H. Shriver, whose contributions from the first have been major and entirely appreciated.

David M. Brownstone
Jacques Sartisky

Chappaqua, New York
New York City

Other Books by David M. Brownstone

David M. Brownstone is the author of more than 20 books. His books on personal finance and business include:

The AMA Handbook of Key Management Forms with Irene M. Franck (forthcoming)
The College Money Book with Gene R. Hawes
The Complete Career Guide with Gene R. Hawes
The Dictionary of Business and Finance with Irene M. Franck and Gorton Carruth
The Dictionary of Publishing with Irene M. Franck
The Investor's Dictionary with Irene M. Franck
Law and the Computer with Irene M. Franck
The Manager's Advisor with Irene M. Franck
Money Wise
Real Estate and the Computer
The Real Estate Dictionary
The Sales Professional's Advisor with Irene M. Franck
The Saver's Guide to Investing
The Self-Publishing Handbook with Irene M. Franck
Sell Your Way to Success
Successful Selling Skills for Small Business
Where to Find Business Information with Gorton Carruth

Contents

1
In Uncertain Times
Like These . . .

In times like these, it is very easy to flow with the tide, to accept what *is* as what *will be,* and to forget that one of the few things you can really count on in your lifetime is change. Sharp change; often unanticipated change; the kind of change that tests lifelong assumptions and plans.

On the financial side of life, which is what this work is about, enormous changes have occurred within our own lifetimes. Millions of Americans still alive and active lived through the boom years of the 1920s and the crash of 1929, which changed so much for so many. Tens of millions of us were formed during the bad years of the Great Depression of the 1930s. Most of us now alive have had personal experience with the long postwar boom that culminated in the heady years of the mid-1960s, when everything seemed possible and the good times were never going to stop. And all but the youngest of us saw the good times stop, followed by a decade and a half of fluctuation in the American economy around a stagnant center, first with enormous inflation, then heavy unemployment, and now huge national debts, together creating a situation in which we, our children, and their children are and will be at great risk.

The fact is that the overwhelming majority of managers and other middle-income people working for private business and public organizations are far worse off than they were during the economically good years of the 1960s. Inflation saw to that, with prices almost tripling in 15 years and incomes nowhere near keeping up. The American stock market saw to that, with the average real values of stocks going down sharply after the 1960s —so sharply that, as of this writing, the blue chip stocks composing the Dow Jones Industrial Average are in real dollars worth about 40% of what they were worth 17 years ago. College costs saw to that, rising far more steeply than even the pace of inflation, as they continue to do.

The truth is that the "well-paid" young middle manager who back then would have routinely bought a good, solid house for a growing family today is not likely to be able to afford such a house, unless there are two "well-paid" breadwinners in the family. The same kind of middle-income family, a little later in life, faces huge college costs, may have a second or even a third mortgage on a smallish house or condominium, and probably pays huge amounts of interest on large debts. Later, the same people, now in their fifties, are quite likely to be supporting their aged, indigent parents and at the same time putting their children through expensive colleges, rather than using their highest earning years to build up their own retirement funds. Still later — unless they have seen what all this can lead to, planned and executed well, and broken out into quite different economic air — they are likely to be indigent parents themselves, being supported by their children or becoming the unwilling, unwanted wards of an uncaring state.

Nor can any of us depend on a combination of Social Security and corporate pensions to see us through. Social Security, which has by law been indexed for two decades, is likely to be under attack for the rest of our lives, for it is an enormous and growing drain upon an America that is not so rich as we thought it might be, and will not be so rich again soon. And some corporate pensions will deliver what they promise, but some will not, as the same economic pressures that beset governments and individuals continue to beset companies. Even now, many companies are reducing their contributions to corporate pension plans, to save money and enhance their profit pictures; as that trend intensifies, many more pensions will join those now at grave risk. In addition, many pension plans are now being converted into extremely risky employee stock ownership plans (ESOPs), often to resist adverse takeover attempts. And many of those takeovers result in asset stripping, which is the dismemberment of healthy companies with the loss of thousands of jobs that should not otherwise even have been threatened.

But it is relatively easy to see that these risks are all here now, and that more such risks lie immediately ahead. The personal need — and the challenge — is to surmount them. And this is, of course, what a book on personal financial planning for managers and other middle-income employees must be all about. That is certainly the aim of this work — *to help you see the risks and opportunities clearly, to help you develop a body of approaches and techniques that will enable you to do successful lifelong financial planning, and to analyze the whole range of financial choices before you, so that you can make the profitable, asset-building, security-building moves you need to make.*

Managers and other corporate employees pose an interesting set of problems for the financial planner, for with managers nothing is automatic. Independent professionals and small-business owners are considerably easier to assist, in a way, for the system works for them, building their assets and protecting them as they go through their normal paces. The small-business owner who builds a successful business is at the same time building a major lifetime asset, perhaps transferring the capital developed from business to business over the years but always trying to increase the size of that asset. The business itself therefore becomes the central economic fact in a small-business owner's life and the basis upon which all personal lifetime financial plans are made. Similarly, the independent professional, such as the doctor, lawyer, or accountant, builds a practice that is itself a business, though not necessarily as salable without its owner as are most profitable small businesses. In financial planning terms, the result is basically the same, though: the professional practice becomes the basis for all personal financial planning.

For managers and other salaried employees, it is by no means as simple and favorable a picture. In today's business world, you may work for several companies during a moderately successful career in management and wind up with a few shares of stock, small fixed pension payouts from those plans that have vested, and nothing more in the way of built-up assets directly stemming from your corporate working years — if there has been no default on pension promises made by corporations; if everything is working as originally set up.

Of course, you may come away from your corporate years with substantial amounts of valuable stock and a sound pension payout, even one partly or wholly indexed to the inflation rate. Many have. The problem is that you cannot *know* that you will, except very late in your career, if then. In contrast to the business owner and independent professional, who have some degree of choice and therefore some control over their economic destinies, the employee may, for reasons entirely beyond personal control, quickly lose what seemed for years a sound, stable set of employ- ment-connected assets. As so many managers and others em- ployed by sick companies in sick industries have found out to their dismay in recent years, *the only assets you can count on are those you own right now.* Those are the only assets you have any chance of building over the years.

Building a stake that will help you to do what you want short term and protect you long term requires working at it every day. Those who settle comfortably — they think — into the euphoria induced by a corporate benefit-and-promises blanket are all too often due for a rude and sometimes catastrophic awakening when that blanket is removed, whether temporarily or permanently on retirement. Putting it a little differently, the material part of the corporate American dream — the lifetime attachment to one, two, or three companies, rewarded by the good life now and golden retirement years later on — was always just a dream for most of us. Now, it is a good deal more obviously so, and even the least financially aware of us must realize that it is time to learn how to do sound lifetime financial planning.

For people who will not or cannot build a meaningful personal economic stake, the hazards can be considerable. Not necessarily, of course. Many managers and other employees will quite literally be long-term lucky and do very well financially without serious personal planning. But you cannot plan for such luck, any more than you can plan to win at a Las Vegas crap table. Yes, you can pick your company and industry carefully — but you can also see a sound company or even a sound-seeming industry turn bad later in your career, lose a job and find it difficult to get a new one in hard times, decide to try it on your own in a small business, or become disabled. The day-to-day, year-to-year task is to build your assets as quickly and safely as you can. In these very chancy times you can be pushed under the American rug if you don't have enough of a stake to see you through difficult personal times. The long-term need is to build both a substantial stake and a later-years career; for most of us these will make the difference between living reasonably comfortable and fulfilling later years and living poor and in despair, as de facto wards of our children, the state, or both.

The Keys to Successful Financial Planning

Some years ago, in a financial planning book directed to a somewhat wider audience *(Personal Financial Survival)*, we put forward several basic understandings, which served as assumptions upon which much of that work was based. These apply to this book and its audience as well, although now we will put them a little differently and in somewhat different order.

1. Barring such catastrophes as nuclear and biological warfare, we and our children will live far longer lives than had been apparent as recently as even a generation ago. Millions are living well into their eighties and nineties now, and far more than ever before are over one-hundred years old. That trend can be a blessing or curse, depending upon how we as individuals and as a society handle it. But the fact is that it exists and is accelerating, with enormous consequences for all of human society and for each of us.

2. We must therefore be prepared to support ourselves far longer than we had anticipated. Yes, society will have to be better organized as far as the needs of the very old are concerned, and we are ourselves going to be among those very old. But no, we cannot expect society to take care of us until very near the end, if then. America was never quite the cornucopia it seemed to be, and we cannot expect the country to support millions upon millions of us for 20, 30, or even 40 years beyond retirement, no matter what promises may have been or will be made by our politicians. In our world as it exists today, it is clearly absurd to suppose that you will be able to work for 40 or 45 years and then get any very substantial pension from the government for another 40 years. As America is evolving, quite a number of things are giving way on the economic side; one of them will be the level of Social Security payments, which can reasonably be expected to become lower in

real dollars in the next several decades, as will private pension payments.

3. The value of the dollar will go down over the years and decades to come. That is a long-term and multinational trend, and it will not be reversed. It may be expressed as inflation, which is the historic American mode, or it may be a matter of both inflation and currency revaluation, complete with exchanges of new dollars for old. In the long run, it doesn't matter much which techniques are used; the net effect will be that the dollar will buy less. Even at the current low rates of inflation (around 5% at this writing) much of the dollar's value will be lost between now and what can very easily become poverty at 85 or 90. It is quite likely, though, that the dollar will lose its value much faster than that, given the huge national debt and trade deficits now being incurred every year. Governments repudiate debts; stable governments, like ours, repudiate their debts only partially, by paying them back in dollars worth much less than the dollars initially borrowed. With a national debt that will in a few years top $2 trillion, the United States will have no choice but to repudiate by repaying in less valuable dollars; that is inescapable. All of which will put greatly increased pressure on those receiving public and private pensions, and make it absolutely mandatory to reconsider the questions of "retirement" and income-producing later-years work.

4. The concept of retirement at 65 or anywhere near that age is unfortunately quite outdated, in light of the above understandings. For business owners and independent professionals, that poses no insurmountable problem; they will very easily stay on, as so many have been doing all along and even more in recent years. But for managers and other corporate employees, that can pose very great problems indeed. It makes the question of changing basic approaches to corporate and government retirement absolutely essential; and as a practical matter it becomes urgently necessary for many to plan postretirement careers carefully.

5. Despite all this, we must plan to survive and prosper now and later in an economy and a system that are basically the same: a set of mixed private-public ownership forms, with the mix changing back and forth over the years as needs and political ascendancies change.

6. However strongly any of us feel about the proper role of

government in matters of social responsibility, the only prudent way to proceed is to plan the financial side of life exceedingly well. By so doing we can take care of both short- and long-term personal needs and fulfill many of our lifetime's desires as well. Care and skill in financial matters can help us provide well for ourselves and for others close to us; lack of that care and skill can destroy all hopes and plans, leaving us worrying about money every day of our lives.

Becoming Skilled in the Financial Marketplace

Much will depend on how skillfully we seek sound financial advice, and how consistently well we learn to move on our own in the single, unified financial marketplace that has emerged in recent years.

Not so long ago, right up into the late 1970s, there was no such thing as a single financial marketplace. Instead, as far as individuals were concerned, there were several key players. Banking was done by bankers; they made a profit on lending your money to others, and they got as much of your money as possible to lend by selling savings accounts, checking accounts, and certificates of deposit of varying durations. Some also made money on trust and related services. Securities sellers sold securities, mostly stocks, bonds, and mutual funds. Insurance people sold insurance, with some life insurance sellers also selling mutual funds, and lately also tax-sheltered investments of several kinds. A relatively small number of practitioners thought of themselves as financial planners, and set themselves up to recommend and sell a considerable range of financial instruments, trying to tailor each plan somewhat differently to suit individual needs; to do so they had to make a series of pioneering arrangements, cutting across traditional financial service lines.

Today, a combination of unsettled economic conditions, the historic real-dollar stock price decline of the 1970s, and the deregulation of the financial marketplace have led to the emergence of quite a new situation. Now, pretty nearly everybody sells pretty nearly everything financial. Yesterday's stockbroker is now likely to be employed by a "financial supermarket," and to be intent upon selling you stocks, several kinds of bonds, many kinds of mutual funds, options, futures, pension plans, mortgage-backed securities, and tax-sheltered investments of many kinds. This new breed of broker may either refer you to the banking and insurance salespeople just down the hall, or offer to handle those needs, too. Yesterday's conservative banker is today likely to be eager to sell you all the same kinds of things, as will yesterday's insurance specialist.

That is all very well — for the incomes of now-freed financial sellers. It is not always so good for increasingly bewildered individuals, trying to do some effective lifetime financial planning. Twin, interrelated problems have emerged as the new financial marketplace has taken shape. The first is that, with a large number of highly competitive institutions now in the field, new kinds of financial instruments are being created very rapidly. The second is that most sellers are not much better equipped than they were before they became all-purpose financial sellers. The stockbroker who had a hard enough time trying to keep up even halfway competently with conventional stocks and bonds is hardly likely to have become expert in all the investment vehicles now available, any more than the insurance seller and the banker have become multipurpose experts.

Knowing this, it is more important than ever to develop a body of personal financial management skills of your own. To seek and find good financial advice is essential; it is equally essential to be able to make all the main decisions yourself, applying your own knowledge and skills to the information and advice you have received from others.

Financial Planning: Your Own Small Business

All this financial planning requires learning and keeping up. And that takes time, especially if your basic training has been along other lines. But learning and keeping up are requirements in any business, including both the main business at which you spend your days and your subsidiary business: managing the economic side of your own life.

That, certainly, is the way to see it. *Your personal financial planning and execution are a business, to be understood, orga-nized, developed, and built into a lifelong success, just like any of the other businesses with which you may be associated during your career.* You should no more think of trying to run your personal financial business unprepared than you would consider opening a restaurant or garden store without preparation. Actually, becoming skilled at personal financial business is just about as important as becoming skilled at what you do for your main living; the truth is that both sets of skills are indispensable for lifelong success.

Taken together, the matters discussed in this book are a guide to effective lifelong personal financial planning. Having said that, let us be very clear that a single book can be only that — a guide, a set of approaches and techniques to be applied to a set of economic situations, jobs, and markets that are always in flux. The only way to be successful in personal financial planning and execution is to stay with the process all your life, continuing to keep up, learn, and make the right decisions in a timely fashion. There is no magic at all, here or anywhere in the financial world, and certainly no advice that will help you to get rich quick. Far from it. The main thing here is to learn how to make the right financial decisions, and to keep on making them for a very long lifetime.

2
How Your Needs, Wants, and Choices Will Determine Your Financial Success

If you want to win, you have to know what the game is. And although running the financial side of life is analogous to running a small business, the financial side is not all there is to the game; for most of us, life is far more than the single-minded pursuit of profits and asset growth.

Putting it a little differently, financial planning properly serves personal needs and desires. All financial planning and execution is easier if you develop and keep a clear view of personal short-, medium-, and long-term financial goals. To do that you must have a clear view of what you perceive as your own needs, what you want to accomplish beyond satisfaction of perceived basic needs, and what you are willing to do to accomplish satisfaction of both needs and wants.

For some people in this culture, questions of desire become paramount, taking precedence over satisfaction of what others consider needs. The dedicated painter, actor, or writer may be willing to settle for low income, substandard living accommodations, too little money for children's educations, and the probability of impoverished later years. Nobody in the arts wants it to be like that, but many artists, striving to be professionals in their chosen fields, know they have little choice if art is to be properly served.

Managers face the question of very small incomes as a matter of choice only when they are considering either leaving the business world or gambling very heavily with their finances and careers. You may come up against the question, though, in other ways. You might be offered a new job that will yield more money and responsibility but that is unattractive to you. You could also find yourself in the classic, truly terrible situation of continuing to hold on to a job you hate, simply for the money. Sometimes it is a matter of weighing your own needs and desires against those of people you love, as when you hang on to a job in a bad situation and in hard times, for the sake of getting your children through school or your spouse trained and started on a new career. Sometimes — all too often — you may find yourself rationalizing fear of change, and holding on in a bad situation quite unnecessarily. And sometimes, you may fall into the trap of holding on to what is only an inflated lifestyle, pursued with people you would not miss if they all faded away tomorrow.

The personal key, and therefore the lifelong financial planning key, is to know what it is all about — for you and for those you love. It is essential to differentiate between your needs and your desires, to track and understand those needs and desires as they develop and change over a lifetime, and to develop a body of career and financial plans that accurately reflect your understanding of who you are, where you are, where you want to go, and how you plan to get there, in the short term, some distance out, and in the long term — that is, for your entire lifetime.

What Managers Can Reasonably Expect to Achieve Financially

Some things are routinely considered to be needs by managers and other corporate employees. Expectations have changed, even in the last few years, but such people can still reasonably expect to be able to:

• Own their own homes, even though today they may be condominiums or small single-family houses, rather than yesterday's large houses. Such home ownership is doable.

• Maintain, with current income, a standard of living that

includes adequate food, clothing, transportation, health care, and other such obvious necessities, plus some modest provision for recreation and holiday expenses. "Need" here includes more than a bare-bones austerity budget.

• Send their children, if any, through a basic four-year college course. Today that may, and often should, be a low-cost public college, rather than a high-cost private institution. Even the low-cost college may make parent and student borrowing necessary, but the basic expectation — and ability to make it happen — is the same.

• Cover themselves and their families against insurable catastrophes, with adequate life, health, accident, property, and liability insurance. Some of what is thought to be adequate coverage is instead illusion, as we will later discuss, but the basic expectation is there, as is the ability to buy enough of the right kinds of insurances, once needs are understood.

• Put something of their own away for their later years, on top of any public or private pension plan coverages they may have. That is likely to be doable, too, but in many instances only as a result of considerable spending restraint and sound lifelong financial planning. Indeed, in a wider sense, satisfaction of all these needs depends upon restraint and sound planning, for to overspend here is to come up short there, and to fail to guard against potential catastrophe now may be to experience it later.

Don't Confuse Need with Desire

Some of the most intractable of our money problems come from the habit of too easily moving from need to desire. All too often, we think of desires as needs, justify them in that way, and then straightforwardly move ahead into the most horrendous financial errors, some of them the kinds of mistakes that can haunt us all our lives. For example, we properly see ourselves as "needing" housing and a decent lifestyle — and then go ahead to buy far-too-expensive homes with mortgages piled one on top of the next, the second and third mortgages carrying even higher rates of interest than the too-high first mortgage. We rationalize all that, with talk about appreciation in the value of high-quality housing, and that is somewhat so. But that appreciation is in a single investment, the house, and any sensible financial planner will caution you not to put all your eggs in one basket. That is especially true for managers, by the way; a job loss or a transfer can force home sale at the wrong time, resulting in the loss of all your paper gains on the house, and then some. But people who buy expensive houses they cannot really afford usually know all that; they choose to ignore it in pursuit of bankruptcy masquerading as the upwardly mobile version of the American dream.

Similarly, and usually much intertwined with such matters as houses, day-to-day overspending can and for many does easily become a way of life. That is, as we all know so well, the conspicuous consumption trap, when necessary clothes become designer suits, necessary cars become very expensive high-prestige sedans, and a little holiday becomes a hugely expensive international jaunt paid for on the cuff. Actually, maybe we all really don't know so much about the conspicuous consumption trap; if we did, not so many of us would overspend, undersave, and routinely go into debt over mere consumer goods. The truth is that conspicuous consumption is entirely irrational; it is a disease that is injurious to economic health, and millions of us are infected with that disease. What nonsense it is to suppose that anyone "needs" an expensive holiday badly enough to go even more deeply into debt to finance it. Or that you or anyone else "deserves" a perfectly useless and very expensive piece of clothing or hardware, when what you already have is still perfectly serviceable. Or that you can "afford" a beach cottage just because you have or can easily borrow the money to buy it. How terribly old-fashioned — and terribly true — it is that what you spend now will not be available to save, invest, and grow, and that real material needs have very little to do with the more expensive desires generated by our consuming society.

Quite the opposite. What we have been very painfully learning as individuals and as a people in the last decade or so is that our earnings are not infinite, our capital is more limited than we had supposed and becoming slimmer every year, and we must make choices. You need only to step outside to see that our roads, bridges, and industrial plants continue to fall apart, and that our cities work less and less well. You need only look at some entirely available numbers to see that our debts are piling up, that many of our main financial institutions are in trouble, and that we become in many major industries less competitive every year. Similarly, you need only look at the economic situations of many seemingly affluent Americans to realize that spending now will mean deep trouble later; indeed, that spending yesterday is bringing deep trouble today.

No, very few managers and other corporate employees are in worse trouble than most unemployed steelworkers; it is those steelworkers and millions more who are in trouble now and will be in deeper trouble later in their lives. But what is becoming increasingly clear is that a great many now seemingly affluent people are going to be in deep trouble, too, as the years directly ahead begin to unfold — unless they recognize the situation and its dangers, and very quickly begin to do some astute financial planning.

The American Family: A Case Study

Take for example this fairly typical American corporate family; call them Bob and Wilma Jones. They met in college, back in the early 1960s, and were married two days after President Kennedy's assassination. They had been planning to wait a little while, until after graduation, but somehow just then it seemed like the right thing to do. Neither of them would have put it as ponderously as this, but in a sense their marriage then was an affirmation of the continuing validity of the American dream.

Whatever the reason for the timing of it, it is entirely fair to say that they then proceeded to live happily ever after. Bob went to work, has had a modestly successful business career, and is currently assistant divisional purchasing manager at one of the midwestern plants of a large industrial company. He's making $40,000 a year, and is in line for more responsibility and the pay that goes with it in years to come.

Wilma had babies — three of them, a careful two years apart — who are named Mark, Luke, and Janet. All three of their children are bright, inquisitive, and clearly headed for great things; they are much loved, and Bob and Wilma are going to see to it that they go to their alma mater, the wonderful little college in Pennsylvania where they met. That includes Janet. Neither Wilma nor Bob ever paid much attention to women's liberation questions back in the 1960s, but both are very clear that Janet has to have the best education that money can buy, including graduate school, so that she will be as competitive as anyone else out there in the job market.

Wilma went back to work a few years ago, and now she's a middle manager, too, handling market support functions in the regional office of a computer service company. She will move up over the years; right now, she makes $22,000 a year, and that's not bad for someone who has very recently come back into the labor force.

The extra money has been wonderful. It was pretty tight in the early years, with Bob not making much and Wilma at home, but now it's a lot easier. Since Wilma has started working, they've been able to move into a more suitable house, with enough room for all of them, and some proper entertaining facilities, besides; they are not really big spenders, but after all, two people on their way up have to do a little entertaining once in a while. They've also traded in both of those old cars they were running; lately, there haven't been any of those frantic calls from somewhere between home and work to rescue either of them out of a car that has stopped for a red light and won't start again. And they've even managed to take some vacations; one was a vacation of a lifetime, all the way to Greece with all three kids in tow. Expensive, but it was worth it.

They know about conspicuous consumption; that is not what has been going on here. All they've been doing is a little catching up. There are two good jobs here, and nowhere to go but ahead. They don't have much money saved, there are car payments to make, and the second mortgage they had to take to swing the down payment on the house was at a higher interest rate than they had expected — variable rate, too. But you do what you have to do. And, of course, they know they will have to do some borrowing to get the kids through college, but there will surely be some financial aid available one way or another. Besides, their house is proving to be a wonderful investment; it is going up in value every year, and in a few years there will be enough extra value in it for them to be able to take an equity loan on it to help with college costs. They're both bound to be making more money by then, anyway. Besides, these are good people, and sound people, and people who are in their own way partaking of the fruits of the dream that is their birthright.

Yes, certainly. They are also quite clearly what a banker friend of ours once called "walking bankrupts," planning to get even deeper as the years go by.

If anything at all goes wrong and either one of them is out of a job for as little as six months to a year, they will be unable to meet their current obligations and equally unable to borrow money. If either of them wants to try a different kind of career or perhaps a small business, there won't be enough money. Even if one of them only wants to take a not-very-secure but very promising new job, it may be imprudent to do so, for if it doesn't work out they may be unable to survive. As it now stands, Wilma and Bob are trapped in corporate lockstep, dependent upon both jobs and unable to make any kind of move. And they have trapped themselves, with just a few minor, hopeful, bad financial moves. They have spent too soon, without having built up any meaningful savings and investments, without having developed any of the financial reserves that spell freedom. They have also built a situation in which they must continue to overspend, unless they make a quite radical change in current lifestyles.

But even if nothing adverse happens, it will soon become worse — much worse. For no pay increases they can secure in the next few years can begin to pay for the enormous college costs they intend to incur. They should be sending their children to excellent and entirely available public colleges in their state, for one third to one half of the cost of their old alma mater, a very expensive private college. It wasn't that expensive when they went to school there, back in the late 1950s and early 1960s, but it sure is now. What would cost $4,000 – $5,000 per year per child in a public college in their present home state will be $12,000 a year at the private college when their first child starts college, rising to something like $16,000 – $20,000 per year eight years later, when their last child, Janet, finishes school. How much college costs will rise in those eight years will depend only partly on the rate of inflation in those years; college costs can be expected to rise more swiftly than the rate of inflation throughout the period, as they have for a long time now.

It will therefore cost Wilma, Bob, and their children — for the children will have to borrow enormous amounts of money to make it through — a total of something like $150,000 – $200,000 for those three four-year college educations, plus $50,000 – $75,000 more for the interest they will have to pay on those huge loans for many years after college. Allow for some reduction in these costs because of some small contribution from Bob and Wilma's current incomes, from children's college and summer jobs, and from a very small amount of no-need grant and scholarship money; and with the interest payments you still come up with at least $150,000 that will have to be spent for those entirely unnecessary, bankrupting private college educations. The ultimate irony of it, by the way, is that the home state university is quite likely to be as good as or better than the private school, by every measure of academic worth, for that is also what has happened since Bob and Wilma went to school.

All this is without the cost of graduate school, which is another and very expensive ballgame. In our time, the four-year college degree is for many professions only openers; it is the graduate degree that takes you where you want to go.

Any solutions? Certainly. They can sell the too-expensive house and buy a smaller one, or perhaps an equally large and useful one in a less expensive area. They can use any money left over to start a savings and investment fund, which should include Individual Retirement Accounts for both Wilma and Bob. The cars can be paid off in due course, and then held and repaired for many years, for the money spent on repairs will be minuscule compared to the yearly payments avoided. More affordable holidays can be taken, using money generated in surplus-cash years. And Wilma and Bob have to talk with each other and with their children about college and college costs, long and seriously. It may be painful, for they have by now probably built up expectations that will have to be redirected, but it will be far less painful in the long run than bankrupting themselves and causing their children to saddle themselves with huge debts right from the start of their adult lives. For putting aside the question of paying for graduate school, the difference between sending children through expensive private colleges and sending them through at least equally good and much less expensive public colleges will be in most instances a very real $35,000 – $50,000 per child, once you take into account inflation and huge interest charges on borrowings.

Parents astute enough to convince themselves and their children that the public college choice is right will still be wise to develop a savings fund dedicated to coming college costs. Yes, you may be able to borrow part of what you need when the time comes, but you should not base your plans on it, for personal and societal circumstances may have changed greatly by then.

Managers and other corporate people with children headed for college should be putting some thousands of dollars a year into college funds. Even public college educations are quite likely to cost at least $5,000 per year per child, plus an inflation factor, and not figuring in graduate school costs. Parents with coming responsibilities that great will be wise to put at least $5,000 a year into their college funds, figuring that if they start early enough, the impact of college costs may be bearable. For example, $5,000 per year put into a fund accreting after-tax at the rate of 8% per year for 10 years will create a fund of a little more than $78,000 — enough to go a long way toward solution of college costs. As of this writing, a sound deferred annuity, with its combination of tax advantage and yield, might give you an even better compounding interest factor, as might a Clifford Trust or a high yielding and quite liquid medium- or long-term federal government bond, as might many of the other investment possibilities discussed later in his book. But the money has to be there when you need it; college funds should be conservatively, rather than speculatively, invested.

Will people make the kinds of moves we recommend here, even if they are self-evidently the right ones? We don't know. Probably not, at least for such lifestyle matters as houses, cars, and vacations. Perhaps yes, on college choices, for the costs have become so prohibitive that yesterday's choice is today's impossibility for many, even for many relatively well-paid corporate people. Our hope is that astute people will not get themselves into this kind of fix, and that if they have done anything like this they will reverse course. Without money, there is nothing to save and invest, and all talk of sound lifelong financial planning presupposes the ability to generate enough cash to build a meaningful savings and investment fund over the years.

Many managers and other corporate people can and do generate savings and investment funds, and recognize the need to build their assets in a long-term way, seeing clearly that with financial independence comes a certain kind of freedom and a good deal of lifelong security. They seek advice, make up their own minds, watch their money, try to understand what is happening in a fast-changing financial world, and try to make right and timely moves. None of it is particularly easy; all of it requires a certain amount of prior personal spending restraint, so that funds for growth will be available. In our view, all of it is well worth the doing, even in an increasingly chancy financial world, for the alternative is to depend on government and private pension plans, which cannot be counted on.

3
The Secret of Successful Planning: Preparation

If you want to win, you have to prepare for it; indeed, you have to overprepare and stay overprepared. That is as true for the part-time business that is the financial side of your life as it is for your full-time career.

In the working world, you are to a considerable extent as good as your sources of information and insight. That is why so many managers and other business people spend so much time and money on keeping up with developments in their fields, on highly paid professional advisers, on tracking the progress of their own businesses, and on rather sophisticated short-, medium-, and long-term planning. In many American businesses today, the meetings and constant paper-shuffling that accompany all that information gathering are carried to absurd excess, getting in the way of the planning process rather than helping it. But that obscures without changing the essential need for astute planning, which has very little to do with endless, compulsive, buck-passing meetings and the torrent of paper that threatens to drown so many managers today.

In a way, it is unfortunate that so many managers have come to view the planning process in their companies with such ill-concealed disdain. That disdain is certainly understandable, for what we have been seeing for the past decade and more has been the development of the "rolling" five-year plan (or even longer); all too often, in practice that means spending a great deal of time every quarter and even more every year completely revising an entirely unrealistic long-term plan, to meet the current profit needs of hard-pressed top managements trying to weather difficult times. The company that has made a perfectly stupid major investment in a consumer fad, mistaking it for a long-term trend, will have major problems and have to drastically change forecasts; the recent computer games phenomenon is such an example. That has always been so; but in recent years we have also seen once quite healthy companies buffeted about by such out-of-control matters as Japanese-government-sponsored competition and protectionism, foreign currency fluctuation, huge interest-rate fluctuations, and the constant veering of a troubled American economy around a stagnant center. All that makes for the kinds of unstable work situations that occasion many of the cautionary comments in this book; it also makes managers and other business people unnecessarily dismissive of their own excellent planning abilities.

American managers and business people — Americans altogether — are excellent planners, given half a chance. The history of the last two centuries makes that abundantly clear; indeed, that ability to plan, execute, and grow whatever we believe needs to be grown is an extraordinarily important part of our intellectual infrastructure, and is recognized as a huge asset all over the world. That is not national pride speaking; we prefer to think of ourselves as citizens of the world. But we do believe it to be a fact, and by any measure the most important personal financial planning fact of all when speaking with managers and other business people. *The same skills that bring you long-term success in your business life will, if you have the wit and tenacity to adapt them, bring you success in your personal financial life.*

Creating a Steady Flow of Sound Advice and Useful Information

It all starts with knowing how to get sound advice and good information, on a day-to-day, constant-flow basis. That means finding excellent, trustworthy, long-term financial advisers, and learning enough on your own to be able to evaluate their advice on the basis of knowledge developed from your own excellent information and insight.

In financial planning, as in all businesses, good information starts with published sources, which can, if used properly, supply both the contexts within which financial decisions must be made and also a great many of the specifics about a substantial number of the moves you may be contemplating.

For example, anyone considering investment in an oil stock is able to learn a good deal about the world oil situation and any recent major events affecting a specific company, and to follow the day-to-day price moves of the stock, all from a single source, *The Wall Street Journal.* Don't be too concerned about that publication's objectivity, by the way. Its editors may take a rather conservative, business-oriented position editorially, but that does not stop them from taking objective, often quite critical positions on the specifics. The top management of a major oil company at one point in 1984 was so annoyed as to stop cooperating with the *Journal*—a most reassuring sign for anyone who needed such reassurance. You need not be concerned about the publication hiding anything from you that might affect your investment decision.

In fact, it is the starting point for everyone in the financial marketplace and should be for you, too, with your part-time financial businessperson's hat on. Subscribe. Follow general trends and specific interests, become familiar with the whole financial world, and keep on doing so for a lifetime. Spend the money and the time; it is basic to your financial success. It will not stand alone as an information source, nor will it substitute for astute financial advisers. But it will supply context, and enough specifics to enable you to develop opinions and check your information, insight, and opinions against those of others.

Putting it as plainly as possible, an innocent can be taken in by investment fads and unscrupulous sellers, but no one who reads *The Wall Street Journal* carefully and consistently over a period of years will long stay innocent. Carefully and consistently, that is, *and* with all your management training and skepticism brought to bear. An unread or too-slightly used major information source is useless. Then all you do is lull yourself to sleep, using the subscription to the source as an alibi for not putting in the necessary hard work of analysis. Good managers are good learners, analysts, and problem solvers in any business, including their own financial business, if they work their skills hard enough.

It also pays to buy strong, detailed, sometimes rather expensive information and insight in areas of major investing interest. For example, those with strong interest in the stock and bond markets may spend hundreds of dollars a year on quite expensive books and services, such as those provided by Value Line, Dow Jones, Zweig, and other investment advisory publishers. As of this writing, such publications used as investment advisory tools are tax-deductible, but even if they were not, it is essential to have some of them readily available. Without proper information, you cannot possibly develop your own informed opinions, and you must be able to do just that as you develop the lifelong small business that your personal investing must be.

Similarly, the investor who decides to pay a good deal of attention to nearby real estate opportunities had best find out what professionals in the local real estate industry read, and thereby guarantee access to proper published information and insight. Such local publications as the New York metropolitan area's *Realty,* Connecticut's *Commercial Record,* the New Jersey *Building and Realty Record,* and a large number of regional and local business newspapers, such as California's *Orange County Business,* are excellent ways to stay informed in local real estate markets. For longer range investing, such national publications as *Real Estate Review, Real Estate Today,* and *Real Estate Tax Ideas* are available, but in truth the individual investor going into long-distance real estate investments will have to rely very heavily upon professional advisers, as we discuss later on in this book.

For an investor who decides to limit focus to such opportunities as local real estate, local small businesses, and savings accounts, the main necessary publications will be the local ones, perhaps supplemented by a weekly investment newspaper like *Barron's.* Entirely necessary or not, though, we still believe that subscribing to *The Wall Street Journal* is a good idea for anyone in the process of building up a substantial personal financial stake, as the wider financial and business coverage then available will provide a proper context within which even very close-to-home decisions can more effectively be made.

Libraries

Beyond those finance-related periodicals you may want to buy, you should be able to find rather easily a large number of information sources, many of them as close as your local branch library. Certainly, most corporate libraries and almost all business school and regional public libraries will be able to supply basic information about most of the investments you might wish to consider.

For guidance to information sources, Brownstone and Carruth's *Where to Find Business Information*, Lorna Daniells' *Business Information Sources*, and Grant Cote's *Directory of Business & Financial Services* are standard, quite comprehensive books, and available at most libraries. Any one of them should easily take you to all the main sources of current financial information.

In the libraries, you will find such basic information sources as the whole line of Moody's services, including *Moody's Bank and Finance Manual, Bond Record, Bond Survey, Dividend Record, Handbook of Common Stocks, Industrial Manual, Investor's Fact Sheets, Municipal and Government Manual, Over-the-Counter (OTC) Industrial Manual, Public Utility Manual,* and *Transportation Manual.* Many of these are topped with newsletters and supplemented frequently in looseleaf, and in aggregate supply much of what you might want to know about specific investments in the areas listed.

Similarly, you will find a major and in many areas directly competing set of reports, published by Standard & Poor's. These include *American Stock Exchange Reports, Bond Guide, Daily Stock Price Record, Dividend Record, Earnings Forecaster, Fixed Income Investor, Industry Surveys, Municipal Bond Selector, Over-the-Counter Stock Reports, Register of Corporations, Directors, and Executives, Standard Corporation Records,* and *Standard New York Stock Exchange Reports.*

In many libraries, you will also find such publications as Wiesenberger Financial Services' *Investment Companies,* carrying detailed information on mutual funds, and such smaller mutual funds books as the Investment Company Institute's annual *Mutual Facts Book* and Hirsch's annual *Mutual Funds Almanac.*

You may have some difficulty in finding basic data in the relatively new futures and options trading areas, but such books as the Dow Jones commodities and stock options handbooks will be found either in libraries or business bookstores, or may be bought directly from their publishers.

On the other hand, you should encounter no difficulty at all in finding books and services dealing with life and health insurance. In those areas, the main problems are those of selection, with many new publications every year, and many law and regulatory changes, especially when there is a new tax law. Some libraries will have such sources of ongoing information as Prentice-Hall's looseleaf *Life Insurance Planning*. And in addition to the book you are now reading, you will find such standard works as Gregg and Lucas' *Life and Health Insurance Handbook*, published by Dow Jones-Irwin, and Consumers Union's *The Consumers Union Report on Life Insurance* quite useful.

In short, learning to use the available resources of the library will take you to much of the information you may seek on a specific investment. In this regard, you will find reference librarians greatly helpful, and eager to be asked for help. It does take a little work, a little familiarization with the tools and techniques of looking for the information you need; but once you are indeed familiar enough to find your way around in the materials, you will have acquired an invaluable lifelong skill.

There is more, of course; much more. *Where to Find Business Information* lists over 5,000 sources of business information, most of them properly seen as also carrying investment information; in itself it is somewhat selective. No one can be current on every investment, but everybody can effectively reach for basic information on any investment.

Databases

Those managers who have access to financial and business information databases through office or home computers can learn a great deal about some kinds of possible moves through astute use of those computers, without even having to leave their chairs. For example, it is possible to reach into *Dialog's* massive set of databases for a considerable body of information about any widely held and traded public company, finding information about the company, its products and markets, its prospects, the price fluctuations of its stock, and a good deal more. It is possible to reach into *Nexis* for articles relating to the same matters. It is also possible, by using such databases, to get information about the individual and corporate sponsors of such operations as real estate and natural resources enterprises before going into them. More and more information vital to savers and investors is becoming readily available through home and office computer access, and those who arrange such access for themselves can greatly profit by using it.

As of this writing, managers using company-supplied and paid-for access have a considerable advantage, for individuals who have to pay for that access often find it rather expensive. But the costs are coming down, both of home computers and database access through those computers, and major organizations such as IBM and AT&T are beginning to compete hard for what will eventually be a massive set of office and home database access markets. When millions of people seek such access from their offices and homes — and that time is not far off — prices will really tumble. You are unlikely in the near future to turn reflexively to your computer screen for general financial and business news, or even, as many investment professionals now do, for routine updating on the investments you are currently following. But even now, those who can find database access should take the time to use their computers to research projected moves as thoroughly as they can.

Finding Good Advisers and Making Them Work for You

As you become fully competent to develop your own informed opinions about investments and other financial matters, you become better and better able to secure, understand, and evaluate advice directly offered by others, and to get and hold good financial advisers. Unless you become astute in these matters on your own, you have no chance in the world of assessing the objectivity and astuteness of others.

You certainly will be working with outside professionals, as do people running any kind of business. No matter how conservative and modest your asset-accretion program, you will probably find yourself working with accountants, bankers, brokers, insurance sellers, lawyers, perhaps realtors, and probably independent financial planners over the years. All will have a good deal to contribute, if you know enough to be able to ask them the right questions and clearly evaluate their answers. If you don't know much, then none of them will be of much use to you in the long run, except for doing some mechanical things. And if you don't know much, some of these kinds of people can do you a good deal of harm, for an increasing number of them have their own axes to grind.

For example, a good accountant can become a trusted lifelong tax adviser, going beyond tax-return preparation to develop tax-saving recommendations of many kinds. As so many accountants will tell you, that is what a good accountant really wants to do; they are all too often frustrated in such attempts by client inertia and failure to enter into the lifelong financial planning process. Quite true. But the not-so-good accountant — and there are some — may take clients into questionable tax-avoidance devices, very often collecting finder's fees from brokers or promoters for doing so. There may be nothing particularly wrong about the fee collection, as long as clients are clearly told what the arrangements are. What can go very wrong is that, while the good accountant will investigate the tax-avoidance arrangement very closely before recommending it to clients, the not-so-good accountant may pay a good deal more attention to the finder's fee than to client welfare. And only if you develop your own informed opinion will you be able to distinguish between the good proposal and the bad one — and between the good accountant and the accountant who may be far from good for you.

Similarly, yesterday's trusted banker may in today's financial marketplace be selling as well as advising. Yes, the banker always sold the desirability of keeping your money in banks, but today that banker may be selling municipal bonds, insurance, and a good deal more. When big banks have whole departments set up to sell their depositors highly questionable municipal bonds, it is clear that you must, as never before, be prepared to make your own well-informed investment decisions.

Make no mistake about this: in the financial marketplace, you are in the last analysis on your own. You *must* know enough to make your own decisions astutely. Make no mistake about this either: both action and inaction require knowledge. To hesitate and fail to make a move because you don't know enough can, in many financial situations, be as damaging as making the wrong moves. If you are going to have some money and other assets, you are going to have to know enough to manage well on your own.

That is as true for high-earning managers as it is for those who make much less. At least once a year, the newspapers break a big story about some truly astonishing collection of celebrities, politicians, and corporate executives who have lost large sums of money through investing in the latest get-rich-quick or tax-avoidance scheme. Often it is a combination of both; recently, it was a very complicated and sophisticated set of straddle operations wrapped round with a tax-avoidance device, to which a large number of such people had been led by their professional advisers. Although in other situations the device seems to have turned out reasonably well, in this instance it turned out very badly.

Here, the investors signed notes for 100 cents on the dollar, put in 25 cents on the dollar, and on paper — they thought — owed 75 cents. Then they took full 100-cent tax deductions in the year they put their money into the investment. On that basis, they were prepared to lose the 25 cents in cash they had put in, for the tax benefits would, for these high-income people, offset any losses. But Congress had recently plugged that hole in the tax law, and the notes they signed were real notes, as they found out when the whole thing went bad. As of this writing, most of the investors probably now owe far more than the cash they put in, and litigation proceeds. Indeed, if the whole thing turns out as badly as it possibly can, many can ultimately find themselves paying 50 – 75 cents *more* on top of the 25 cents they put in, plus very high lawyers' and accountants' fees, plus court costs. How they and their professional advisers will fare is anybody's guess — and all for unthinkingly following some professional advice that was, to put it as gently as possible, extraordinarily adventurous.

That sort of experience underscores the need to know enough and pay enough attention to your own financial affairs so you can make your own informed decisions, no matter how high-priced the professional help you have secured. Do not misread this, though; professional help *is* needed in the financial marketplace. That help is available in varying degrees and competencies from a considerable range of professional financial planners, accountants, lawyers, bankers, securities sellers, and insurance sellers. An increasing number of managers are working directly with professional financial planners, either through their companies or on their own. Most managers involved in financial planning, however, continue to start through their accountants, though some, especially in smaller places, start with their lawyers and local bankers, as was the pattern earlier in the century. A surprising number undertake to do their financial planning mainly through securities sellers, who are increasingly putting themselves forward as financial planners, although relatively few have the kind of broad-gauged experience necessary to do successful long-term financial planning, and many do not even have a wide enough range of financial products to sell to accomplish effective financial planning.

It is not at all easy to find and hold on to sound financial advisers in a world that often seems full of ill-informed sellers. But good people-picking is always hard, whether in your main business career or in your part-time financial business. It is also essential. All the financial planning forms in the world, computer-generated or otherwise, are not worth as much as one sound adviser working with you over the years. And after all, a skilled manager has a leg up on almost everybody else when it comes to good people-picking, for that is one of the key elements in managerial success.

The analogy holds up for some little distance further. The good people-picker in management knows how to search for the right people, interview them, make sound — not always correct, but sound — choices, and work with those who have been picked. The good picker of financial advisers does essentially the same things — seeking out, interviewing, picking, and working with financial advisers, with the objective of finding the kinds of advisers who can successfully be worked with for many years.

Professional Financial Planners

In some corporations, financial advisers are picked by the firm and managers work with them without charge, as a company-supplied benefit. When that kind of benefit is provided by your company, use it to the hilt, for then you are often getting the kind of help that you couldn't possibly afford on your own. Frequently these are highly qualified financial planners who, because they are working on a fee-only basis rather than generating commissions for themselves, would have to charge you thousands of dollars for the advice rendered if you were an individual client. Professional financial planners developing complex plans for rather well-to-do clients may charge anywhere from $5,000 to $30,000 for their original plans, plus yearly fees for continuing advice. Advice developed for corporate employees, often on a group-lecture basis and often with tailored individual plans as well, might cost somewhat less, but would still be prohibitively expensive for most managers if they had to pay for it out of their own pockets. So, by all means, take advantage of that kind of advice, trying to develop a full-scale financial plan at the outset and seeking continuing advice as long as it is available.

The cost of securing this kind of full-scale professional financial planning advice may be prohibitive when it is offered on a fee-only basis, as is often done by planners working with corporations or with wealthy individual clients. You can certainly buy a computerized "plan" for as little as a couple of hundred dollars, but that is scarcely the same as developing a detailed lifelong plan of your own in direct consultation with a highly skilled professional financial planner.

The true cost of such complete financial planning presents a real problem to individuals on their own — and to financial planners as well, who want to give excellent, highly specific long- and short-term advice to individuals, but who can scarcely begin to charge enough for such advice if it is given on a fee-only basis. Yet you have every reason to be cautious about taking investment recommendations from those who stand to profit through commissions generated by implementation of their own recommendations, and most professional financial planners understand that very well, too. The solution — and it is sometimes necessarily a rather tentative one until you and your financial planner have come to know and trust each other fully — is to come to a financial planner with some of your financial goals at least partly defined, and knowing that one way or another your financial planner will need to be adequately compensated. If that means generating some commissions for your financial planner, that should be acceptable to you — as long as you have in the early stages become satisfied that the planner you are beginning to work with is acceptable to you in terms of integrity, knowledge, experience, personal compatibility, and services available.

There are no "bargains" when it comes to paying for financial planning advice, but it is possible to pay too much for a high-priced consultant when what you may need is someone who will develop a long-term common-sense program with you and then proceed to implement and adjust that program with you over the years. Similarly, there is little sense in developing a "program" with someone who is really only a seller of a particular kind of investment; your adviser must have the capacity to meet or at least to adequately help you to implement your whole program.

There are thousands of seasoned, ethical financial planners working in the United States, most of them members of either the International Association of Financial Planners, The Institute of Certified Financial Planners, or both. There are also increasing numbers of financial planners employed by banks, to work with individual customers in search of financial planning help; and by large accounting firms, though the financial planning function in those firms is often carried out by accountants, rather than by financial planners. There are also, as in every field, some who are not so very ethical. By and large, there are as many ethical and unethical financial planners as there are ethical and unethical accountants, lawyers, bankers, and brokers; as always, you are obliged to find people you can work with, respect, and trust.

Financial planners and their organizations offer a considerable variety of services and fee structures; you may buy anything from a computerized printout to an extremely complex set of recommendations, with accounting, legal, and money management fees included. The client either pays the planner a fee, as sole compensation; or pays a fee plus commissions through recommended transactions; or pays no fee, with the planner's compensation coming solely from commissions. Given the real cost of developing sound personal financial planning advice, it is realistic to expect to pay some modest fee for initial consultation and to engage in commission-generating transactions if the advice given is taken. Some excellent planners will charge modest fees, and some will not; in a way it hardly matters to you, for the quality of the advice given will not depend on the presence of a fee. Far from it; a modest fee is usually a screening device that helps the planner sort out serious potential clients from those who might otherwise only waste extremely valuable time.

We speak here of a modest fee for rather complex face-to-face advice, by the way, not for the computerized printout approach. Someone offering you a computerized printout for $200 may well be making money on the printout transaction itself, while a skilled financial planner who spends a couple of hours with you and then charges you the same $200 is losing his or her shirt, if that is as far as the planning relationship goes. And the planner knows it — as should you. That early interview is aimed at securing a long-term client, whether there is a charge for it or not, and is entered into by the planner with only that long-term relationship in mind.

You, too, must properly seek such a long-term financial planning relationship, for no matter how good you may be on your own, you cannot be as well served by yourself alone as you will in the long run be served by combining your skills and insights with those of a skilled financial planner. The planner wants to know how serious you are, and whether you are compatible with each other. You, in turn, are trying to learn enough to be able to make an informed decision about trying to work with the planner.

That decision usually rests a good deal upon how well the planner has been recommended. A great many first contacts between potential clients and planners start with direct recommendations from accountants and lawyers, and sometimes from bankers, brokers, and insurance sellers as well. A good many more come through recommendations from friends or colleagues, who are usually satisfied clients of the recommended planner. Some come cold, as when a potential client responds to an advertisement or has called one of the two national financial planning organizations for a recommendation of local members. (You can do that by querying the International Association for Financial Planning, 5775 Peachtree-Dunwoody Road, Suite 120-C, Atlanta, Georgia, 30342, (404)252-9600, or The Institute of Certified Financial Planners, 3443 South Galena, Suite 190, Denver, Colorado, 80231, (303)751-7600.) Clearly, a strong recommendation from a respected professional or equally respected friend or colleague will count heavily, while a call upon an unknown will be treated far more cautiously. A recommendation stressing the amount of money the planner has made for someone in speculative investments probably should make you run the other way, because good planners are not product salespeople touting specific investments, but rather very sober, long-term thinkers who will try to help you define and then reach your financial and personal goals.

A good recommendation can be very helpful. On the other hand, it is imprudent to lose sight of the need to assess any financial planner carefully and independently, however well recommended. Even if your accountant is sitting in the same room with you and a warmly recommended financial planner, you should ask a considerable series of questions, the same questions you would ask if you had just come in off the street and the planner were a complete stranger.

Here are some key matters to examine, when considering what may become a very important and possibly quite long-term relationship with a financial planner:

• If you are being recommended by another professional, such as an accountant, lawyer, banker, broker, or insurance representative, will the person recommending you get any sort of payment for the referral? There is nothing particularly wrong about that sort of referral fee, but it is certainly something you want to know about going in, and from whoever is doing the recommending, rather than from the planner, who should not have to reveal this if someone else has not been willing to do so. Many professionals will freely tell you about a referral fee without even being asked, but if you ask and the response to your question is evasive, you may have a problem, with recommender or planner or both.

• If you are being recommended by anyone, you will want to know how long and how well the recommender has known the planner, and to try to learn everything you can about the planner before your first meeting, just as if you were about to interview someone for a key job in your company.

• When you call the planner to make an appointment, ask that any available printed material be sent to you before the meeting; allow enough time to receive and read the material before the meeting.

• At that first meeting, you should ask about the experience of the planner, both as a full-scale financial planner and in any other finance-related matters. In this kind of consulting relationship, relevant experience counts a very great deal, and unseasoned neophytes are only that, no matter how well formally educated.

• Having said that, you also want to know about the education of the planner, for professional association certifications and college financial planning degrees and courses can be very helpful, if some basic experience is there.

• What kinds of clients does the planner have, in terms of their occupations, income levels, and resources? If quite a few of them are like you, then you may be talking with someone who will easily and helpfully respond to your goals and needs. If not, you may be dealing with someone who is a bad fit, no matter how skilled and personally congenial.

• What specific referrals to satisfied existing clients will the planner supply? If none, walk away, with all deliberate speed. If some, be very sure to call them to discuss as much as they are willing to discuss, asking them the same kinds of searching questions you would ask anyone recommending the planner. This kind of careful call is highly desirable, no matter how strong any initial recommendation.

• Will someone else in the office actually be handling your planning? If so, then your basic queries must include that person, even if that requires a full second interview.

• How will the day-to-day, week-to-week relationship actually work? Whom will you call when you have a question or comment, or want to make a move? Will the planner be calling you to suggest moves, as laws and investment situations change?

• What will your financial plan look like? This is the planner's cue to offer to show you some reasonably appropriate plans developed for other people in your general circumstances, of course without revealing their identities.

• How often will you and the planner update your plan? The answer should be at least once a year, with you supplying everything the planner needs to do the job well.

• What will it all cost? This should be a very complete discussion of initial fees, commissions for the several kinds of financial planning moves you might make through the planner, and recurring costs, as for a yearly plan review. It should not at all be taken for granted that all transactions will flow through the planner's office, though many will. For example, you may very well want to use a discount broker for some kinds of transactions.

• After the initial meeting, discuss what you have learned with others, including your professional advisers and whomever else you think might be helpful.

• Should you decide to go ahead to make a financial plan, also carefully discuss the plan ultimately made with the same kinds of people. In financial planning, some of the earliest recommendations a planner makes may involve some of the most important financial moves you will ever make. These early recommendations often require financial restructuring in such vitally important areas as life and health insurance, major investments, and retirement planning. They are coming from someone you cannot yet know very well, no matter how carefully you have investigated and directly queried the planner, and should be treated very carefully indeed. While remembering that inaction is itself often a very costly error, ill-considered action is at least as great a threat.

Getting the Most from Your Accountant

Whether or not you work directly with a professional financial planner, you are also quite likely to work very closely with your accountant on financial matters. Actually, one of the key roles a good accountant can play is to introduce you to an equally good financial planner, so that you may work with both accountant and planner over the years.

For many, it has been and will continue to be the accountant who performs the main financial advisory functions, bringing in other professionals as needed. This is understandable. It is your accountant who "does the numbers" with you every year for your tax return, and who — if you are wise enough to seek help — will work with you to minimize taxes now, make asset-building plans for the future, and insure against potential catastrophe. Like a good financial planner, a good accountant is, in a very real sense, a substantial personal asset. Such relationships are worth developing and attentively building for decades, if possible.

To a considerable extent, how you work with your accountant

depends upon how you understand the tax preparation process. If you see the process as merely a matter of getting a distasteful task over with at the least possible cost, then you might as well use a trained tax preparer with a computerized tax preparation program and let it go at that. The tax preparer will probably cost you considerably less than the accountant. The accountant is probably using a similar computer program, anyway, as the whole preparation process and taxing system has become so complex that it is almost impossible to do it by hand and do it really well — that is, to take all the preferences and options into account, so that you come up with the least expensive solutions. (A digression: beware the impulse to do your tax return yourself, on your brand-new computer, with a nice new tax preparation program you've just bought. Unless you are a tax professional — preparer or accountant — you are highly unlikely to know enough to put the right numbers in and in the right way; as a result, you will probably cost yourself far more in taxes paid than any amount you can save on tax preparation fees. Garbage in, garbage out; wrong numbers in, tax payment obligations out.)

On the other hand, if you see the tax preparation process both as a disagreeable necessity and as a major yearly review and financial planning opportunity, you will find a good accountant and work with that accountant on far more than a tax return. Tax planning and all other aspects of personal financial planning are deeply intertwined; and the planning time you spend with your accountant before each year-end, when planning moves for next year can still be made, can be some of the most valuable time you spend with anyone all year. This is when you figure out the main tax-related investment moves and pension plan arrangements, as well as the main tax-avoidance moves. This is when you can and should track such matters as your total investment asset growth. Those figures should, by the way, be carefully separated from the meaningless net worth figures, which confuse because they include consumable assets that can neither grow nor be turned into investment dollars, but can only be consumed.

You should see your accountant at least twice each year: once in a substantial planning session long enough before the end of the year to enable you to make the moves indicated, and once at tax-return time. The tax-return meeting is far less important than the earlier planning meeting. Indeed, if you have done the planning meeting well, you may not even have to meet at tax-return time; your filled-in input forms may give your accountant all that is necessary to do your tax returns well. It is the planning meeting that is vital, with its review and summing up of the year's financial activities and its look ahead to next year's financial activities and beyond.

The accountant who will refuse to work with you this way is a rare bird indeed, for this is precisely the kind of client relationship sound accountants cultivate. Most lament the fact that so few of their clients do this kind of consistent, astute planning with them. But if you do by some mischance find yourself with an accountant who doesn't have the time to do this kind of planning with you, get another accountant. If it is a matter of a trusted accountant becoming too expensive for you — and this can happen, as accounting careers develop — you should still get another accountant, for you need someone with whom you can work and for whom you continue to be a valuable, wanted client.

In addition to this kind of rather formal planning, it is wise to develop the kind of relationship with your accountant that includes a call for advice on the possible tax and financial implications of projected substantial moves. No, not a hand-holding relationship, in which you check with your accountant before buying a home appliance or making a minor stock trade. But you may very well want to check the tax aspects before buying an automobile or a computer, for the automobile buy or lease decision can have substantial tax implications, as can the timing of the home computer purchase. And you will always want to check very carefully with your accountant before making an investment decision involving substantial tax avoidance; never, never get involved in any kind of substantial tax-avoidance or tax-shelter situation without first consulting your accountant, and you might want to speak to your lawyer as well.

Working with Your Lawyer, Banker, and Other Advisers

Not so long ago, accountants, lawyers, and bankers were all thought of as dispassionate financial and business advisers, and therefore more trustworthy than such interested parties as commission-generating financial advisers, securities sellers, and insurance sellers. Sure, accountants, lawyers, and bankers sold, too, but what they sold were their services, and the integrity of that sale rested to a considerable extent upon their not making money as a result of their advice.

Well, there may have been something to that view in some instances, not so long ago. But the world has changed, and not necessarily for the better. Now, a very large number of accountants, lawyers, and bankers sell and make money on their advice, too. Banks set up major departments to sell financial advice and a wide range of recommended financial instruments, on which they make commission income. Large numbers of accountants and lawyers take their clients to financial sellers of all kinds, and collect finder's fees for doing so, quite legally and often fully disclosing that fact, as they should. In truth, one of the main characteristics of the new financial marketplace is that almost everybody sells almost everything. Therefore, the existence of self-interest and possible conflict of interest can no longer be seen as a red flag and a knockout factor when choosing advisers. Lack of full disclosure or even perceived reluctance to disclose should be that kind of warning and a signal to walk away. But beyond that, your own knowledge and the development of some carefully evaluated experience with such advisers is all you can really count on.

If you have found people you trust and respect to work with, treasure them, lean on them — but only a little — and allow for the possibility that they can make a mistake or two, even though their mistakes can cost you money. But if the chemistry isn't right between you to start with, or if it goes wrong, or if you have some reason to mistrust anyone for inadequate disclosure reasons, by all means move on. Finding new advisers can be difficult and time-consuming; it can initially cost some fee money as well. But staying with advisers whose advice you will not take is worse, for then you have no advisers at all.

How do you find a good accountant, lawyer, securities seller, insurance seller, or banker? Word of mouth, mostly, and by referral from one to another. If you have found one good adviser, you have not necessarily found them all, but you are certainly on the way. That is particularly so if you have found a good financial planner or accountant, for both are the kinds of professionals who routinely reach out for other, related professionals to work with. Of course, as the financial marketplace has become today, if you have found one financial planner or banking organization you trust and respect, you may have found your securities and insurance sellers as well, for the modern tendency is to expand the financial goods and services sold to fill all perceived client financial wants and needs.

We do have some practical reservations about using banking and other large financial planning organizations as primary financial advisers. The potential problem is that of long-term personal continuity. People employed by large organizations like these do tend to move about a good deal, from job to job within an organization and from employer to employer, as is clear to anyone who has watched a parade of local bank branch managers and assistant managers or young stockbrokers go by. That is understandable; developing careers can require that kind of moving about. But it is often far from good for individual clients, who quite justifiably feel misserved by people who cannot possibly find the time to become as acquainted with their goals and needs as they must be to be able to offer sound financial planning advice. Such large organizations tend to be heavily computer-supported, but all the computer-generated reports in the world cannot properly substitute for individual plans carefully crafted and adjusted by experienced individual financial planners or accountants who can and often do stay with their clients for years and even decades. At its best, personal financial planning is far more a very personal kind of cottage industry than an assembly-line affair. Look for financial advisers who will be there for the long haul.

Keeping Organized Records

As in any business, your own part-time personal financial business requires a certain amount of efficient record-keeping. To do financial planning consistently and well, you have to be able to get your necessary records together, keep them together and capable of being reached easily when you need to consult them, and at least minimally track your financial progress.

Many people are now using home computers to help them

handle these kinds of tasks. There are literally hundreds of personal financial planning programs for every kind of home computer, aimed at helping you to accomplish everything from keeping records of day-to-day expenditures and doing personal cash-flow forecasting to automating the way you keep your long-term records of vital documents. If you have a home computer, by all means use it for these kinds of purposes, with only these cautions.

First, that **net worth,** as we discuss in the next chapter, can be a seriously misleading concept. In figuring your progress, strip away the value of all consumables in your possession, and then see where you stand month to month and, more significantly, year to year.

Second, a computer program full of numbers is no substitute for hard thinking, any more than it is in your main business career. To do effective planning, you have to reassess your wants and needs continually as they change over the years and reach under the numbers to understand what is really happening on the financial side of your life. Using a very simple example, a year with a single large paper gain on a rank speculation may look like a good year; but the facts may be quite different when you realize that, aside from that gain, you have been overspending and continuing to pile up personal consumption debts. Even if the gain is realized, you would still be well advised to consider what would have occurred had the windfall not been there. Let the computer help you, but don't let its appeal as a new toy lull you into a false sense of security. And if you don't have a computer, you can perfectly easily keep excellent records of income, expenditure, cash flow, and investment asset growth, just as you could and probably did before the advent of home computers. Some of the many books always available in the record-keeping area may also be useful; two are Richard Stillman's *Your Personal Financial Planner* and H. & R. Block's *Family Budget Workbook*.

With or without a computer, you need a good working office at home, whether that is a separate room or the corner of some other room that does not get too much traffic. In that room, you need a large-enough table space and adequate, lockable file space, into which you can put your current working papers and materials you may need to refer to, such as recent tax records. It needs good light, too; that office is the headquarters of your part-time personal financial business, and you will spend a good deal of time there. It is worth setting up your office at home as efficiently as you would your office at work.

All tax records should be kept at least four years, three of them to satisfy the statute of limitations applicable to most tax matters and one year more because the situations involved may go back a year before filing the return. But there is no statute of limitation on fraud, and many such records also very often involve other, even longer-term record-keeping needs, such as those relating to pensions, insurance, and investment matters. Even receipts, which most of us tend to keep for at most a few years, may be vital for insurance purposes when determining the value of items destroyed by fire or water. As a practical matter, then, it is probably a good idea to keep at least tax, investment, pension, insurance, major purchase, real estate, and financial planning records at home indefinitely, on the theory that you cannot recover them once you have thrown them away and cannot know what you will need and when.

You also need a safe deposit box, for valuable hard goods, securities, contracts, deeds, and key personal records such as birth, death, marriage, and divorce certificates. You may want to keep copies of such documents as deeds and contracts at home, for ready reference. Don't keep your original, witnessed will in your safe deposit box, but rather in your lawyer's safe deposit box or some other safe place. Your box will be sealed by the bank as soon as it is known that you are dead, and your will with it, which can cause small but unnecessary problems for your heirs.

For planning purposes, the main need is to keep everything current and in good working order. It is all too easy to let personal record-keeping go, for it seldom seems like the kind of thing that should enjoy any kind of priority attention. But it must. Consistently effective personal financial planning requires continuous attention to the nuts and bolts.

4
The Fundamentals of Money and Investment

If you want to win, you have to understand the money basics and ask the right investment questions about each projected personal money move. No, that doesn't mean letting the money questions become primary in life, or conditioning every action on its money consequences. Certainly life is more than money. But that is the classic and still the best of all reasons for understanding money and its uses: In this society, fortunately or not, rightly or not, for most of us financial independence is intertwined with whatever measure of real freedom we are able to achieve.

Much of effective personal financial planning rests on understanding several key matters regarding saving and investing. These have to do with **compounding, the forced holding of assets, yield, net worth,** and **leverage.** These are the kinds of matters that for most of us surely produced no more than glassy-eyed inattentiveness and huge covert yawns while we were in school. Just as surely, they are all so basic as to be absolutely necessary understandings if we are to manage the financial side of life at all well.

The Joys of Compounding

What is left in, compounds, first developing growth on principal and then growth on growth. That is simple enough. It is also one of the main motors in the economic life of every one of us and in an increasingly interconnected world economy. We ignore it at our peril, as the truly spectacular growth of the American national debt and the equally extraordinary growth of the international debts of many debtor nations now show us every day.

On the positive side, compounding means that every dollar

we are able to save and invest can grow very quickly, if we place it astutely where reasonably safe after-tax yields will be greatest, and leave the gain in. Where we are encouraged or even forced by the nature of the investment or by its tax aspects to leave the gain in, the ultimate gain is likely to be very large indeed. And in periods where the gains are quite high relative to the rate of inflation, the growth can be enormous.

In this instance, the numbers really do tell the basic story. Just $1,000, put into a tax-advantaged Individual Retirement Account (IRA) yielding an effective 12% yearly for 30 years, grows almost 30 times, to $29,960. On the same basis $1,000 put in *each* year becomes $270,293 in 30 years. A 9% average inflation in the same 30 years would greatly cut the real value of those gains, but you would still come out with about two and a quarter times what you put in, which is not bad relative to the pace of inflation. But an average 6% rate of inflation for those 30 years would cut your real gains by much less, so that you would come out with a little over five times as much as you put in. The numbers come out far better if you use leverage properly, and far, far worse if you use it badly — that is, too adventurously. More on leverage later in this chapter.

The question of compounding and its practical effects is considerably obscured by the way we keep some of the main numbers in the national economy, as distinct from the way most of us understand our personal savings and investment numbers. In the economy, the most watched number is the inflation rate, as measured by the Consumer Price Index. In personal finance, the most watched number is net after-tax yield. But in the economy, the percentage increase in the inflation rate always stays in, while in our personal economies, we all too often spend some of our after-tax yield, thereby making a smaller base upon which to build a stake — that is, a body of growing assets.

Once again, look at the numbers: Assume that you are measuring $1.00. The Consumer Price Index — that is, the inflation rate — goes up an average of 6% a year for 20 years. In the first year, the index becomes $1.06. In the second year, 6% is not 6 cents anymore, but rather 6% of $1.06, or 6.36 cents; and the base on which you are measuring the increase in the third year is $1.1236. By the end of the twentieth year, that $1.00 has become

$3.21, and for the next year that 6% annual rate of increase will be 6% of $3.21, which is 34 cents, rather than the 6 cents 20 years earlier. That is an extraordinary — and perfectly standard — kind of increase over the years. Indeed, it is a much smaller rate of increase than we have experienced in many of the last 20 years. For the year 1984, for example, the Consumer Price Index rose at an annual rate of a little over 4%, while in terms of its 1967 base number it rose about 13 points. That is also, by the way, why we continue to perceive substantial price increases in many areas of life, even in years when the inflation rate is down.

This is all very basic, and we all know about it. Or do we? If we really did, we would pay much more careful attention to holding on to any gains we make, rather than using those gains for consumables. In a very real sense, even after-tax yield doesn't mean all that much, if you spend some of that yield rather than holding on and reinvesting it. A stock whose growth and dividends together yield an after-tax 10% in a year in which inflation is 6% is doing very well — if you reinvest those dividends after making an allowance for tax payments. But if all you do is treat the dividends as spendable ordinary income — as they are treated for tax purposes — then your long-term financial planning will not work as it should. On the other hand, if you are substantially locked into an investment such as your own home or an Individual Retirement Account, then investment growth is equally locked in.

Mortgage payments are an interesting example of how the way we keep our numbers can fool us. A 14% fixed-rate mortgage on an expensive home may necessitate truly huge mortgage payments. If you compare them with home prices that are likely to go up, but not necessarily at anything like 14% a year, you may wonder whether home ownership will really work out well financially in the long run. But the truth is that even a moderate rate of growth in home prices will very quickly build substantial new equities, for the equity buildup has little to do with mortgage rates and everything to do with locked-in compounding. Even at such very high mortgage rates, and even if the tax advantages accompanying home ownership are greatly limited by new tax laws, the underlying demand for housing and certain other major factors in the real estate marketplace (which we will discuss later) will ensure at least a modest growth in the values of well-situated homes. The 14% you may have to pay on a fixed-rate mortgage does not compound, but will instead eventually disappear, as the mortgage principal is paid off — in progressively less valuable dollars at that, due to the long-term effect of inflation. The value in the home will compound, as it has for so many millions of other Americans since the end of the Great Depression, now half a century ago, creating what for many is the main asset of a lifetime.

As to home ownership, once the quite simple, really basic principle of compounding is understood, the only real question that should remain is how to go about acquiring a supportable home in the most advantageous way. In this, as in so many other aspects of your financial life, the key thing to do is to make compounding work for you, as you develop a growing body of savings, investments, and other growable assets. The key thing to avoid is allowing compounding to work against you, as when a consuming lifestyle builds up a quickly compounding body of debts. Because what you have to pay for money is usually considerably more than what you can make on money, a growing bundle of personal debts will usually compound far more quickly than a bundle of assets. *Avoid the spending that creates the debts and work on creating the right kinds of assets; then compounding will work for you.*

Maintaining Asset Growth

It is easy to hold on to the growth in an owner-occupied home. Indeed, it is rather difficult to do anything else, even when you borrow money at ruinous rates, using your home as collateral. In the long run the home just keeps on growing in value, provided it is well-situated. The main hazard is that you will be unable to carry the home, especially if you have borrowed a great deal more on it over the years for such purposes as college education costs.

Similarly, growth in the money you put into a tax-advantaged Individual Retirement Account or Keogh plan is easy to hold. The tax advantages accruing to those who build and hold such plans are enormous, and the penalties for too-early withdrawal of funds are substantial enough to make anyone think two or three times before invading the plan for any but the direst needs. For their combination of built-in hard-held asset growth and tax advantage, owner-occupied homes and these personal retirement plans are by far the best long-term personal investments available in America today.

Some of the modern annuity contracts also offer good accretion possibilities. We emphatically do not mean to speak well here of any of the older annuity arrangements, which built in such a terribly low rate of interest that annuity holders lost tremendous amounts in real dollars as against the rate of inflation over the years, with the result that many are now spending their later years in far worse circumstances than they had any reason to believe they would. There is no magic at all in forced savings or forced held-in gains, unless those savings and gains are accompanied by excellent rates of return that are in some significant way indexed to relevant changes in the economy.

The older annuity contracts, the older federal savings bonds, and the older standard life insurance policies carrying low-interest savings features all well illustrate the danger of fixed-rate long-term commitments. Those who held or are holding such instruments have lost very heavily over the years. As of this writing, the pace of inflation has lessened, but inflationary times may come again, and soon. That is why it is wise to enter into arrangements that automatically hold your gain for you very carefully — the right real estate, the right kinds of tax-advantaged retirement plans, perhaps the right kinds of annuities, and perhaps the right kinds of contributory corporate savings and pension arrangements.

But after that, your main focus should be on the right kinds of rather freely movable investments in this highly volatile period. That means exercising will when it comes to holding in most kinds of gains. First and most important of all, in a planning way, it means very carefully placing your investing money and your spending money in separate accounts, and never mixing the two. You should no more mix them than a lawyer who is holding funds for clients should mix those funds with other monies. In essence, you are holding your own investment money in trust for your own future and the futures of those you love or will come to love in your lifetime.

In the last analysis, of course, it is not investment in vehicles that automatically lock in your growth that matters; all such arrangements can be circumvented. Rather, it is your determination to build some sort of meaningful stake, in uncertain times that are not likely to become much more certain in the foreseeable future.

What Is Yield?

The concept of yield is simple enough, at its most basic; but for long-term planning, yield must be seen in considerably more complex ways.

At its simplest, and as generally used in the financial world, yield is how much an investment pays, on an annualized basis. A one-year certificate of deposit that pays a total of 11% a year in interest, after all daily compoundings and the like, yields that 11%. A corporate bond paying 12% a year yields that 12%.

Only a little less simply, a stock you hold for exactly one year, which you buy for 100 and sell for 106, has yielded 6% in growth. If it also paid dividends in that time amounting to $6 per share, it has yielded a total of 12% in that year. Similarly, a bond purchased and held for the same amount of time would yield a combination of gain or loss on sale plus whatever relation the interest you received had to your purchase price, expressed as a percentage.

When transactions are for fractions or multiples of years, then they are annualized. That means, for example, that on this basic level something held for six months must have its gains or losses doubled to derive yield, and something held for two years must have its gains or losses halved to derive yield.

We have all been sold enough tax-advantaged investments by now to have had the somewhat more complex concept of after-tax yield put before us more than once. It is worth restating here, though, if only because it is still so widely misunderstood. After-tax yield is that portion of yield left after allowance is made for all applicable federal, state, and local income taxes, in your highest incremental bracket. If you would, in the year taxes are payable on a transaction, be taxed at a combined top rate of 50%, then whatever part of the taxable gain is to be taxed at that rate should be deducted from the real yield you derive from the transaction. If all or part of the transaction is taxable at other income tax rates, as for example at long-term capital gains tax rates, then those taxes must be subtracted from the transaction to derive real, or after-tax, yield. Rigorously speaking, other kinds of taxes stemming from the transaction, such as real estate transfer and stock transfer taxes, should also be subtracted from yield. They are, but as associated business expenses, and therefore do not figure in the computation of actual or probable after-tax yield.

Also rigorously speaking, the long-term tax implications of a transaction or set of transactions spanning many years should also be taken into account in figuring probable yield. But although these can and should be a vitally important part of your thinking, it is very difficult to come up with a prospective long-term after-tax yield. It is one thing to compare tax-advantaged bond yield with a fully taxable bank certificate of deposit yield in any given year, or the net after-tax yield of a stock with that of a bond or mutual fund. But to compare any of these closely with the ultimate yield of an Individual Retirement Account or Keogh plan is almost impossible, for the accreted value in that sort of account will be taxable many years later, in accordance with the tax law as it will be then. All you can do, really, is point to the much faster accretion possible in a tax-advantaged account, take a stab at estimating future taxes on ultimate distribution of the account, show that money put aside tax-advantaged will grow far faster than fully taxed money, and suggest that the net of it all will be greatly to your advantage if you hold long-term money in such an account. If you live, that is; if your IRA or Keogh account passes to your heirs, they are likely to benefit far more than even you would have benefited; more on this later.

Similarly, it is almost impossible to factor in the long-term tax implication of home ownership. As the law now stands, you have a large one-time exemption from capital gains taxes on home sale later in life. By the time you get to it, the tax law may have changed a dozen times, and the exemption may be the same, far larger, long gone, or quite differently arranged.

You can, however, do some year-by-year, period-by-period comparison of long-term holdings with short-term holdings, even without actually realizing the value in the long-term holdings. With retirement accounts, the comparisons can be quite precise, dollar for dollar. With such assets as homes, businesses, and collectibles, the comparisons must be rough ones, based on the current market values of similar assets and with the knowledge that much may change by the time you actually want to turn such assets into cash. Still, the rough comparisons are well worth making, as part of your yearly financial self-assessment and forward planning.

There is another kind of yield that is far less tangible than anything so far discussed, and is almost impossible to express in numbers, much less compare with other kinds of investments. But a financial planning book — and especially a financial planning book directed mainly to managers and other businesspeople — should take up this kind of investment. That is the investment in education, and especially in professional education, which may in the short run actually deplete your financial assets but which in the long run can, in the overwhelming majority of instances, pay off handsomely.

Those corporate fringe benefits that provide for full or partial payment of professional education costs are, in economic terms, among the best fringes available. Those expenditures directed to the professional education of a spouse returning to the work force after years spent in childrearing are among the best investments of a lifetime. Those very large amounts of money spent in educating children in good public colleges and good — although sometimes expensive — graduate schools are enormously beneficial to the economic prospects of those children, although they may be great drains on the finances of their parents.

For example, a spouse returning to the work force as an entry-level, unskilled office worker may be able to make money at the rate of $10,000 – $15,000 per year a few years into such a low-paying career, and a few thousand more per year as skills develop the slow, hard way — on the job. But the same person, after an investment of as little as a few thousand dollars in cash and some thousands of dollars in foregone income, can get a perfectly good MBA, can double or even triple that entry-level income, and in the course of a career can make five times as much as an unskilled returnee. There are now a substantial number of state universities offering MBAs, with surprisingly low tuition and fee charges. For example, state residents can attend the graduate business school at the State University of New York in Buffalo for a very low $2,150 a year, as of this writing. For state residents, the graduate business school at the highly esteemed University of California at Berkeley comes in at only $1,421 a year. Mississippi State costs $1,238 yearly; the University of Arkansas $1,100; the University of Nebraska $1,035; and the University of Montana $747, all to state residents. All offer perfectly good, entirely negotiable MBAs, and all therefore open the doors to excellent lifelong management and other business careers. Such business schools as Harvard, Stanford, and Wharton cost $9,000 per year for tuition and fees, but you don't need a degree from that kind of expensive school to pursue a lucrative business career.

The fact is that for very little cash and not very much in foregone income, a spouse returning to work can secure an MBA and can then reasonably expect to make $10,000 – $30,000 a year more than the unskilled returning spouse *every year.* In a lifetime, that is hundreds of thousands of dollars more for the quite minimal initial investment required. And that is *yield,* too. Although it can not be gathered, measured, and reinvested in cash, it can be measured in a rough comparative way, and by any such measure it is surely one of the best yields available in a lifetime. In the short run, though, it is all cash out and income foregone, often with considerable negative effects on apparent personal and family worth; for professional education is not the kind of asset you can put on a personal balance sheet when totaling up asset gains every year. But professional education is a very real and extremely valuable personal and family asset; we must not become captives of our own numbers and thereby fail to invest in such long-term intangibles. Keep that yearly balance sheet, by all means, but also do the less precise but entirely necessary work of evaluating the growth of intangible assets. Early professional education, continuing professional education, growing practical professional experience, and personal financial planning skills are all properly seen as such valuable intangibles.

Your Net Worth

The concept of net worth is a wholly different kind of matter, for here we urge careful, consistent, lifelong subtraction of quite visible tangibles from your personal balance sheet. Indeed, we think that calculation of net worth in the standard way is entirely valueless as a measure of personal economic growth. Quite the opposite. Many of those whose net worth has grown a good deal in any given year have also seriously damaged their personal financial positions by putting far too much into consumables, actually lessening the value of those assets that have the ability to grow. Periodically figuring net worth can be a terribly misleading thing to do, especially if you pay any attention at all to that figure.

Net worth is the actual or estimated market value of everything you own, minus everything you owe. It is the cash value of bank deposits, the current market value of such owned securities as can be readily traded, the estimated market value of such assets as homes and businesses, and the estimated market value of all your goods, such as cars, clothing, furniture, and the like. It is, in this respect, much like a business balance sheet, in which the difference between all other current assets and liabilities appears as owners' equity.

An individual's net worth estimate must, by its very nature, be quite imprecise, for much must be estimated and actual values depend on circumstances as of the time of sale. A home may be worth even more than you think, but if you have to sell it in a hurry, it may be worth much less on actual sale. The gain in a security may be there if you sell it today, but may be gone tomorrow if you sell because a company, industry, or whole market goes bad. There is nothing surprising about any of that; business net worth estimates are only estimates, as well. A recently built chemical plant running along at full capacity may be worth a great deal this year. Next year or the year after, closed after a disaster, it may be worth less than nothing, being only a tax and maintenance burden.

After that, though, the analogy between a personal net worth statement and a business balance sheet breaks down. Business assets are generally used to make money; but only *some* personal assets are used to make money. The others are consumables; you will use them up, not sell them at a profit. It is the inclusion of such consumables in net worth statements, and therefore in personal financial planning, that is wrong and misleading. Even the inclusion of necessities in net worth is a planning error; for financial growth purposes, the necessary clothes you wear and car you drive are merely consumables, which you will wear out, rather than sell. Even a car carrying a residual value should be seen this way, for you will probably use any such residual value to acquire yet another consumable car.

It depends a great deal upon how you use your money. The money you put into an owned home creates a growing and measurable asset. The same amount of money, put into a rental that is equally a home, creates nothing of measurable value and adds nothing to assets. Put into an Individual Retirement Account, $1,000 a year in due course creates an asset worth hundreds of thousands of dollars. The same $1,000 a year, spent on cosmetics, beer, or any other discretionary consumable, creates nothing. Outside of necessities, these things are to a considerable extent a matter of choice and understanding.

It is true that millions of Americans make so little money that they cannot meaningfully save and invest; we may want to do something about that, as individuals and as a whole society. But managers and most other corporate people certainly can save and invest, if they will, and they should look hard and consistently at their consuming habits. That means understanding net worth for financial planning purposes to be quite different from the kind of net worth we state when applying for a loan. It means measuring, for financial planning purposes, only those assets that have investment value, and excluding the rest. After getting a hard figure for net worth in investment value terms, you can and should add any of the kinds of intangible items previously discussed, but that comes later, and serves only to qualify and explain some items in your asset growth picture.

Financial planning net worth should include bank accounts, real estate, securities, personally owned businesses, built-up insurance policy values, personal pension plans, and any other stores of value you own, such as collectibles, gems, and gold. It should not include Social Security and corporate pension plans, unless those corporate plans are vested and carry determinable payouts. It should not include consumables. It should include all personal debts. Then net worth becomes a concept worth using and tracking for financial planning purposes.

See the box for an outline of the kind of simple financial planning net worth statement you should do at least yearly.

Calculating Net Worth for Financial Planning Purposes

	Now	One Year Ago	Change
Bank accounts, including CDs not in retirement accounts	_____	_____	_____
Stocks, bonds, mutual funds, and other securities	_____	_____	_____
Home, other real estate, at fair market value minus mortgages and anticipated selling costs	_____	_____	_____
IRA and Keogh accounts	_____	_____	_____
Company pension, profit-sharing and deferred-compensation accounts payable, if you were to leave today	_____	_____	_____
Insurance policy cash buildups	_____	_____	_____
Other owned businesses, if salable, at anticipated market value minus anticipated selling costs	_____	_____	_____
Other stores of value owned, excluding consumables	_____	_____	_____
Total	_____	_____	_____
Minus all debts, other than mortgages	_____	_____	_____
Net worth	_____	_____	_____

To see how you have done in relation to inflation, deflate the net worth figure by the amount of inflation for the one-year period, and then compare net worth now with net worth one year ago. Over the years, this kind of net worth statement can become a very realistic and extremely valuable financial planning tool.

The Pros and Cons of Leverage

Every Yankee skipper who ever borrowed money to buy cargo to take around Cape Horn to China was using leverage. So, too, was every company that ever borrowed money to finance expansion and every homeowner carrying a mortgage on a home that has appreciated in value. For leverage — that very basic, often misunderstood, and terribly misused concept — is only the use of borrowed money to make money. That's all there is to it at root. The principle is that the use of borrowed money magnifies both the gains and losses you can experience on your own invested money.

If you have $1.00 to invest, buy something that costs $1.00, and make 20 cents on your invested dollar in a year, you have earned 20% before any applicable taxes. Similarly, if you lose 20 cents that year, you have lost 20% of your investment. But if you borrow $4.00 at 10% interest, buy something that costs $5.00, and make 20% in that year on your investment, it works out like this:

Your own cash investment	$1.00	
Borrowed	4.00	
Purchased investment	$5.00	
Profit at 20% in that year		$1.00
Interest to pay at 10% of borrowed $4.00		.40
Profit on transaction		$ .60
Percentage profit on own $1.00 cash investment		60%

Not bad. That 60% profit is three times as much as the 20%

you would have made if you had not borrowed the money to invest. That's leverage at its best, and that's what makes it enormously attractive. It is not an entirely unrealistic example, by the way, for this is precisely the kind of thing that has happened to millions of American homebuyers for most of the last half-century. They were forced to borrow mortgage money to swing home purchases, often paying 20% or even less as down payments, and found themselves quite accidentally the beneficiaries of both a long-term rise in home prices and the unwittingly astute use of maximum leverage. That is why an initial $5,000 – $10,000 actual cash investment in a home 30 years ago has resulted in ownership of a home that today may be worth $150,000 – $300,000.

But that's the best sort of thing that can happen, and it explains the tremendous attractiveness of the concept. Leverage is also a great seducer, capable of leading both the terribly innocent and the highly skilled to ruin. Here is the same example, but with a 20% loss, rather than a 20% gain.

Your own cash investment	$1.00	
Borrowed	4.00	
Purchased investment	$5.00	
Loss at 20% in that year		$1.00
Interest to pay at 10% of borrowed $4.00		.40
Loss on transaction		$1.40
Percentage loss on own $1.00 cash investment		140%

Not so good; in fact, terrible. A 140% loss is seven times as much as the 20% you would have lost if you had not borrowed the money to invest. In fact, you lost everything you had on the transaction, and had to find 40 cents more to pay interest on the money you borrowed. The same 20% that, as gain, produced a 60% three-times gain produced a 140% seven-times loss, and all because of the interest you had to pay on the money you borrowed. Paying the interest took 40% off the top of your profit, and added 40% to your loss. That's leverage, too.

Actually, in such an example you would today often be paying higher rates of interest and making less money, even when you are turning a profit. Beyond that, on certain kinds of highly leveraged transactions, which we will discuss later in this book, you will also be paying high commissions to brokers, making it even more difficult to make money with leverage. The truth is that individual investors who attempt to maximize gain through the use of substantial leverage must learn how to play leveraged investing games very skillfully and carefully. Those who do can make a good deal of money, and often relatively safely. Those who do not are almost certain to lose their shirts, in the not very long run. We will discuss the several highly speculative and very foolish uses to which leverage is put by some investors as we discuss different investments later on in this book.

Assessing Your Own Financial Needs and Risks

To be able to learn on your own is, first of all, to learn how to identify and ask the right questions consistently. If, as we believe, you are ultimately always on your own in the financial marketplace, then one of the most useful things this book can do for you is to identify the right questions to ask yourself about every projected investment move, so that you can indeed apply those questions to the wide variety of investment situations and decisions we must all face in our lifetimes.

Here are some basic questions to ask yourself about such projected investment moves. All should be very carefully asked, until they are put so reflexively that you no longer have to think about them. For many of us, some or all of these questions are already second nature, and that is as it should be. But for many others, these kinds of searching questions are asked haphazardly, partially, and sometimes not at all, often with personally damaging results. We will first list them all together to supply an overview, and then discuss them one by one.

- Am I making a fully informed move?
- What are the risks?
- What is the likely after-tax yield?
- What are the alternatives?

- How fast can I get out if I want or need to?
- Will I have too many eggs in one basket?
- Do I know how to make the move at the least possible cost?

Am I Making a Fully Informed Move?

This question might also be put: *Do I know all I need to know about the specific investment itself?* If you are buying something specific, such as the stock of a single company, the debt obligation of a single government or corporate issuer, or a specific piece of real or personal property, you should be satisfied that you know a good deal about that specific investment — its history, its prospects, the quality of the people managing it, the total situation of which it is part. That someone else has made money, or that you have a tip or rumor, or that your trusted broker has made what is essentially an unsupported recommendation, is not enough. That it fits wonderfully well into someone else's planning pattern is not enough. When you make an investment, it should be on the basis of *your own real knowledge,* and for your own well-conceived and well-understood reasons.

Similarly, when you buy professional management, as when you buy into a mutual fund or the kind of syndication or limited partnership that runs many properties, you should know enough about the organization and its management to be able to make an informed decision. As all skilled managers know, not all managers and not all companies are equal. That, after all, is why there are winning competitors in every industry, and why some investment organizations do so much better or worse than other, equally well-funded and well-staffed organizations.

You would surely not want to make a voluntary career move to another company without knowing a great deal about where it has been, how it is doing now, where it wants to go, how likely it is to get there, and under whose leadership. By the same token, you would surely not want to place substantial funds under the management of others and their organizations without asking and getting good answers to those kinds of questions. And that is what prospectuses, company marketing people, and standard reference sources are all about, from the buyer's point of view. What is extraordinary is that so many skilled corporate people do not use them enough when making important investment decisions. To develop the habit of informing yourself fully on every aspect of a projected investment is one of the main positive financial reflexes of a lifetime. Actually, the question "Am I making a fully informed move?" cannot be properly answered "Yes" unless you have already answered all the other questions that follow.

What Are the Risks?

It is vital to ask yourself this question very early in the investment decision-making process, and very seriously indeed. If you don't, or if you defer the sometimes hard work of ascertaining risk, you may focus far too much on how much money you are going to make, and wind up losing a good deal of money instead. Astute sellers understand how that works very well, and will usually leave it to you to raise the question of risk. Occasionally, a scrupulous seller will behave otherwise, but it is nothing you can count on.

Don't misunderstand us here. There are no riskless investments, and not even any relatively risk-free investments that you can buy, tuck away, forget about, and cash in on many years later. Every investment carries some degree of risk, and all risks are enormously magnified for those who are negligent about watching their investments. It is up to you to determine how much risk is involved, and how much you are willing to take to gain the possible rewards, within the context of your financial plans and goals. Throughout this work, we indicate possible risks and rewards, and lean toward limitation of risk as generally a proper stance for lifelong financial planning. But much of your investment decision-making will depend upon your own assessment of risk, and upon how much you are willing to risk for what you perceive as high returns on investment. Where you and we can and should agree completely is on the need to inform ourselves well enough to develop sound opinions on what the risks and potential rewards really are.

Disagreements in this area can lead to great differences as to where to put money. For example, the dedicated survivalist who believes that the country and the world are headed for another Great Depression and perhaps even toward atomic war soon, should pay little attention to most of the advice given here. We recognize the possibility of the development of another Great Depression, but scarcely see it as just around the corner. Rather, we see an American economy fluctuating around a stagnant center, which is quite likely to move into the next century with most of its current opportunities and problems still in place. We understand the possibility of atomic war, but cannot see any benefit in urging others to turn their backs on the possibility of prevention of that war, to what we see as sterile and ultimately impossible-to-achieve survivalism.

Similarly, we see some kinds of investments, such as commodities futures and raw land trading, as highly speculative, in this or any period. If you believe that the American economy is about to emerge into clear air with the kind of booms we experienced in the 1920s and 1960s, then you may very well see these kinds of speculations as major opportunities. We would rather see you throw your money away at a Las Vegas crap table; the odds are probably better, you will probably have more fun, and it won't waste as much of your time.

One rather important thing to bear in mind about the question of risk is that there is no neat little table of risks and rewards you can consult in making investment decisions, with the smaller risks yielding the smallest rewards and the largest risks yielding the largest rewards. That sort of thinking works to a very limited extent as to bond yields, largely because of the impact of the bond rating services and the presence of very large sums of professionally managed money in the bond marketplace. And it works to a certain degree in stocks, with small, untried companies in fast-growing industries sometimes presenting somewhat greater yield possibilities and almost always much greater risks than large, blue chip companies. And it works to an even more limited degree where there are residual values, as for gold; the speculative runups and downturns experienced in gold and silver within the last decade make it clear that no risk – reward equation works for making investment decisions in this area.

Even in bonds, the risk – reward approach must be used carefully. Surely, a short-term direct federal debt obligation is as safe as anything can be, and is also likely to pay less than many other less safe obligations. But a longer-term federal bond may be safe as to interest and unsafe as to its real yield possibilities vis-à-vis other bonds, should interest rates rise during its lifetime. And another example: Many municipals, with or without their present tax advantage, pay less than some rather well-rated corporate obligations, while at the same time being far more risky than those corporate obligations.

You must also be able to see clearly what kinds of risks you may be taking on. Those investments that carry the risk of some loss may be entirely acceptable, as long as there is some reasonable assurance that you will not lose your shirt. Those investments that carry possible disaster with them may not be acceptable at all, no matter how great the possible rewards. The illustration we used when discussing leverage is a good example of the latter, with the risks of loss involved going considerably beyond the money invested. But a long-term federal bond that ties up money on which you could be earning a little more interest may, in some periods, be a perfectly acceptable risk. And gold may be acceptable in a particularly turbulent period, for it has intrinsic value that in the long run will move with the pace of inflation, although it carries some negatives with it as well.

In risk matters, then, first of all look for the potential catastrophe, just as you do in insurance matters — which are, after all, only a different order of risk. We will discuss risks and rewards throughout this book, as we move into the different kinds of investments.

What Is the Likely After-Tax Yield?

As previously discussed, this question needs to be asked directly, in terms of how much of the yield of an investment will be left after the taking of taxes, figuring those taxes at the highest bracket rates you anticipate paying in the year in which the investment is made or sold. Some investments have long-term tax implications and possible indirect yields, as in the example of the spouse's benefits flowing from an education. But what is really measurable is the short-term after-tax yield. The after-tax yield question, therefore, should be seen as a short- and medium-term estimate coupled with some necessarily very general long-term estimates.

Looking at it that way, it is relatively easy to make some fairly close short-term after-tax estimates. The tax component can be figured for such direct payments as bond interest and dividends without too much trouble, subject always to unanticipated windfalls and tax law changes. It is a little harder, but still possible, to make some fairly sound estimates of the after-tax yields of tradable securities in which you have gains or losses, assuming sale within a few years of purchase, and very much subject to changes in taxable income and tax law. For tax-sheltered investment vehicles, it is relatively easy to make such estimates in periods of tax law stability and almost impossible in periods of major change. But for such quite long-term vehicles as optioned stock, homes, Individual Retirement Accounts, and annuities, it is best to figure yield as if it were not affected by eventual taxes at all, for these kinds of assets accrete their values tax-free for many years. Only if you are close to realization of gains in such assets, or know that you will be realizing any gains within a few years of acquisition, should you seriously try to figure after-tax gains. For example, someone who is 25 years old now and putting money into an Individual Retirement Account cannot possibly know how taxes on the gain in that account will be handled two generations on. However, the same person at the age of 55 can and should (probably with the aid of a financial planner or accountant) figure the tax impact of that year's account contributions.

What Are the Alternatives?

Figuring tax impacts and after-tax yields is essential if you are to make informed comparisons of investment alternatives, for without knowing the probable after-tax yields of investments carrying roughly the same degree of risk you cannot make sound investment decisions. For example, as of this writing a federally insured six-month bank certificate of deposit paying in the 10% range is a far better purchase than a short-term federal Treasury bill paying nearly 2% less. Yet only a few years ago, when bank interest rates were set by law at much lower rates, millions of investors bought the then-higher Treasury bills. In safety, they are true comparables, making the buying decision an easy one as the situation changed.

The main thing here is to understand both which investments are comparable in terms of risk and reward, and how the alterna-

tives fit into your own investment plans. A rather good investment in local real estate you know a lot about may be no riskier and
a good deal more lucrative than an investment in a sound stock,
but you may have to hold on to the real estate investment for some
years, while you can get out of the stock very quickly. If you want
to and can hold on, the real estate may be the investment for you,
but if you will need to use the money for a house or to pay for a
child's education next year, you may decide on the stock or some
sort of comparable security.

You must know about the risks, though, for what may look
like comparables — and may be sold as comparables — are not
necessarily comparables at all. A state-insured bank in California
may be willing to give you 1% more than a federally-insured bank
in your home state. That may look very good indeed, until you
realize that the state insurance is not at all as good as the federal
insurance, and that if the bank goes under you may have to wait
for years to get your money. If the California bank were federally
insured, it might be a good buy, but it is not. A high-flying new
industry stock may far outperform the blue chips, but that's no
reason to buy that stock; there may be no real comparison between the two stocks in terms of risk. Every seller will tell you
about potential rewards, but the risks are not always so obvious;
you must know about both risk and reward to measure alternatives.

How Fast Can I Get Out If I Want or Need to?

This is the very standard question of liquidity. For this discussion, we are assuming the context of a working financial system, rather than a deep economic crisis; what is easy to turn into
cash or other portable stores of value now might be unconvertible
then. We are not, then, discussing a situation in which the currency of a failed government might be worthless, the stock of its
companies wholly without value, and the promises to pay (embodied in bonds and other debt obligations) mere pieces of paper.
Rather, we are discussing how quickly individuals turn their
assets into cash or cash equivalents to suit their individual purposes in a working economic system.

The potential liquidity of an asset is an important question, both for personal planning purposes and for effective handling of assets in the financial marketplace. On the planning side, as indicated in the above example of real estate versus stock investment, too little liquidity can defeat your purposes. At the same time, making liquidity your primary concern is justifiable only when you really do think that you may need to turn assets into cash very quickly in the face of very adverse conditions. For those living in turbulent societies from which they may have to flee at any time, or in societies plagued by enormous inflation rates, liquidity and safety go hand in hand.

Too little liquidity can also trap you in specific investments and in kinds of investments that you might not like to continue to be in. The thinly traded or untradable stock resulting from exercise of a stock option, the real estate, oil and gas, or other limited partnership that is going bad but that you cannot sell, and the home that you must sell because of a transfer but should not because of the state of the real estate market, are all such potential traps. Too little liquidity can also trap you with assets and without cash, as so many business owners know. We will include the matter of liquidity in our discussion of the several kinds of investments.

Will I Have Too Many Eggs in One Basket?

This is the question of investment diversification, so dear to the hearts of mutual funds salespeople. It is for individuals sometimes a false question, because of the practicalities involved, though there is some limited value in diversifying among some kinds of investments.

As a practical matter, most managers — for that matter, most people in all trades and professions — inevitably have most of their eggs in one basket; if anything goes seriously wrong with that basket, all else changes, and much for the worse. That basket is your career. If you are out of work or disabled for any great length of time, you are likely to become effectively bankrupt — in fact, if not in legal form.

Even so, this is still a basically proper question to ask yourself, after putting aside the career-related and need-related assets. It raises the questions of risk and yield again, in a different way and sometimes about the kinds of investments that we would not otherwise question. It suggests risk, mostly, such as holding too much stock in your own company or in yesterday's blue chip, which is now a troubled company. Johns-Manville and Union Carbide come to mind as companies with special problems; so does U. S. Steel, a beset company in a troubled industry.

This question also brings up the matter of comparative yields. To keep your investment money safely in short-term and often government-insured vehicles is entirely right in very difficult and unstable times. To do so in better times may be unnecessarily conservative, and cost you a good deal in foregone income.

Do I Know How to Make the Move at the Least Possible Cost?

Finally, you should ask the question of cost. For some, the choice of a discount broker instead of a high-priced broker can mean a saving of hundreds and even thousands of dollars a year. For others, the search for a no-load or low-load mutual fund can mean similar savings and the freedom to move your investments about as you should, rather than holding them too long to avoid additional transaction fees and finally having to take big and unnecessary losses.

For some, a careful examination of costs can mean go or no go on the investment itself. For example, the real estate or other limited partnership in which the general partners are, in one way or another, managing to skim 25% – 30% off the top of your invested money before it really has a chance to begin earning for you is very likely to be a terrible investment. Unfortunately, there have been some such deals in the past few years, with many investors taking large losses that could have been avoided, had they carefully read and understood even the offering prospectus.

In some investment situations, the transaction costs are so high that any individual investor really understanding them should not for a moment even *think* about making that kind of investment. The oustanding modern example is the truly enormous set of transaction costs resulting from brokered commodities speculation. When you are facing "normal" yearly brokerage commissions amounting to one third of the entire amount of cash you have put into the account, and know that in many accounts yearly commissions actually amount to more than the amount of cash you have put into the account, it must surely be apparent that you are facing a deck stacked the wrong way. In the not so very long run, the only possible winner will be the broker.

It pays and pays and pays to search out the ways to make your investment moves at the least possible cost. This is a question that should always be asked.

5
Making the Most of Your Compensation Package

For purposes of lifelong financial planning, what you earn as pay for work is in some quite significant ways the least controllable of all the major economic factors in your life. Lifestyles, homes, educations, and a large body of savings and investment choices are substantially controllable matters, but pay for work is far more often seen as a matter of doing the best one can, always reaching for greater responsibility and the total compensation package that goes with doing the big job excellently. Nor are most of the other elements of the total compensation package — benefit packages, pension and profit-sharing plans, and the like — particularly controllable either, except to the extent that voluntary contributions to some plans may be allowed. You can negotiate some of them, such as moving costs and perhaps participation in stock option plans, as you negotiate pay on taking a new job, but only within a rather narrow range, for these items are relatively uniform matters of corporate policy, except at the very highest levels of the company.

Yet it is worth understanding exactly what your compensation is worth and how to make the most of it — current cash pay and everything beyond that. In today's rather confused, fast-changing world of corporate compensation, there are major tax-advantaged opportunities proceeding side by side with expensive, worthless, conspicuous-consumption fringes; superb insurance coverages that can turn into enormous traps for the unknowing; and long-term promises that may, in some instances, turn out to be impossible to keep. There is also a highly volatile tax and regulatory situation regarding several important aspects of the total corporate compensation package, with many changes proposed in Congress and many more in preparation. All that being so, many of the specifics discussed here will change, perhaps even between when we write and when you read — but the principles will not change, and what you should look for and seek to understand in your own compensation situation will not. Putting it a little differently, only the specifics can be expected to change; the main understandings, opportunities, and hazards should remain basically the same.

The Value of Cash

The first of these key long-term understandings is rather painfully obvious, yet at the same time needs restating again and again, for it underlies all the other choices. It is that you will need a lot of cash to make it come out all right in the end, to pay for everything and still have enough left over to do meaningful lifelong financial planning. Today, even modestly satisfactory lifestyles cost a good deal of money, when you put together all the costs associated with homes, cars, medical expenses, recreation, holidays, and day-to-day living. And when you add such extraordinary items as college educations and the care of aging parents, the bundle of cash you need can become shockingly large. It is. The figures for consumer credit in use and home mortgage delinquency continue to mount. Times have been difficult for over a decade and a half now, and many seemingly good incomes show it.

The real incomes of many managers and other corporate employees have suffered greatly in this period, in terms of both take-home pay and what seemed, not so long ago, to be reasonable expectations. Corporate incomes have been far more vulnerable to difficult times than those of some other groups; for example, independent professionals have been able to adjust fees, trim costs, and move better with the times than people employed by the many American companies faced with low profitability and obsolescence in this period. The numbers tell much of the story here, and it is easy to apply them to your own situation, once they are before you.

As of this writing, the Consumer Price Index, which was until some years ago called the Cost of Living Index, stands at 315. That means that, using 1967 prices as a base of 100, it costs 3.15 times as much to live now as it did then. There are some arguments about that, of course; for example, we believe that this index somewhat understates the real rise in living costs since the base year of 1967. If you are reading this book some years from now, that index will probably have risen. However, for purposes of the comparisons here, the 315 index figure will do; just bear in mind that as you are reading these pages, the comparisons are probably even worse than shown.

There is another adverse factor as well, even harder to quantify but very real. That is the enormous impact of hidden inflation in these past two decades, in which the quality and quantity of the goods and services we buy have been severely debased. We now "save" public money with repaving jobs that need to be redone almost as soon as they are completed, and build homes with two-by-fours that have long since ceased to measure two inches by four inches. Were the real impact of hidden inflation quantifiable enough to be added to the cost of living figures, that 315 to 100 might very easily become 400 to 100, or even more.

But even if we accept "only" the 315 to 100 relationship as a given, some truly terrible things happen to the real incomes of most managers and other corporate people. A salary of $31,500 in 1985 dollars becomes worth just $10,000 in 1967 dollars. A salary of $63,000, which is a very good salary today, is worth only $20,000 in 1967 dollars, which was not such a very good salary then. In truth, a manager who has spent the last 18 years fighting all the way up from $20,000 to $63,000 has in real terms — in cost-of-living terms — gained nothing at all, but rather has only kept up with the pace of inflation.

Once those very basic income numbers are understood, much else begins to make sense. Then it is easy to understand why a family with two "highly paid" managers can today live only about as well as a family with one well-paid manager lived back in the 1960s. Then we can understand why families with two young wage-earners and no children often cannot even afford the kind of house either one of them would have been able to buy then, and why there are so many tiny condominium dwellings, and tinny little cars, and why so many parents and children are effectively bankrupt after paying for college. No matter how the numbers are kept and adjusted in Washington, it is surely abundantly clear that the overwhelming majority of American managers and other corporate people are not able to buy nearly as much with their salaries as they could in the mid-1960s.

At the same time, corporate people today live in a far chancier world than the world of the 1960s seemed to be. Then managers felt they worked in a world of unlimited growth, and had a choice between staying put in a healthy, growing company at progressively higher real rates of income and then retiring to affluent golden years, or of aggressively moving from company to company, always upward, eventually to head a company in which they held a pile of valuable stock. Now, those are still perfectly sound and achievable goals, but for some the ultimate realities may be quite different. Now you must allow for the significant possibility of protracted unemployment that is not at all of your own making, of involuntary career change and lower pay in mid-career, of optioned stock that may turn out to be very nearly worthless in the end, and of pension promises that cannot be kept.

All the foregoing is by way of pointing out that, although compensation must for maximum personal benefit be seen as a total package, *never lose sight of the cash element.* For all but the highest paid of corporate people, cash now must be the main focus of all compensation attention. Putting it a little differently, *do* negotiate hard for and astutely use every meaningful noncash element of the compensation package, but *don't* trade cash for fringes unless they are very good and sure fringes indeed. Above all, think two or three times before trading cash for wasteful or meaningless fringes, or for long-term benefits that may very well not be there later on. As a matter of simple prudence, focus on cash now while welcoming tax-advantaged fringes now and tax-advantaged payouts later, for it is only cash now that can be relied upon to pay your bills, meet your coming obligations, and provide you with a growing lifelong stake. All the rest is important, no doubt about it; but cash is by far the most important element of the compensation package.

The Total Compensation Package

Looking at it from a company's point of view, the total compensation package must be seen as a body of pay, benefits, incentives, and promises for the future, all together aimed at providing adequate to excellent inducements for good people to come and stay with the company at the lowest reasonable cost. When the company or outside consultant engaged by the company explains that total compensation package to its employees, therefore, the explanation is almost inevitably couched in selling language, aimed at convincing employees that the package is an excellent one — not just competitive but considerably better than the packages offered by comparable companies. That is understandable; you cannot really expect a company to tell its employees that it has reduced its pension plan contributions so much that future payment promises are now in jeopardy, or that the company-dominated trustees of the plan have somehow managed to use large amounts of your retirement money to help the corporation's sagging building program or defend the company against a takeover.

Your view of the total compensation package must be rather a different one; all too often it must be arrived at by means of skeptical distillation of company claims. To truly see the compensation package, you must be able to assess:

- What you really have, right now, in pay after taxes.
- What you really have in investment funds derived from your employment, in money that you could walk away with, right now.
- What you are receiving right now in fringe benefits that you would otherwise have to buy yourself.
- What you are receiving in fringes that are essentially worthless to you, items you would not otherwise need or buy if they were not provided by the company.
- What you are promised for the future, how likely those promises are to eventuate, and what they may be really worth if they do.
- What you are gambling for and what risks, if any, you run with the gamble.

The Tax-Advantaged Portable Personal Pension Plan

If in any year you make a dollar and, in your top combined tax bracket, walk away with only half of that dollar, you are making only 50% of the top dollar in your earnings. If you make $50,000 that year, and walk away with an after-tax $40,000, you have made 80% overall, rather than 50%. But it is best to look at the top dollar, for if you can replace that half dollar with an untaxed full dollar, you have doubled it. And if you can do that with a dollar every year and compound that dollar tax-free, at least until some later date, the cumulative difference is enormous. That is clearly the essence of all tax-avoidance and long-term tax-advantage thinking; making that happen can mean the difference between having only a little and having quite a lot in your later years. It can and should be applied to all long-term financial planning; at present it is very easily and lucratively applied to the corporate incomes of those who can put aside even small portions of their salaries for long-term accumulation.

As of this writing, the **401 (k) plan** (also known as the salary reduction plan) allows employees to put up to $30,000 a year of pretax salary into the plan. The money in the plan accumulates tax-free until withdrawal, as in a personal IRA or Keogh plan. Many companies link these with company-contributory plans, putting a large additional multiplier into the tax-avoidance and accumulation picture. The ultimate benefit of all this can be enormous, for it is then possible to turn a 50-cent top dollar into as much as $2 from the start, with vastly larger compounding then occurring over the years. A simple and very conservative example: $4,000 in top combined-income tax-bracket dollars becomes $2,000 in your pocket. That $2,000, all invested and yielding an after-tax 10% will, in 30 years, become almost $35,000. The same $4,000 in salary, matched by a company contribution of $4,000, becomes $8,000, and at the same 10% for 30 years becomes $140,000. If you put that $2,000 into taxable investments, netting after-tax perhaps 7%, it will grow to only $15,000, and the difference is then as between $15,000 and $140,000. Clearly it is worth finding a way to put some of your salary aside and into such a plan, with company contributions here acting as a pay raise, as you put money into the plan. The net effect is that you have at least $4 for $1 in real take-home pay, or even $9–$11, and that all those dollars are thereafter rapidly growing tax-free.

One very great advantage of the 401(k) plan is that as it now stands you can withdraw money from it without penalty in case of "hardship"; and hardship is so loosely defined as to include home purchase and family college education cost needs. That is a big enough hole in the early withdrawal penalty provisions of the law as to make those provisions very nearly meaningless, and no serious bar at all to anyone seriously intent upon withdrawing money from the plan without penalty. You can also borrow money from the plan. In these important respects, the 401(k) is, for individuals, far superior to the IRA and Keogh plans, for in fact you are here creating with tax-free money a fund that grows tax-free and is for all major purposes entirely within your control. Anyone who can participate in a 401(k) plan should, as long as it is available. Here is one of the junctures at which all the lifestyle and major spending choices converge, for if you are a walking bankrupt, you will not have enough room in your economy to take advantage of what is truly an enormous accumulation opportunity.

These specific 401(k) plans are currently under attack and the rules are likely to change, but at present you own the money you have in them, with the money accompanying you when you leave employment or retire. Ten-year forward averaging on your taxes comes into play on lump-sum withdrawal, also the ability to roll them over into Investment Retirement Accounts (IRAs) and thereby keep them going until you are 70½, if you wish. We deal with IRAs further on in this book.

These plans offer you a substantial measure of control over the funds accumulating in them. In this, they differ very greatly from the great majority of corporate pension and profit-sharing plans, which are trustee-administered, with the trustees often very substantially influenced by the companies setting up the plans. In many instances the choices are somewhat limited, but most plans will offer at least money market fund, bond, stock, and other mutual fund alternatives, and sometimes also flexible annuity, deferred annuity, and life insurance premium payment possibilities. They will tend not to offer speculative opportunities, but when dealing with what should be seen as long-term tax-advantaged money, that is all to the good. If you want to speculate, do it with money that is not so extraordinarily well positioned for growth because of its intrinsic tax advantage.

An alternative offered by many small companies — an alternative to this and all other pension and profit-sharing arrangements, as well — is the **simplified employee pension** (SEP), which

offers even more control, though not without some potential disadvantages. This arrangement allows a company to pay substantial sums directly into your own IRA. Up to $30,000 or 15% of your
salary, whichever is smaller, can be paid in every year, with no
minimum contributions and withdrawals under standard IRA
rules. But, at this writing, these have no ten-year forward averaging provisions; that means a lump-sum withdrawal when you
leave a job is taxed as received all in one year, and therefore at a
very high rate.

This is a complex and changing picture, much affected by
current tax law and national deficit funding arguments; the main
long-term fact here is that the principle of the tax-advantaged
portable personal pension plan under your own control is in the
process of being established in these years, and particularly in the
forms of the 401(k), SEP, IRA, and Keogh plans. The names of the
devices will change, as will the specifics of those devices; the
principle can reasonably be expected to remain. That is an enormous new development on the American financial and economic
scene, providing managers and other corporate employees with
large new opportunities for effective personal financial planning.

Valuable and Not-So-Valuable Fringe Benefits

Some of the noncash elements of compensation are clearly quite
valuable. Chief among them are the **health care insurance** coverages, which in many instances include everything from basic hospital and surgical all the way through every cost related to any
kind of illness, including some coverages that are almost impossible to get on your own at any affordable price, such as dental,
doctors' office, and nursing home costs. Many companies even
supply quite meaningful disability insurance. As we discuss in
Chapter 6, there are substantial hazards connected with termination of such company coverages, hazards so great that under certain circumstances they can entirely sink you economically. But
while you have those coverages, they are very useful, for to buy
them on your own, as a sole buyer or as part of an outside-of-em-
ployment group (such as alumni, religious, or fraternal organiza-

tion), would probably cost $2,000 – $3,000 per year for family coverage. Even then, as we mentioned, some kinds of coverage you could not even buy on your own, so while you have them, some of these company coverages are particularly valuable. Also, not all the premiums you pay when on your own are entirely deductible from your income taxes, making the pretax dollars you would have to pay even higher than the seeming cost of the premiums. In this area, the value-of-total-compensation figures supplied by so many companies every year to their employees are, if anything, understated rather than overstated.

In one area, these health insurance coverages are sometimes negotiable, and that is on termination of employment. Should you face involuntary termination, by all means fight hard for continuation of full health benefits, if at all possible for a year after termination. That is particularly vital if you have not previously set in place some major medical insurance of your own, as that extra year of company coverage can then help you to avoid the extremely dangerous preexisting conditions trap, covered in Chapter 6. Even if you will, after termination, be covered by a spouse's health benefits, fight for your own coverage continuation. A year is a long time, and it is possible for a spouse's coverage — or a spouse — to disappear prematurely.

As you will also see in Chapter 6, we don't think terribly much of **company-supplied life insurance.** For long-term planning purposes you will have to buy life insurance on your own anyway, and just as much of it as if the company-supplied life insurance did not exist. That company coverage is worthwhile only if you can move from company group term coverage to individual term coverage on an absolutely guaranteed basis and at term life insurance costs on termination of employment or of the plan by the company. That is quite an unusual provision in a company group term life insurance policy, for the premium rates on the group term are developed from averages of the many lives covered, and individual policies require both different kinds of premium rates and often medical examinations, as well. A few life insurance companies have begun to offer policies with such guaranteed coverage and cost to companies employing 300 or fewer people, all white collar; should that kind of coverage spread, our view of company-supplied life insurance might be reevaluated.

You might see **continuing professional education** as another kind of insurance, one that ensures that you will be able to continue to grow and earn, as the world of American management very rapidly changes about you. Seen that way, company contributions to the cost of your continuing professional education are a valuable fringe, and one that you should take full advantage of. As of this writing, such contributions are, for tax purposes, completely deductible for the company and not income to you, but this benefit is currently under attack. To whatever extent the benefit continues to be available, use it.

There is also a considerable body of **perquisites** — "perks" — available in varying degrees to managers and other corporate employees, some valuable and some merely wasteful. Many of the costs associated with changing jobs are potentially valuable and often negotiable matters. On termination, items like severance pay and continuing office presence and support, as well as outside placement counseling services, are all worthwhile noncash elements of the total severance package. On initial hiring and internal transfer, such items as moving expenses, minimum price guarantees on homes sold, and mortgage subsidies are all valuable and often very substantial additional elements of compensation.

So, too, are such perks as financial counseling and professional association dues. Anything really useful the company pays for is a straight addition to your compensation package if it is something you could also get a tax deduction for; it is worth even more if it is something you would have to pay for out of after-tax dollars.

The operative word in the paragraph above is "worthwhile." A perk that satisfies nothing but the desire to consume conspicuously is impossible to see as worthwhile, and can serve only to bulk up total compensation costs needlessly, to nobody's benefit. For example, an expensive company-supplied car may seem like a wonderfully prestigious fringe benefit, until you figure out how much better you might be able to do running your own less expensive car, being reimbursed by the company for mileage and related costs, and facing no leased-rate additional taxable compensation on your earnings statement at the end of the year. There is nothing at all wrong with running a moderately priced several-years-old vehicle on company business. We are in a period in which the expensive new company car should be going the way of the three-martini lunch; lean companies and lean-and-hungry managers and marketers do not need those kinds of dubious benefits, any more than they really need country club membership and expensive business lunches, dinners, breakfasts, and between-meals drinks. All that is only foolish, unproductive overspending, the kind of thing that all too easily moves from business to the personal side of life, making conspicuous consumers out of previously quite sane people. Value the worthwhile fringes high; value the conspicuous consumption fringes at zero.

Do note that many of the worthwhile noncash elements of your compensation package are indeed negotiable on termination, and should be bargained for very hard. You do have a bargaining position, especially if you are being terminated for no demonstrable fault of your own, and that bargaining position can be a very strong one, based as it is upon fairness, past company practice, and the implied threat of litigation. As a practical matter, you have nothing to lose by pointing out that a proposed severance package is pathetically inadequate and that you are quite prepared to employ a strategy that calls for discussing the matter at very great length, every day, with everyone from your immediate superior to the chairman of the board. On that basis, you are quite likely to win substantial concessions.

On such termination, you should be prepared to fight hard for substantial severance pay; extension of your present full health, life, and any disability insurance package for one full year after the date of termination; a stretchout on the repayment schedule of any loans, including home down payments, you have from the company; an indefinite continuation of any guarantee the company has made on any mortgage or other loan; company-supplied out-placement assistance from an independent consultant; and continuing office presence and support for some months after termination.

How much severance pay you can secure will be a major matter to negotiate, and it is worth negotiating for much as you would negotiate pay on the way in. Generally, what is offered should not be considered enough; that the company is following a carefully worked-out formula, which it wishes to apply to many people being fired, should not mean a thing to you. Similarly, some of the noncash elements of the severance package, notably the insurance portions, are vitally important.

Pension Promises — Are They for Real?

Pension and profit-sharing plans are essentially out of your personal control. You may, of course, make a very general kind of evaluation that causes you to go with this company or that, in part because of pension or profit-sharing arrangements and your view as to how those arrangements are likely to work out for you in the long run. Between IBM and a faltering steel company, if direct pay is equal, the better choice is likely to be IBM, for its better prospects; not the least of these is that IBM is likely to be there to pay off on its long-term promises. In long-term personal financial terms, then, the main question here is how wise it is to rely upon long-term company pension and profit-sharing arrangements.

The answer to that question depends upon the kinds of arrangements your company has made, how much you have built up in the plan and for how long, how well the plan is funded, how healthy your company and industry are, and how long it will be before you reach the age at which funds are to be distributed to you. Putting it a little differently, some plans supply fund ownership quickly, while most do not, and the closer you are to ownership and actual control of funds, the surer you are of receiving them. Note that you may be able to borrow up to 50% of the value of your vested interest in pension and profit-sharing plans, if certain conditions are met. We suggest that you check with your company's pension consultants to see if this is feasible and advisable.

If you are participating in a profit-sharing plan, one that builds up funds in profitable years that are yours after a certain period of employment, then you may have a fund growing that is as much yours as any that would be under your own control, except that yearly contribution and investment decisions will be made by the company and the plan's trustees respectively. In those circumstances, termination of employment also can mean distribution of accrued profit-sharing proceeds, which you may then take as ordinary income with forward averaging for tax purposes, or roll over into another retirement plan or into an IRA. Here, as elsewhere, the tax law is changing, but the principle of tax-advantaged profit-sharing will remain the same. At this writing, you can also withdraw from profit-sharing plans without penalty, paying taxes on withdrawal amounts as ordinary income, and borrow from your own plan as well, with the interest you pay yourself going back to you on ultimate plan distribution. That can provide a peculiar tax-avoidance wrinkle when interest is deductible, but consult your accountant before trying it, as this aspect of the law is in flux.

"Qualified" corporate pension and profit-sharing plans— that is, those that are so organized as to meet federal legal requirements—are tax-advantaged plans. Company money put into them comes out of pretax dollars, and the funds created thereafter grow tax-free. When only company money is going in, the plan is a "noncontributory" plan; when employee money goes in as well, it is a "contributory" plan. That employee money is not tax-advantaged going in, as it comes out of after-tax income, but grows tax-free until distribution thereafter.

Such plans are federally regulated. The basic enabling act is the Employee Retirement Security Act of 1974 (ERISA), and the regulating federal agencies are the Internal Revenue Service, the Department of Labor, and for some kinds of plans also the Pension Benefit Guarantee Corporation, which has so far worked rather effectively to ensure that almost all previously made pension promises have been kept. That was not the case in earlier years; one notable instance concerned the now-defunct Studebaker Corporation, which left its pensioners high and dry when it went out of business, with very little money left in its pension fund.

The careful regulation and ensuring that is now the rule is all to the good. Even so, however, many adverse things can happen between pension and profit-sharing plan promise and ultimate fulfillment, so many that it is imprudent to rely upon these plans to provide large portions of your needed later-years income. Although a long-term pension plan may yield a great deal of capital and income in your later years, our view is that what we need to see us through our later years is a combination of the tax-advantaged portable personal pension plan, personal accumulation, and later-years work, along with some money from Social Security and corporate pension plans. People who rely upon a combination of

Social Security and corporate pensions to see them through — and all too many of us are doing just that — are making what can turn out to be a very serious error.

In the new world of American business, a world characterized by personal hazard, opportunity, and job volatility, rather than by safety and job longevity, managers and other corporate people move about a great deal. Not so long ago, it was a little unusual for someone to turn up with a resume showing five jobs in fifteen years, so unusual that further employability was put in question. Today, it is quite normal; everyone realizes that people do move about a great deal more than they used to, and often for reasons quite out of their control. However, it may also mean that you are in five long-term pension plans in fifteen years, and that none of them have "vested" — that is, you have no pension rights at all from any of them. Or you may have a total of five jobs in forty years, and still be vested in only two or three, with smallish amounts due to come to you from those pension plans later on in life.

On the other hand, you may stay put and the pension plan may leave you. In 1984 and 1985, the newspapers were full of stories about company plans that have been severely cut back or in some cases simply terminated. When terminated, people with vested benefits in them have continued to be covered — for as much as they had built up, which is often not very much. When cut back, the question of ability to pay, to keep promises solemnly made to employees, has been very seriously raised.

Even when plans were neither cut back nor terminated, people in many companies and industries must, in all prudence, have questions about how well promises made can, in the long run, be kept. It is all very well to point to the size of pension funds already in existence, but a company-dominated pension fund that uses a great deal of the fund's money to purchase the company's own building or to free up company funds to withstand possible raiders has just run the risk of seriously compromising the fund and its promises. The pension fund of a troubled company may be highly vulnerable to company manipulation. In difficult times for many companies and whole industries, that kind of manipulation is to be expected, some of it quite legal and none of it in the best interests of people depending on the funds for later-years income.

Aside from such manipulation, your pension fund can be very

badly mismanaged, and not at all illegally. Investment decisions are matters of skill and judgment, qualities conspicuously missing in all too many professional investment managers, who may woefully underperform in several financial markets at once. Throughout the 1970s and early 1980s, for example, many fund managers who insisted on putting substantial sums into the stock market made consistently less than they would have had they simply put the money into savings instruments. A fund that is understrength and may not be able to keep its payment promises should be strengthened by new infusions of money from its company, but whether or not that new money will be forthcoming when needed must always be a matter of conjecture.

Even if all goes well and the pension plan is well funded in terms of its promises, the nature of those promises may be misunderstood. Most pension plans pay fixed amounts to retirees on the basis of age, length of time with the company, or a combination of both; they are therefore called "defined benefit" plans. Sometimes, the defined amounts to be paid are set without relation to Social Security payments. Sometimes they are a fixed amount that includes Social Security payments, with the amount paid by the company going down if Social Security benefits go up; then the plan is described as "coordinated" with Social Security payments.

When the fixed or defined benefits paid are not "coordinated" with Social Security, they are subject to the same kind of erosion from inflation suffered by all fixed incomes. That can be very serious erosion indeed, as we will discuss more fully in Chapter 10 of this book. But when those benefits are "coordinated" with Social Security, the promised pension may be little more than a hoax, for indexed Social Security payments may become as large or very nearly as large as the promised combination of corporate and Social Security pension payments; in that case, the total payments will provide little more than a life of poverty for people with only those payments to rely upon in their later years. We are here describing only what has already happened to many retirees in the last decade and a half; it can happen in any period of high inflation and indexed Social Security payments.

Long-term corporate pension and profit-sharing plans can be wonderful sources of later-years income. For many, who have worked long for strong companies with meaningful plans and good funding, they are today — with Social Security and the income from lifetime accumulations — making it possible to live decently in retirement. That will be true tomorrow as well — for some. The problem is that you cannot really know whether or not one of those someones will be you, many years from now. You will need to create your own personal pension plans and accumulations, and to keep on earning, to be sure that it comes out all right in the later years.

Stock Options

Management compensation comes in several additional forms. There are various kinds of stock options, cash bonuses, stock bonuses, bargain stock and other bargain property arrangements, many performance compensation modes, and a series of variations on those and other themes. For long-term personal financial planning purposes, only the stock option should be considered here, as the others carry no element of choice with them. That your company chooses to provide additional compensation for individual or group performance may be good for its employees, but has nothing to do with their personal financial planning, since it is out of their planning control. But whether to take advantage of a potentially lucrative — or perhaps potentially too-expensive — stock option offer is very much part of such planning, quite often a major part. In aggregate, the corporate stock resulting from exercised options can become a very important part of your accumulated stake, *if* the stock was bought at the right price and has appreciated as hoped.

The principle of the stock option is that employees designated by the company — and only those employees — are offered the right to buy company stock for a stated time at a stated price. If the stock goes up between the time of the offer and the time of purchase, and stays above that purchase price until sold, the employee makes money on the exercised option. If the stock does not go above the offering price, the option lapses, unexercised. If the stock goes up, is bought, but then comes down, the purchasing employee may choose to sell at a loss or hold, hoping for a better price later, as in any other securities purchase.

Some of the specifics of the law may be changed in 1985 or 1986, but as of this writing there are two basic stock options generally offered to upper and some middle managers, and to some other corporate employees. They are the **incentive stock option** (ISO) and the **nonqualified stock option,** distinguished from each other by their differing tax treatment. For tax-avoidance purposes, the ISO is by far the better of the two, as there is no tax on the transaction until the stock is finally sold, and then at low capital gains rates. Should Congress change capital gains rates treatment, the no-tax-until-sale aspect alone will make the ISO still very attractive.

The nonqualified stock option generates an immediate tax on any gain realized on exercise of the option, and at full ordinary-income tax rates. If there is any gain on ultimate sale of the stock, that gain is also taxed as well, at capital gains rates. However taxed, though, this too is a very good additional compensation opportunity and can also be a means of getting and holding "a piece of the action," a meaningful share in your own company at what amounts to bargain prices.

If they are bargain prices, that is. There is no problem with stock that has not appreciated; failure to gain in a losing stock market was one of the main reasons stock options became quite unpopular as a compensation device in the 1970s, the other being the less favorable tax situation that existed before the 1981 tax law created the ISO. Nor is there any problem with stock that has appreciated a good deal and seems to have a very good chance of holding its value, at least until you can sell. Note that your ability to sell in a timely way may be limited by the terms of the option, or that the then-current tax law may require holding for a period to qualify for tax advantage on sale.

The problem comes with the option stock that may or may not hold its value; that problem is magnified if you must, as is common, borrow to be able to afford the stock purchase. For then if the stock goes down, you must either sell at a loss and find some way to pay off the balance of your borrowings, or hold losing stock while continuing to pay off your loans. That is what happened in the 1960s to a rather substantial number of corporate executives who thought they were simultaneously getting a meaningful piece of their own corporations and getting rich. They bought the fast-rising stock of their own companies in a rising market, putting their money where their careers and convictions were — and lost their shirts. For stock is stock, whether yours or someone else's, and markets fluctuate.

The stock-option decision must be made even more carefully than any other stock-purchase decision; for in any other stock you can buy one day and sell the next, while in optioned stock you must hold, and often for quite some time. If you do decide to take advantage of a stock option offer, consider the history of the stock, whether or not it is actively traded, and the market's estimate of its prospects; then add your own often-excellent insider's estimates. Also take into account any debt service on borrowing you may have to incur between purchase and ultimate sale. After that, it may still come out very well; then you should buy. Clearly, if it does not come out well, you should not buy; company loyalty is entirely superfluous when you are deciding to purchase a stock option.

The **stock appreciation right** (SAR) offer is an entirely different matter. With an SAR, you receive a sum — in stock, cash, or both — equal to the amount of increase in the market value of company stock during a specified period. You put up no money, and your exercise of the right is a foregone conclusion if the stock has indeed appreciated during that period. In most situations, you need not even borrow money to pay the taxes (at ordinary-income rates) due on the transaction in the year in which it occurs, for the company supplies cash for the tax payments as part of its additional compensation award. Stock appreciation rights can and often are also tied together with stock options, with the SAR cash payments helping to make it possible to exercise the stock options without borrowing.

6
Catastrophe Insurance

Although company-supplied insurance of several kinds can offer a good deal of premium-saving coverage during your years of employment, it is private insurance — insurance you buy yourself — that you should rely upon for long-term protection against the impact of personal catastrophes.

Very great risks can stem from reliance upon company-supplied insurance. Holes exist in company coverages, and massive traps can be sprung if you should become unemployed, change jobs, or decide to go on your own. You also always face the risk that your company will change its mind about the kind and size of the insurance benefits it will offer its employees, possibly leaving you high and dry if you should by then have become uninsurable in any important way.

We speak of insuring against the impact of catastrophe, because that is the essence of the insurance transaction, whether you are dealing with life, health, accident, fire, or casualty risks. Whether or not you insure yourself against the cost of replacing a broken window in your car is a minor matter, in which relatively small replacement and insurance premium costs are to be compared. Whether or not you choose to buy life insurance with a savings, interest-sensitive, or investment component is a more important matter, and can be a key investment planning decision, but it is still minor relative to the kinds of hazards that accompany being uninsured or greatly underinsured. Whatever else you do with your money, it is absolutely vital to use as much of it as you must to cover catastrophes, for otherwise all hopes, plans, and accumulations can be negated in a moment, with a single blow.

Life Insurance

Almost no greater tribute to the power of the seller's art exists than the habit of reflexively calling insurance that pays upon the death of the insured "life" insurance. It is death insurance, of course, and the money paid to beneficiaries lessens the economic impact upon them caused by the death of the insured.

One greater tribute, perhaps: all life insurance sellers of traditional contracts should at least daily thank the unsung genius who first hooked up life insurance and savings, developing policies called "whole life," "straight life," and "permanent life" (all synonyms) and all policies carrying "cash surrender values"—that is, savings buildups in the policies. By so doing, that genius made it possible for insurance companies to collect premiums far greater than those needed actuarially for funding their death insurance policies, investing the difference, and paying a small portion of the investment proceeds into the policies on behalf of their insureds, while pocketing the balance. The profits so spun off whole-life policies bearing cash surrender value made the companies very rich indeed. Millions of individuals still have these kinds of policies, and some are still being sold, although in this period the trend has decisively turned toward two other kinds: "term" life insurance, which is pure death insurance, without the cash surrender value, and to "universal life" or "variable life" policies, which bear far more favorable cash surrender values.

The interest rates paid on universal and variable life policies vary, usually yearly, and are based upon fluctuations in the value of the securities portfolio in which a substantial portion of premiums is invested. Their rate of return is generally set yearly by the insurance company, though in some policies it is tied to a stated index. In most instances, you can get your cash surrender money out for a small fee, in the $20–$30 range; or you can borrow it out for a small net interest charge, in the 2%–3% range. The cash surrender value builds up in the policy without yearly taxes being levied upon it, and is therefore greatly tax-advantaged. That is why it is often best to borrow your money out when you want it, rather than taking it out, for on takeout you may have tax liabilities.

For the life insurance industry, this is a period of great change, and new, highly competitive insurance policies emerge rapidly. There is no longer any need to buy disastrously low-paying traditional cash surrender value policies; indeed, they are offered less and less, and they become harder and harder to sell.

Today, you can buy quite inexpensive term life insurance or one of the many kinds of variable and universal life insurance policies. What type to buy should be one of the main matters you take up with your financial advisers.

Group Life Insurance

Companies buying group life insurance for their employees as a fringe benefit are buying term insurance, without cash surrender value buildups. These policies provide that employers will pay premiums on such insurance, and that beneficiaries named by covered employees will be paid specified death benefits, with coverage kept in force as long as the company chooses to keep it in force. These insurance contracts also usually provide for conversion of the individual life insurance should employment terminate or the company decide to drop the fringe benefit, but often with significant limitations (more on those limitations in a moment).

As of this writing, up to $50,000 of such insurance can be company-supplied, with premium payments handled for tax purposes as a company business expense and without the value of those premiums being taxable to employees. Premiums paid for life insurance over $50,000 must be taken as additional income by employees. It is also possible for employers to continue paying life insurance premiums for employees after retirement, as part of a retirement compensation package, although this is unusual and rather expensive for the benefit achieved.

Conversion over to an individual policy after termination of employment means converting over to a noncancellable life insurance policy with the same insurer, with no medical examination required. Unfortunately, most insurers require that conversion be to policies bearing cash surrender value, which are far, far more expensive than group life term policies; that makes the conversion "opportunity" something of a trap. It is a trap that acquires quite considerable significance if you find on termination and conversion that you have some kind of physical problem that makes you uninsurable by another company, so that you must take the conversion or nothing. And if by then you are in your fifties or even your sixties and still feel that you really need life insurance, the premiums you will have to pay for relatively small amounts of insurance will seem prohibitively high.

The main thing to bear in mind about company-supplied life insurance, though, is that *for practical lifelong planning purposes it is in most instances essentially a worthless fringe benefit.* For planning purposes, the essence of life insurance is that it must be something you have so firmly that nobody can take it away from you, short of national disaster and a change of governmental system; it is a very basic kind of catastrophe protection, underlying all else. But company-supplied life insurance that may disappear if the company chooses to discontinue it, or may be too expensive to continue if you leave the company, is scarcely such bedrock protection. Nor is $50,000 much life insurance any more.

In our view, it is best to ignore such company-supplied insurance altogether and buy on your own as much insurance as you feel you need, as early as you can. Whichever kind of policy you buy, let the insurance-buying decisions proceed without reference to any company-supplied life insurance you have. Group life is properly seen as a kind of potential extra for beneficiaries, rather than part of the stuff of bedrock protection.

The only exception to this rule is the kind of new policy previously mentioned, which provides for full conversion to individual coverage with no additional medical examination or change in premium cost, and which is usually accomplished by originally issuing the insurance as a group of individual policies, rather than as a single group policy. In such instances, the company-supplied life insurance does indeed become part of a portable personal lifetime pension plan and benefits package.

How Much Life Insurance Should You Buy?

No fixed set of rules governs how much life insurance you should buy, nor are there even terribly good rule-of-thumb guidelines in this area. The minimum amount of life insurance you should carry will depend upon your anticipated needs, your estimate of how the course of inflation is likely to proceed, and your guess as to how insurable you may or may not be later on, when needs and inflation estimates may be different. All this adds up to suggesting that it is wise to err on the side of buying a good deal of insurance in the early years, while you are entirely insurable, at the best rates being offered, rather than running the risk of not being able to buy as much as you may need later. For the truth is that, if you have even a small family to protect and the rate of inflation rises even modestly over a period of decades, the amounts of insurance you need are quite large; but they need not be expensive to secure, especially at the younger ages.

For example, a 30-year-old manager with $50,000 in company-paid life insurance and no plans to marry may feel that there is no particular reason to buy any additional life insurance at all. Perhaps; but five years on, that 30-year-old may be married, have one small child and another on the way, be the sole support of the family, and have become uninsurable. Then, at best, it will have to be the company insurance and nothing else, and $50,000 is pathetically inadequate in those circumstances. No matter how you look at the probable course of inflation and education costs, a surviving parent with two very young children and perhaps not very much in the way of marketable skills is likely to be in deep trouble if the family's main support dies young and terribly underinsured. A young family with two children can look forward to as much as $100,000 in college costs in later years, and the surviving parent can reasonably expect to need $10,000–$20,000 a year *more* than can be earned for a decade or more. In this situation, $500,000 in life insurance would not be too much; $250,000 should be seen as minimal.

On the other hand, the same family 30 years on will probably need much less life insurance. There are likely to be two wage-earners and far more assets then; and children will have grown up, been educated, and gone out on their own. At age 60, as little as $40,000–$50,000 of life insurance may do very well, mainly for beneficiaries to have liquid cash and possibly for estate tax purposes. Estate tax questions have become much less important for most people since the value at which estates become federally taxable has gone up very greatly and there is no estate tax paid upon the death of the first spouse. However, it is still possible to die with a million-dollar business or a piece of real estate constituting the main portion of your estate, causing your survivors to have to sell at big losses, unless you have given them some liquidity in the form of life insurance proceeds. You cannot always plan to provide that kind of liquidity in other forms, either, for unanticipated personal costs and more general economic conditions can frustrate your plans at a time when you are in no position to do much about the situation.

Clearly, then, it is prudent early in life to buy more insurance than you necessarily "need" at the moment of purchase, and equally prudent to reevaluate your insurance needs every step of the way thereafter, anticipating that you will need less as the years go by and your responsibilities are met. Term insurance lends itself to that kind of reevaluation, going up in price as you age. A one-year renewable policy is usually the least expensive kind of term insurance.

Some life insurance is literally thrust upon us, by the way, usually in the form of life insurance guaranteeing payment of our loans. Mortgage, personal loan, and credit line life insurances are all examples. They are there, but should certainly never be figured in as part of long-term life insurance planning, for as the loans are paid off, the insurance disappears.

The truth is that most of us simply cannot afford to buy anything but term insurance, if we are to buy as much as we really need. The truth also is that those who buy cash surrender value, interest-sensitive, or variable life insurance all too often find themselves uneasily carrying considerably less life insurance than they really need. That underinsurance, rather than comparative costs and investment yields, is the main hazard posed by purchasing anything other than term life insurance. The main slogan of the term life insurance seller was for many years "Buy term, and invest the difference." Today, it should be "Buy term, so that you can buy as much as you really need." Further, "Buy universal or variable, if you also want to use your policy as a tax-advantaged investment instrument."

To protect your survivors as best you can against the economic impact of your death is basic to any lifelong financial planning. To join an investment component to that basic insurance is entirely optional, and the decision to do so should be thought of purely as an investment decision, with such investment aspects as net after-tax yield, liquidity, and safety your prime considerations. The investment decision has absolutely nothing to do with the insurance decision here, for you can protect yourself with insurance without also treating the insurance policy as an investment instrument.

As an investment, a conventional straight or permanent life insurance policy has very little good going for it. If searching for its positive features, you can fairly say that it offers forced savings for those so unable to handle the financial side of life that they must seek forced savings — but that is scarcely a recommendation for those who have purchased and are now reading a book on lifelong financial planning. It also accretes tax-free (at the low rates set by the insurance companies) until and if you ever cash in the value in the policy — but so do IRA and Keogh accounts, and at far greater rates of accumulation. You can also borrow at low rates against accumulated cash surrender values — but only because the companies make so much money on the investment returns they don't pass on to you.

Those are rather dubious positives, and the negatives far overbalance them. With a conventional life insurance policy that has a cash surrender value, you are locked into a low-paying, long-term investment in a period characterized by wide fluctuations in available interest rates, and in which the main requirement is to stay short term, medium at most. If you already have such a policy, you may have to stick with it, should you have by now become uninsurable due to health problems. If you are healthy, though, you may find a new policy less costly because of the application of new life expectancy tables, especially for non-smokers. And healthy or not, it might be wise to check the amount of cash surrender value built up in the policy and the rate of interest the insurance company charges on borrowings from those cash values. There may be better after-tax yields available, even taking into account the interest you would have to pay, and you may want to borrow out much of your cash surrender value.

People with substantial assets may want to take advantage of the new universal life and variable policies, sometimes mixing term coverage with these to reach optimum coverage and desired investment objectives. If you are quite affluent, you should certainly also take your particular planning situation to a competent financial planner, who will help you develop the right insurance plan within the context of a total financial plan.

Annuities

An annuity is an individual or group life insurance contract between an insurance company and a policyholder in which specified sums are payable either at times set by the insurance contract, or on the prior death of the annuitant (if that occurs first), but to which any mortality considerations are incidental; the essence of the contract is its underlying interest, investment, and tax-advantage considerations.

An annuity is in reality a tax-advantaged investment fund in which yields and capital appreciation accumulate tax-deferred, while an exclusion allowance can shield annuitants choosing some kinds of settlement options against the full impact of taxes on payout. Should the annuity be paid to beneficiaries on the death of the annuitant, its proceeds bypass probate and its associated costs. Current law also permits annuity beneficiaries to roll over annuity proceeds or in certain plans to continue the insurance contract, thereby retaining the original tax-deferred benefits of the deceased annuitant.

Annuities may be purchased by individuals or by such tax-qualified plans as corporate pension, profit-sharing, and thrift plans; as IRA and Keogh plans; and as tax-sheltered instruments available to employees of educational institutions and nonprofit associations. Purchase of an annuity under any of the tax-qualified plans provides an income tax deduction in the year of purchase (as well as tax deferrals until receipt of proceeds), bypass of probate, and rollover opportunities for the beneficiaries of deceased annuitants.

Annuities can be purchased as single lump-sum contracts or as add-on contracts, in which payments are periodically added, in varying amounts.

Until the early 1970s, the overwhelming majority of annuities were wonderful sources of profit for the life insurance companies selling them and disasters for those who bought them. Many who have retired in the last decade and some now about to retire have for many years held annuities on which they have faithfully paid premiums and which have been accreting in value at a ruinous 2%–4% a year, while inflation raged and available interest rates soared. In real dollars, the losses to such annuity holders have been enormous, often spelling the difference between modest comfort and poverty in their later years. Plainly, that kind of annuity has no place in astute financial planning even when, as now, the companies pay somewhat higher returns on money invested.

More recently, however, new forms of annuities have developed. Modern annuity owners are now able, as specified in their contracts, to call for return of all or part of their annuity fund monies almost at will. Modern annuity policies now carry fully market-competitive rates of interest. And front-load sales charges on annuities have all but disappeared, so that annuity funds now begin to earn money as soon as they are paid over to the insurance company. For these reasons, the annuity has once again become a widely used instrument in financial planning, seen by many as a safe, high-yielding, tax-advantaged, and essentially liquid investment.

Modern annuity contracts come in two basic forms. The first is the **deferred annuity,** in which premiums form an investment fund that grows tax-free in the years after the money is paid in and before the annuity legally matures. The insurance company holding the annuity contract and its fund guarantees annuitants a specified rate of return, which is usually set yearly but in some instances may be set for as long as four- or five-year periods. Companies competitive in the one-year-guarantee area normally pay a high first-year guaranteed return, usually paying 50 to 100 basis points (0.5% to 1%) higher than comparable term bank certificates of deposit and Treasury bills. Companies whose interest rates are guaranteed for as long as four or five years normally offer yields 0.5% to 1% lower than contracts offering the one-year guarantee. Some companies do not fix interest rates in this way, but tie yields to specified indexes or instruments such as Treasury bills.

However interest rates are established, generally such deferred annuity contracts have no front-load sales charges (that is, charges on initial purchase of the annuity). They generally do assess back-load charges (that is, charges on cashing in the annuity before maturity), normally going from 7% down to zero over seven years; waive all sales charges on the death of the annuitant; and waive sales charges on withdrawal of 10% of the investment fund every year. Contracts usually provide that if a company's interest rate falls below a specified figure (usually 1% to 2% below the original yield) in future years, all monies can be withdrawn without sales charges. This is usually called a **bailout rate.**

The second form of annuity contract is the **variable annuity,** in which the value of the investment fund that is the annuity varies with the value of the investments in the fund, and the annuitant chooses the basic kind of investment for the annuity fund. An annuitant may elect to take a fixed rate offered by the company, but may also choose to invest in any of a wide range of stock, bond, and money market mutual funds as well as in Treasury bonds.

There is considerable variation in sales charges among companies offering such variable annuities, as well as up to ten-year back-load charges and money withdrawal restrictions. There are also in some instances additional death benefits and therefore mortality costs built into the contract. Annuitants may also borrow money from these annuity funds, usually at favorable interest rates. And the annuity funds fluctuate with the fortunes of their underlying investments; that is the nature of the investment made here.

There are hazards in annuities, as so amply demonstrated by the Baldwin-United situation, in which many policyholders lost a good deal of their invested money when it turned out that the company could neither meet its guarantees nor repay all the money it was holding. You may want to consider putting some of your money in an annuity, but you should buy one only from a very large national insurance company or from a company licensed in a state that tightly regulates its insurance companies, such as Pennsylvania or New York. You should under no circumstances buy an annuity from a small or even medium-size company headquartered in a lightly regulating state like Texas, no matter how attractive the rates of interest offered.

Life Insurance: Some Important Details

Net yields and tax deferrals on modern annuity policies may make them attractive buys, as long as you take proper care as to the companies from which you purchase them. On all of them, you will want to look at the variations offered, in such areas as guaranteed interest rates, track records on the rate of return on investments, front-load and back-load sales charges on purchase and liquidation, the several kinds of settlement options, and the terms of conversion into an immediate annuity. These are the kinds of questions to bear in mind when approaching any decision to purchase life insurance, and today they are more important than ever, for in the new financial marketplace a large number of new kinds of insurance arangements are now being generated. Competition is keen between the several kinds of insurance and investment sellers, with many new kinds of life insurance and investment packages being developed for sale by banks, securities firms, and insurance companies. Low-paying whole life and annuity policies are now being replaced by financial sellers with higher-paying and much more complex combined insurance and investment arrangements, all developed with both investment and tax aspects in mind.

Several other choices are connected with the purchase of a life insurance policy. One important choice is designation of one or more beneficiaries. If you own the policy, the choice is yours; if someone else owns it, the choice is theirs, as this choice goes with ownership. The only requirement of the insurance company is that any beneficiary named must have an insurable interest in your life, meaning that beneficiaries must demonstrably suffer loss because of your death. With that single restriction, the policyowner can name and change beneficiaries at will, except when the beneficiary is named by the owner as irrevocable. That is sometimes done when the life insurance purchased is funding a legal obligation, such as a loan repayment.

A number of possible choices revolve around how insurance proceeds are to be paid. Proceeds paid all at one time are called **lump sum payments;** the installment modes of payment are called **settlement options.** Sometimes, insurance policy proceeds might well be left for the insurance company to pay in installments, rather than all at once, as when beneficiaries are incompetent or thought to be irresponsible, or because of divorce and separation agreement terms.

A settlement option is legally irrevocable, and you cannot force the company to change this method of payment once it is chosen. Most companies provide up to 30 variations of settlement options in their contract. Unless you have a specifically defined objective for choosing a settlement option, it is wise to choose the lump-sum distribution. This gives you immediate control of all the funds and the opportunity to fine tune the use of your money; it also allows you to consider other types of fixed-dollar investments that are equally safe and tax-advantaged and may pay a higher yield than the settlement option rate being offered.

On the other hand, in the rapidly changing competitive financial services industry some life insurance companies are offering short-term settlement options, such as five years, with a relatively high rate of interest while the money is paid out in installments over the five-year period. With a tax-favored annuity exclusion allowance protecting your taxable proceeds, this may be an excellent option.

It is wise to take the "waiver of premium" option on insurance policy purchase. That involves paying a little more so that the insurance company will pick up premium payments as long as a policyowner is disabled, even if that is for the remaining life of the policy, with premium payments beginning again when disability ends. In insurance this is caled a **prior option**. It is usually available for purchase through age 55; the "rider" and its cost usually terminate after age 60.

Another such prior option is the purchase, for a small additional premium, of a guarantee that the insurance company will sell you tated additional amounts of insurance for a stated time beyond your original purchase, without medical examination or any other kind of qualification. Not very many insurance companies offer this choice, but it may be well worth your while to take it, if offered.

Getting Around Uninsurability

People with substantial medical problems may find it very difficult to buy any life insurance at all in standard ways and from safe companies. You can always find a company somewhere in the country that will take your premium money, but that is scarcely the same as being insured, if the insurer is a fly-by-night, poorly capitalized and lightkly regulated company. Putting it a little differently, a small company that takes on a lot of por risks is hardly likely to be there to pay beneficiaries when the time for payment comes. What you must look for are insurance arrangements that merge a whole range of risks, as does group life insurance, or arrangements for which you perhaps pay more but with companies that are quite likely to be there when needed.

For some people, shopping around will turn up a sound insurance company willing to take you on as a standard risk, meaning at standard rates. A borderline physical problem that causes three companies to turn down your insurance application may cause a fourth company no difficulty at all. Standards vary; at any given time, there will be some perfectly sound companies that want business badly enough to set a somewhat elastic standard. You may also encounter a company that has had different mortality experience than most or that is experimenting with new standards.

Few companies have very elastic standards, though. If you have a substantial problem, you are unlikely to secure insurance at standard rates. You may, however, be able to secure good life insurance as a substandard risk, meaning that you will have to pay higher rates for your coverage, and probably that the amount of insurance you are able to buy will be more limited than you would like. But substandard risk coverage is far better than no insurance at all, and within the bounds set by the policy, the insurance will be there if needed.

In some states, people who are otherwise uninsurable can buy **guaranteed issue policies.** These are rather high-cost policies that will pay on death but only within conditions specified in the policy. They are characterized by long waiting periods and other limitations, but are worth examining if available in your state. For example, a contract offered by some companies will not pay the face amount of the contract if death occurs within three years of the date the policy was purchased, but will pay the beneficiary all premiums received plus interest in those circumstances. After three years, the face amount is paid upon death.

It is also often possible to find group life coverage through alumni, fraternal, and professional groups, requiring no medical examinations and with reputable insurance companies. There may be limitations on the amounts of insurance you can purchase and some waiting periods, as well, but this kind of life insurance is one of the best ways to cover yourself if you are otherwise uninsurable.

Group life coverage also applies when you are covered by mortgage and other loan insurances, or when you accept group insurance offered through such sellers as credit card companies. For those who encounter difficulty in securing adequate life insurance coverage, the whole process becomes a matter of piecing together adequate coverage in a number of unconventional ways, rather than going to a broker and buying a single policy. But especially for those with medical problems, developing that kind of piecemeal approach can be a vitally necessary aspect of long-term financial planning, and worth doing well.

Choosing the Right Life Insurance Company

The entire life insurance transaction rests upon your belief that the company will be there to pay your survivors when you die, or pay you cash benefits contracted for during your lifetime. In reliance upon that promise, you are willing to pay premiums for what may be decades. If that promise turns out to be worthless, then a bedrock protection upon which you and those you seek to protect rely is not really there; in that case all plans may be negated, and along with them your future and the futures of those you love.

Choosing a safe insurance company therefore becomes a very basic kind of priority, and watching that company to see that it continues to stay safe becomes one of the quite mundane, absolutely necessary things we do in our lifetimes. Insurance companies understand that, and spend a great deal of their advertising money creating big, safe images to help them sell insurance more successfully. Many state governments understand that, too, and require strong capitalization, while strictly regulating insurance companies licensed to do business in their states. Some state governments do not; Texas, for example, was long delinquent in insurance company regulation. The federal government does not regulate insurance companies; that is why you must take a company-by-company approach to insurance safety. Ask your agent to provide the Best's insurance evaluations of the companies you are being asked to consider.

When you buy life insurance, be very sure to buy it from a company that is both tightly regulated and strongly capitalized. That means buying it from a major national company, long since licensed to do business in all the highly regulated states; or from smaller companies headquartered in states like Pennsylvania and New York, which view regulation as part of necessary protection of state citizens. Don't buy life insurance — *any* life insurance, no matter how cheap or how cleverly advertised — by mail across state lines, or from companies you do not know in states that regulate lightly. The small Texas or Arizona company that offered such favorable rates or so obligingly sold you life insurance without a medical examination when you had a hard time buying it anywhere else is not likely to be there decades later, when your survivors need the proceeds for which you have been paying premiums for so long. For that matter, the company may not be there next year, if your death is untimely; some of those little, almost unregulated companies come and go with startling speed. Buy your life insurance from reliable companies, carefully looking at company size and headquarters location.

Health Insurance: Protecting Yourself and Your Family

Medical care costs continue to rise, far more steeply than inflation. We live in a time when even modest medical problems can generate substantial medical bills, and major illnesses routinely generate tens and even hundreds of thousands of dollars of medical expenses. When the costs of an uncovered or underinsured illness can be a far greater personal catastrophe than the illness itself, then health insurance is catastrophe insurance.

Health insurance costs accurately reflect the accelerating medical costs underlying them. As of this writing, merely adequate health insurance for a family of four, including only Blue Cross-Blue Shield hospital-surgical coverage, major medical, and modest disability coverage, will cost $3,000 – $4,000 a year.f Excellent coverage, such as that provided by some corporations for their employees, going far beyond the basic coverages to include some doctors' and dentists' bills, hospital indemnity payments, and psychiatric care, can cost the companies offering them a good deal more.

In those circumstances, it is entirely understandable that many managers and other corporate employees figuratively throw up their hands, rely upon company health insurance coverage, and hope for the best. Most figure that, at worst, they will at some times in their lives be unemployed for brief periods, and will then need to cover themselves and their families by interim converson of corporate plans into individual plans, followed by fresh company coverage when new jobs are started. People often have some vague disquiet about what might happen if unemployment were to last long, and about how much coverage they might be able to get on such a corporate-to-personal conversion; and of course they realize that they would have to really do something about it all if they ever went on their own. But that's all—just disquiet. For all too many managers, personal health insurance purchase is an issue quickly shoved under the rug. If you get sick, the company insurance will cover it; what is there to discuss?

There is a good deal to discuss, actually. Because sometimes the company coverage doesn't cover, and sometimes the converted company insurance doesn't coverenough, and sometimes you may be on your own, high and dry because your health makes it impossible to buy the insurance you desperately need just when you need it most. All those situations can turn into personal disasters, destroying all assets and negating all plans; all can happen, if you misperceive the extent to which company coverage protects you, and when.

Basic Hospital-Surgical Insurance

Many millions of corporate employees are covered by company-supplied basic hospital-surgical plans; Blue Cross-Blue Shield is the most widely used. When your basic company coverage is from Blue Cross-Blue Shield, you need not worry about what may happen if you leave your company, since Blue Cross-Blue Shield provides for transfer over to other group and individual Blue Cross-Blue Shield plans without medical examinations and without the insertion of any noncovered waiting periods for possible preexisting conditions.

Many company plans, however, are far better than the basic Blue Cross-Blue Shield coverage, providing for such benefits as payments for doctors' office visits, dental care, psychiatric care, drugs, and outpatient and posthospital care. Some simply pay for substantialy all health care costs, after a small yearly deductible amount employees pay out of their own pockets.

All that is very much to the good for those currently employed, but can develop substantial problems for those who for any reason leave the company. You can usually arrange for continuation of your previous company's health coverage after employment ceases, but generally at very high cost and with severe benefit limitations. You can, when on your own, buy Blue Cross-Blue Shield basic individual coverage without medical examination, but you may not be covered for preexisting conditions — medical problems in existence before you enter the Blue Cross-Blue Shield plan — until a substantial waiting period has elapsed.

When you go directly from one job to another, or are unemployed for only a month or two, you may have no interim period at all between company coverages, as there is usually a grace period between termination of employment and termination of company-supplied health insurance. But even when that is so, there may be a gap in coverage as far as preexisting conditions are concerned — a serious matter.

For example, you may suffer a minor heart problem, short of a heart attack, while employed by a company with a wonderful health care plan that pays for almost everything even remotely connected with the problem. You may leave that company, find the health care continuance available very expensive and coverage laughably inadequate, and move directly to Blue Cross-Blue Shield coverage, without medical examination. Six months later, still unemployed, you may have a heart attack, and find that neither your old company insurance nor your new individual insurance will pay your enormous medical bills. One claims that the heart attack is not a continuation of the old heart condition and the other invokes the preexisting-conditions clause to deny coverage.

Someone going directly from one company to another, without any seeming break in coverage, may face precisely the same situation. This matter of being trapped by preexisting-conditions clauses poses a major hazard, even when dealing with basic medical coverage, for in these years even a brief hospital stay, without surgery, can result in several thousands of dollars' worth of bills. Two weeks in a hospital, a relatively inexpensive operation, and some necessary postoperational care, can easily come to $5,000 – $10,000.

If the basic coverage your company supplies can be transferred over to individual Blue Cross-Blue Shield coverage, without medical examinations and without preexisting conditions traps, then you need do nothing about additional basic coverage.

If there are two wage-earners in a family, both covered by company-supplied basic insurance, but not transferable to Blue Cross-Blue Shield, the preexisting conditions trap may be less of a potential problem; but do *check your insurances to see if family coverage picks up without a waiting period.*

If you are alone, or are the family's sole wage-earner, or if both covered wage-earners plan to leave their jobs at the same time and coverage is not transferable to Blue Cross-Blue Shield, then it will be wise to seriously consider buying the least expensive individual Blue Cross-Blue Shield coverage available. Some people will do this; most won't. For a single, highly employable manager in excellent health, the additional protection may not be worth the expense. Putting it a little differently, such a person may decide to self-insure for basic — but only basic, not major medical — coverage of preexisting conditions in these circumstances.

On the other hand, a sole breadwinner with a large family may reasonably take quite a different view, for then the prospect of being uncovered for even a moment may be appalling. And if you have serious medical problems, you will certainly be wise to buy basic Blue Cross-Blue Shield coverage as soon as you know the problems exist, go through any waiting periods for preexisting conditions, and carry the insurance from then on — regardless of any company-supplied insurance — except when you are employed by a company with basic Blue Cross-Blue Shield coverage.

Major Medical Insurance

In the area of major medical insurance, which continues to pay after basic hospital and surgical coverages have been exhausted, uninterrupted coverage is an absolute must. There is no transfer without waiting periods for preexisting conditions and under some circumstances you may have to go through a medical examination when you are no longer able to pass one.

Insuring against the catastrophic impact of huge uninsured or underinsured medical costs is one of the cornerstones of all modern financial planning. Given the high and rising costs of medical care, it is no longer possible to seriously consider handling major medical costs out of personal assets. Even the very rich, who might be able to do so, would be badly advised to try; prudent asset management demands major medical insurance purchase.

Today, a single heart problem can result in several heart operations, each costing tens of thousands of dollars, which with associated costs can total hundreds of thousands of dollars. A single protracted bout with cancer, complete with operations, chemotherapy, and long hospital stays, can easily aggregate a half million dollars in medical bills. A long stay on life-preserving machines can all too easily build up a million dollars in costs. Uninterrupted major medical coverage is a lifetime must, and that coverage has to have a very high top limit to meet possible needs. You can self-insure to some extent, by taking rather high deductibles and thereby somewhat reducing premium costs, but it is essential to cover yourself for medical problems that may take you right up into the million-dollar range for single illnesses.

We say that it is essential *to cover yourself* because it is so extraordinarily dangerous to rely upon company-supplied major medical insurance for lifetime coverage and financial planning. Here is what can happen if you rely solely on company coverage:

• You can be completely covered by company-supplied major medical, leave the company at some later time, after you have become uninsurable, and be entirely unable to purchase any new major medical insurance, because you cannot pass the medical examination required for any meaningful individual major medical coverage. In the overwhelming majority of instances, you will also find that the continuation individual major medical insurance you are able to buy — if any — from your previous employer's insurer is pathetically inadequate and terribly expensive. In those circumstances, you are very badly underinsured for major medical problems; at best, you may be able to buy some sort of "excess major medical" policy not requiring a medical examination through an alumni, fraternal, or professional organization, which picks up coverage after you have paid $15,000 – $25,000 of the bills for each illness, and also probably has waiting periods for preexisting conditions. You may also purchase major medical coverage directly from an insurance company. Look for a "guaranteed renewable" contract, although the premiums will be higher and the medical requirements may be more stringent. This is a particularly dangerous situation for people who are unemployed for any considerable length of time, or who have decided to go out on their own, outside company benefit umbrellas altogether.

• You can leave the company, immediately go to work for some other company, and still fall into the preexisting-conditions trap, no longer being covered by your previous employer's insurance and not yet being covered by your new employer's insurance, which requires waiting periods — usually one year, and sometimes more — before preexisting conditions will be covered. In those circumstances, you are actually *not covered* for preexisting conditions, and that is a hole in your basic catastrophe protection big enough to bankrupt you, no matter how strong your financial position seems to be. Check that one out, by discussing it with whoever handles your company's health insurance plans. The answers you get may send you out to buy some individual major medical coverage tomorrow.

• You may not leave your company at all, but instead find your company leaving you as far as some essential health insurance protections are concerned. In many sick industries, and in many companies even in healthy industries, top managements are scaling back the whole benefits package. In particular, and because of the rapidly escalating cost of medical care as reflected in medical insurance costs, they are cutting back on health insurance benefits. For example, a company that decides to save some money by cutting the top per-illness limit on its major medical insurance can very easily leave you underinsured in the crucial upper-limit area. Then, when you move to fill the gap by buying excess major medical, you are likely to be vulnerable to the preexisting conditions clause for a year or more. If really major problems arise in the interim, you could be wiped out.

At present, there is no really good solution to all this, short of national health insurance, and that does not seem very likely in the near future. Health care costs continue to rise very sharply, and the shambles that is our private major-medical coverage system gets worse each year. The only real, though expensive, solution is to buy a major medical insurance policy of your own as early in life as possible, getting by the medical examination hurdle while you are healthy, and to hold that policy in force indefinitely, either until society makes different arrangements possible or until age brings existing Medicare arrangements into play. Even then, you are unlikely to drop the policy entirely, but will make other, less expensive arrangements in light of whatever government-subsidized insurances are then available.

Alternatively, and less expensively, you may decide to buy only excess major medical insurance, reasoning that you can rely upon some kind of company coverage for most or all of your working life and are willing to take a chance on the kinds of potential gaps in coverage we have discussed. But life is long, goals change, and even if your goals do not change you may be out of work involuntarily for longish periods of time. If you recognize the need for major medical coverage and the potential gaps, it is wisest to buy meaningful coverage, and that is especially so for those who have the needs of other family members to worry about.

When you do buy major medical coverage on your own, be sure, just as with life insurance, to buy it from a large, well-known, tightly regulated company, one that is likely to be there when you need it. Buy it on a "guaranteed renewable" basis, meaning that the company will not be able to cancel it as long as you keep current on your premium payments and can raise your premium rates only if all other premium rates for that whole class of policies are also raised. That will not protect you if the company decides to pull up stakes in your state — and that has happened; that is why it is also so important to buy any individual policy from a large national company that is likely to stay in business in every state.

It may be possible to buy your major medical insurance through a well-established alumni, fraternal, or professional group. If so, seriously consider doing so, for the rates, the coverage, and the probability of keeping continuing coverage may all be better. In some instances, that coverage may also be on a no-examination basis, although with a preexisting-conditions clause, and for some preexisting conditions the waiting period may be one to three years. That is not the kind of gap in coverage you want, but if you are starting now and have a medical problem, it is a lot better than nothing. Be careful to buy such group coverage through a very well-established organization, though, for if their insurer drops out of the field in your state, they will be in a better position to arrange for a new insurer to take over the group coverage. A small group may find it impossible to keep its plan going, leaving you without coverage and unable to buy it on an individual basis.

Should any major medical insurance you buy top out at less than $1,000,000 per covered illness, by all means try to buy an excess coverage policy. If it is from the same insurance company, it may be called a "piggyback" policy, because it starts where the main major medical coverage ends. Such policies are relatively inexpensive, because they are so seldom used that the risk is spread very widely over those insured. Excess coverage policies are quite often available through organizations.

We have so far deliberately avoided discussing the cost of major medical insurance, largely because costs are rising so fast that whatever we quote when writing this book is likely to be far lower than what will be when you are reading it. And also because such insurance is expensive, and we wanted to make the case for buying it before running the risk of turning you away prematurely.

As of this writing, a couple in their early forties with children can expect to pay roughly $1,200–$1,600 per year for major medical coverage totaling $1,000,000, with a $2,500 deductible. A couple in their early thirties can expect to pay $800–$1,200 yearly for the same kind of coverage. Older people can expect to pay considerably more, and the figures are changing fast and adversely for all age groups. The coverage purchased is not likely to be nearly as good as that available as a fringe benefit from a substantial company, but it is very likely to qualify as very good catastrophe insurance, above and beyond any company coverages.

Yes, these are heavy costs; but no, there is no other way to ensure lifelong major medical insurance protection, and with it the integrity of your lifelong financial plans.

Disability Insurance

Substantial medical problems can also bring with them prolonged disability, and that, too, can be a kind of economic catastrophe. There are federal disability payments that can be meaningful, especially where there are minor children in the family of the disabled wage-earner, but for a former manager's family of four they may total only a quarter of lost income, or even less; $10,000 instead of what used to be $40,000 won't go very far.

Many companies also have disability insurance arrangements. Some of these plans have payments coordinated with federal benefits, to provide a fixed income; as federal payments rise to at least partly keep up with inflation, company payments diminish. Individually purchased plans are seldom so coordinated, but rather provide for a specified fixed income, regardless of what other company or government disability payments may be received.

You should certainly consider the purchase of individual disability insurance, but always bear in mind that it is expensive and that as needs change coverage should be reevaluated. At 35, if you're trying to protect young children and perhaps a nonworking spouse, substantial personal disability insurance may be quite in order. At 55 or 60, with children grown and out on their own, spouse employed and perhaps earning just as much as you are, company and government disability insurance together may do.

When you do buy disability insurance you should, as always, seek to obtain it from a very substantial insurance company. Aside from the level and price of coverage, you will have other buying decisions to make. Waiver of further premium payments in the event of total disability is a good choice. The privilege of purchasing more insurance without new medical examinations is also probably a good choice, as are the purchases of a cost-of-living rider and a residual or partial disability benefit.

There are three kinds of individual disability policies, and they vary in premium cost with the firmness of the coverage offered. **Commercial policies** allow the insurance company to increase the premiums or cancel the policy at will at any anniversary. **Guaranteed issue policies** may not be cancelled by the insurance company, but premiums may be increased if the premiums of this class of policy are increased for all policyholders. **Noncancellable policies** may not be cancelled or have their premiums increased as long as you pay stated premiums for the period specified in your insurance contract.

You should not buy addons, such as accident and extra hospital-surgical coverages, in this kind of contract; it is best to keep the buying decision as simple and clean as possible, and use the money available to buy the best possible contract and maximum disability benefits.

Property and Liability Insurance

To round out our discussion of insurance matters, we must take up some aspects of property and liability insurance, as they relate to protection against catastrophes. We will touch on a few aspects, as most property and liability matters are routinely covered by standard homeowner's (or renter's) and automobile insurance policies, the provisions of which are best discussed with your insurance agent.

One potential catastrophe lies in the area of underinsurance for a homeowner's liability to others, as when a visitor slips on your icy walk, becomes totally disabled as a result of your provable negligence, and sues your insurer — and you — for $1,000,000. If the claimant's suit succeeds, with an award of $500,000, and your homeowner's policy specifies a top payout limit of $250,000, you are probably going to be wiped out. The problem is that many homeowner's policies still do specify too-low top limits, having failed to reflect the increasing size of awards in personal injury cases — and the fact that there are a lot more personal injury cases than there used to be. Check your liability limits, and if they are too low buy additional coverage. Many insurers routinely offer homeowner's liability coverage up to $1,000,000, sometimes calling that coverage an additional "umbrella" policy, and sometimes offering it as an extension of existing coverage. The additional coverage usually costs only a few dollars a year, and is well worth it.

Similarly, check your automobile insurance coverage. In this very litigious society, many accident liability awards easily top $100,000. It is best to carry such coverage in the range of $500,000 per accident, or even higher. The cost of the increased coverage is relatively small for those with good driving records.

An alternative to increasing the liability coverage on your homeowner's and auto insurance policies is to purchase an additional excess liability policy known as an **umbrella liability policy**. It is usually written for excess liability coverages of $1,000,000 –

$5,000,000. It can be written only if you already have basic home-owner's and auto coverage, and provides protection for losses exceeding the liability limits in your primary policies and for unin-sured exposures to liability exceeding a stated deductible. Pre-mium costs run in the range of $100 per $1,000,000 and $300 per $5,000,000.

This kind of umbrella policy, in addition to covering excess homeowner's and auto risks, also covers personal liability away from home. Check very carefully with your insurance company or broker on the minimum amounts of primary homeowner's and auto coverage you must have to be able to buy this kind of excess liability coverage.

An alternative to both of the above may be the purchase of an excess liability policy, which will cover all kinds of liabilities. In this respect it functions much like excess major medical coverage, and doesn't cost very much, because of the spreading of the risk is spread.

People who own homes are routinely insured for fire losses; you usually cannot get a mortgage without it. But sometimes the insurance carried is too small, and that is especially so when home values have been rising quickly. In some states, insurance that is smaller than a fixed percentage of replacement costs may result in much lower insurance settlements than are really needed to fund replacement of burned-out homes. Do not wait for your insurance agent to pick this one up and sell you more insurance, for some-times the agent's coverage reevaluation cycle just isn't fast enough to keep up with home value realities. Reevaluate your own coverage yearly, and purchase additional coverage as needed, to ensure that enough money to rebuild will be there if you should need it.

7

Investing Your Money: Savings, Stocks, Bonds, and Mutual Funds

In terms of investment, using money to make more money, there are many kinds of investment vehicles: stocks, bonds, mutual funds, futures, options, hedges, and speculations. There is also the plain old savings account, through which you lend money to a bank for interest and the bank relends that money to others for higher interest. In this chapter we'll look in some detail at four primary ways to invest: savings instruments, stocks, bonds, and mutual funds.

As a respectable investment, savings accounts are back; they have been ever since the late 1970s, when banks were freed to pay competitive rates of interest, both on demand deposits and on certificates of deposit (CDs).

They are back, that is, where they are *federally insured,* by the Federal Deposit Insurance Corporation (FDIC), the Federal Savings and Loan Insurance Corporation (FSLIC), or the National Credit Union Association (NCUA). We should all be alert to this by now, but it bears resaying: *Don't put your money into any bank that is not insured by the federal government,* unless you are doing it will knowledge that you are taking a much greater risk, one that is acceptable for a greater rate of return. If you can get an extra 1.5% for placing your funds in a less safely insured American bank, and want to do so, go right ahead — but understand that you may wind up with the kinds of problems that beset thrift institution depositors in Ohio in the spring of 1985, when the largest bank holiday (at least as of this writing) since the Great Depression took place.

In the emerging international marketplace, you may want to

go even further, taking larger risks for even larger possible rewards. As of this writing, investment money from all over the world is pouring into the United States, seeking high and relatively safe returns. But the wheel turns; you may find yourself able to put money into a bank abroad in a relatively safe way and for interest high enough to make you want to take additional risks. *But be assured there will most certainly be risks.* Chief among them is the fact that funds placed in banks abroad will not be guaranteed by your own government. Almost as important, the risks abroad will, even in highly developed countries, include the possibility of devaluation relative to the United States dollar, with consequent sharp losses to bear. And in much of the less developed world, the placement of personal funds in banks abroad is an invitation to disaster, as Americans who had placed money in Mexico at high rates of interest found during the 1970s; Mexico suddenly devalued its dollar by 50%, making those bank accounts immediately worth just half of what they had been worth the day before.

For managers and other mid- to high-income people, something potentially adverse is happening right now, and much closer to home. That is the advent of the uninsured **asset management account,** into which many are putting large proportions of their savings and investment money, without giving much thought to whether or not those accounts are protected by federal insurance guarantees. It is an interesting and puzzling development, really. People who consider themselves so ''savvy'' that they would not dream of putting deposit money into state-insured banking institutions are turning right around and putting deposit money and much more into asset management accounts offered by securities firms, also called· universal accounts, that are not even state insured, much less federally insured.

What these people seem not to realize is that these are brokerage accounts, rather than federally insured bank accounts, even though they and bank asset management accounts are identically named and have many similar features. It has been a marvelously effective selling trick to call the securities-firm accounts by the same name as the federally insured bank accounts. But with a securities fraud or simple failure massive enough to exceed private insurance coverage, the difference between asset management accounts from a federally insured bank and from a privately insured securities firm will become apparent — and that is quite likely to happen, in the volatile and fraud-filled financial markets of the 1980s.

It is odd to see these kinds of risks being thoughtlessly taken, too, for right now interest-paying, federally insured bank accounts are, for the first time since the Great Depression of the 1930s, yielding far higher rates of interest than the current inflation rate, meaning that you can let compound interest work for you, securely, with the money in your bank account becoming larger and larger in real dollars over the years, if you give it a chance. That is particularly so for that part of your savings that you are able to put into Individual Retirement Accounts (IRAs) and Keogh accounts, for these will compound tax-free until distribution much later in life, with an extraordinarily favorable impact upon your economic health. The truth is that the combination of high interest and federal guarantees makes bank liquid money market accounts and bank certificates of deposit so good that they are now the standard against which all other investments should properly be measured.

With all the proliferation of "financial products" in these years, there are still only two basic kinds of bank savings accounts. You can lend your money to a bank on a short-term, day-to-day basis, with the right to pull out your money — all of it — on demand. That is a **demand deposit.** Or you can lend your money to the bank for a specified period of time, in most periods at a somewhat higher rate of interest. This is a **time deposit,** and the modern instrument evidencing that deposit is the **certificate of deposit** (CD).

Important qualifications apply to both these kinds of arrangements. With the demand deposit, your right to pull your money out is absolute — if the bank has enough cash on hand to meet your demand. Although banks have federally mandated reserve and cash-on-hand requirements, most assets are out on loan at any given time, which is as it must be. In most periods, that means little for federally insured banks; even when banks have failed, federal regulators have managed to arrange uninterrupted depositor access to funds, as well as ultimate payment of all insured obligations. But in a very difficult period, federal regulators may be able to make only the *ultimate* payment guarantee; that means you may have to wait for quite some time for access to your federally guaranteed deposited funds. That, of course, is what has already happened to state-insured funds in California, Ohio, and Maryland — and by the time you read this work, perhaps in other places, as well. It *can* happen to federally insured funds; that is why it is a good idea to keep some small amount of cash for immediate needs entirely out of the banking system. No, we are not suggesting that you keep a large sum in bank notes, coins, and perhaps gold buried in your back yard; but it might not at all hurt to keep a little cash somewhere other than a bank, for a very rainy day.

In a time deposit, now known as the certificate of deposit, your money is not always available on demand; unless otherwise specified, you may not be able to get it when you want it, even if you are willing to forego some interest to get your money back. When you do lend your money to a bank for a specified time, be sure that the terms of the agreement permit you to get your money back on demand, although at considerably reduced rates of interest. That will be normal practice in almost every bank; but practices can change in pressure-filled times, even though legal obligations do not. *Be sure that you have a right to get your money out when you want it* without waiting until the end of the agreed-upon period of deposit.

Predicting the Course of Interest Rates

The key thing to bear in mind regarding interest rates is that, given the nature and recent history of the financial markets, the only long-term prediction about interest rates anyone can make is this: they will fluctuate. That is because the level of interest rates in all major industrial countries, and especially in the United States, has become a matter of public policy, far more than a matter of market behavior. That puts it perhaps too gently; in truth, our economy is managed — or manipulated, if you choose the more emotionally loaded word — largely through control of fiscal policy, of which interest rates are a key part. The only thing you can be sure of is that, in the long run, politicians can be counted on to manage interest rates to meet their own perceived political needs and their views of the needs of the nations they serve. Interest rates today — and tomorrow — are instruments of national policy and of international economic and political rivalry.

This link between political-economic national policies and the level of interest rates is one of the central facts of our time. But national and international economic and money market factors also affect interest rates, and often in ways that defy the skills of national fiscal managers. In this period, and unless and until new international agreements stabilize interest rates for long periods, those rates can be expected to be inherently unstable and unpredictable. Even in the short term, professionals all over the world are encountering difficulty predicting the course of interest rates. In the longer term, the only possible prediction is that interest rates will continue to fluctuate.

That is as it is now fashionable to say, the macroeconomics and politics of it. From the worm's-eye view — that of the individual investor — this means investing short term in locked-in debt obligations, rather than long term, no matter how attractive the longer-term yields seem. By short term, we mean for one year or less; eschew long-term CDs for 1% or 2% more, for example, and put your money into short-term obligations. Similarly, going into the now rather popular zero-coupon bonds, which "lock in" wonderful yields for decades, is a very large error; more on that shortly, in our discussion of bonds. The only long-term debt obligations you should be in are those that are both highly rated by the rating services, and widely and freely traded.

Understanding Bank Accounts

Some bank accounts are merely matters of convenience; they pay little in the way of interest, usually carry some service charges, and really have little impact upon your long-term economic health. Banks tend to make much of minor service matters; that is understandable, for the services they sell are often so nearly identical as to make your choice of bank purely a matter of geographical and record-keeping convenience. Should you choose to maintain an asset management account, with its large minimum deposits and extra fees, you will receive a good many minor services — rather more than you will find you need. Should you choose a passbook, statement (that is, nonpassbook), or NOW (negotiated order of withdrawal) savings account, or a regular or special checking account, you will — one way or another — find yourself paying in service charges and foregone interest for the bank services involved. It is right to shop around a bit for the bank that, in total, charges least for these services, but the savings are not likely to be so large that you should trade either convenience or efficiency for one that charges less but delivers much less.

On the other hand, some banks, particularly commercial banks, have in recent years taken to charging much higher rates than before for normal bank services, such as check writing, while at the same time creating a two-tier system for bank customers. If you find yourself paying 25 cents a check for the privilege of standing in long lines while people with asset management accounts get preferential service, then it is time to find another bank. There is no reason at all to carry your convenience accounts with a bank that doesn't particularly want your business, when many perfectly fine banks are out there fighting hard to bring you in as a customer. When a merchant offers you high prices and poor service, the proper response is to walk right out of the store; in this respect, treat banks like any other merchants.

There is no particularly good reason to combine convenience accounts and investment accounts, although banks will try hard to convince you to do just that. An investment account, however, has an entirely different and far more central role to play in lifetime financial planning, should be handled with considerable care, and should be moved as needed for current opportunity.

In recent years, the **liquid money market account** has become available. It is an ordinary demand deposit account, usually requiring maintenance of a minimum balance around $500 – $1,000 to continue receiving variable interest rates, and generally paying two or more percentage points higher than the convenience ccounts; that is, in the long run, a much higher rate of interest, because of the way compounding works. Many of these accounts carry service charges, however, which effectively cut the rate of interest being paid, so much so that they are unacceptable when balances are down near the minimums. For example, $10,000 in a liquid money market account at an effective net 8.5% yields $850 in interest. Charges of $30 a year barely touch that amount; the effective net yield then becomes $820, or 8.2%. But with only

$1,000 in the account, yielding $85, a subtraction of $30 in service charges brings the net yield down to $55, or 5.5%; in that case, the account has lost its value as an investment, and you have sacrificed too much for liquidity. In that situation, you can still stay safe and short-term by putting the money into a short-term CD.

Certificates of deposit (CDs) have become a preferred form for millions of American savers, for they combine a high degree of safety (up to the federal deposit insurance limit of $100,000 per account) and simultaneously yield what have for many years been excellent rates of interest. And that deposit limit is in reality no limit at all, for you can open as many accounts as you wish, one to a bank. You can also open two insured accounts in a single bank, if one is an IRA or Keogh and the other a regular account; or you may have $200,000 in deposit insurance in a single bank, if you and your spouse open an account together.

A short-term CD, up to a year, will usually carry an effective yield close to that of a liquid money market fund. Longer-term CDs, in the four-to-ten-years range, will offer proportionally more, up to two or even three points beyond the shorter-term CD. Some, considering this and feeling that they are able to predict that long-term interest rates will not rise sharply, have chosen to "lock in" the higher long-term rates, just as some choose to buy long-term bonds. Our view is clear on this: we urge only a short-term CD commitment. We recognize that reasonable people may disagree, but most people buying longer term do so simply because they are dazzled by the higher interest rates offered, and have given too little thought to the money they will *not* make if interest rates rise sharply while they are locked in to lower rates. It might help to see it this way: If interest rates rise sharply while you are locked in to a long-term CD, you will not be locking in high rates as much as you will be making it impossible to move your money into what may then be far better-yielding forms of investment.

Sometimes, the decision to move money into a higher-paying CD does not revolve around the term of the commitment, but rather around the reliability of the issuer. When all the banking institutions in your area are offering 10.5% CDs, and an institution somewhere else is offering 12% for the same term, what you are probably looking at is either a much greater risk or an introductory rate for something like 30 days — which on a yearly basis may add up to perhaps one tenth of one percent more than you are now getting. Where it is a matter of higher risk, that risk is usually so much higher that it would not be acceptable, if properly understood.

When you do buy a CD, by all means instruct the bank to roll it over for you on maturity — that is, to reinvest it for you in another CD — so that your money will continue to earn for you in the absence of any other instructions from you. That kind of asset management is very much in order; the banks will do it gladly to get the additional business, and will generally charge little or nothing for the service.

Banks and securities firms will want to do a great deal more asset management than that for you, if you will let them. As we have already discussed, **asset management accounts** are now vigorously promoted, by both banks and securities firms. The situation changes rapidly, as they offer more and more services to acquire business, and as the previously hard-held line between the banking and securities industries continues to erode. However, the basic service each kind of asset management account offers is a single centralized handling of all your financial needs and transactions, in return for a yearly fee and the opportunity to make money on many of those transactions.

Asset management accounts commonly generate a single monthly statement of all transactions, stemming from treatment of your financial affairs as a single account. The banks and securities firms offering them almost all offer some kind of credit, usually through a credit card, with the securities firms also offering margin accounts for securities trading purposes. All also offer several kinds of mutual fund investments, whether directly or by the banks, or indirectly through related brokerage firms. And all sweep any revenue from lower-paying investments directly into higher-paying investments, usually mutual funds, as often as daily and not less often than weekly. All such accounts are treated as if they were bank accounts, with checks issued and honored, though many do not return your checks. Many will also hold valuable goods for you, such as gold and securities, trading them on your instructions.

For this service, you will in most instances have to make an initial deposit in your account of $5,000–$25,000 and pay fees, most of which run $50–$150 per year. Both deposits and fees are rapidly diminishing, as banks and securities firms compete for business. You will often also have to pay interest on brokers' loans in margin accounts, high interest rates on any credit card used, and varying fees and charges on mutual fund transactions, depending on the funds involved. In some instances, you will also have to sign some agreements with very fine print — agreements that can cause you considerable difficulty, should you have any trouble meeting your obligations — as when a bank or securities firm through such an agreement becomes able to hold deposited money to satisfy other claims they may have upon you.

The bank asset management accounts are federally insured bank accounts, with a reach out to some securities trading functions. The securities-firm asset management accounts are little more than glorified brokerage accounts and are not federally insured; they also often have the additional disability of being organized and run by high-commission brokerage firms, which will charge you far more for your trades than will discount brokerage houses. If you are an active securities investor, and are determined to use a high-cost broker, perhaps because you value the advice tendered by that broker, then a brokerage-firm asset management account may make some sense; but *do not make the mistake of treating that account as if it really were a federally insured bank account.*

Whether bank or securities firm account, we think it wise to take possession of your own valuables such as stock certificates and bonds, and hold them in your own safe deposit box, rather than leaving them in your account. When you may be borrowing from people, as through a margin account or a substantial line of credit, you will provide collateral only if you must. But if you are not borrowing, it does not make much sense to leave your valuables in someone else's possession. A major securities firm failure might tie up your assets for years and cause you to lose some of them in the end; a bank failure, or even a considerable dispute between you and the bank, might do the same.

The considerable virtue of these asset management accounts seems to be that they supply you with a single monthly statement of all transactions, thereby making the financial side of life easier to understand and manage. That is valuable, and where that is all that is involved, the extra direct fees may well be worth paying. That can be true of some bank asset management accounts, where you pay your extra fees, take advantage of a daily sweep of earnings into a no-load mutual fund, and do not use the high-cost credit card offered. Then you are directly spending only $50 – $150 per year more than you were before, plus some foregone interest on minimum balances required, while slightly offsetting these costs with the proceeds of that sweep into higher-paying funds and getting some quite valuable basic financial planning material in the form of that monthly statement. It is not entirely cost-justifiable, as this is something you can and probably should do for yourself; but for some people, who will not sit down regularly to do basic record-keeping and planning, it may be worth the expenditure.

Investing in Stocks

Stock speculation was the great national pastime of the 1920s; indeed in the years before the Crash, it was a craze. It was almost entirely unregulated then; people bought stocks that went up and up on the thinnest of margins, pouring more and more into their investments until the inevitable day of reckoning came. During the 1930s, and to a considerable extent right on through the 1940s and 1950s, small investors stayed out of the stock market, for memories of 1929 and the Great Depression were still very sharp. In the 1960s, it all began to heat up again, as a brief new boom, lasting no more than a decade, began, blossomed in the mid-1960s, and then came down to earth in the early 1970s. For the stock market, the end of the 1960s boom was not as spectacular as that of the 1920s boom, but it was very sharp, very definite, and took the mass of small individual investors out of the market just as surely.

Nor has the stock market really recovered in this period. The Bellwether average, the Dow Jones Industrial Average, which hit 1,000 in the mid-1960s, reached the 1200-1300 range in the mid-1980s, 20 years later; at that level it was hailed by self-interested financial sellers as hitting historic highs. That was nonsense, of course; taking inflation into account, that average in early 1985 was worth about 400, compared with its 1,000 high in the mid-1960s.

The comparison between stocks and other investments is not as invidious as those figures might make it seem, though; you must take small average after-tax dividend payouts into account as if reinvested, those after-tax payouts varying with the tax brackets of their recipients. But the truth is that all the very safe, rather disdained savings and investment instruments — favored by those who were worried enough to stay out of those boom markets — did better than stocks in that period. The truth is also that most small investors still have not come back into the stock market as individual investors as of this writing, although many do have substantial assets invested in stocks and stock-based instruments.

In a way, it is a little misleading to suggest that the public is still out of the stock market. The pension funds, mutual funds, and insurance companies doing the huge institutional trades that make the modern stock market are using individual funds; the truth is that the public is actually in the market, whether it knows it or not, and whether it likes it or not. Managers and other corporate employees are certainly in the market, as holders of their own optioned company stocks, and often through the investment choices they make in those retirement funds under their own control. And some have the kind of gambling fever that leads people to speculate once again on the thinnest of margins, just as they did in 1929, but this time on such instruments as index and commodity futures.

Underneath it all, and especially for long-term personal financial planning purposes, when you buy shares of stock you make a decision to *buy a piece of a company,* in the hope that the value of the company will grow and with it the value of your shares. You hope to share in the current profits as well, through dividend distributions, and also stand ready to trade as you must. But the main focus of most long-term financial planners who buy into companies is anticipated growth in the value of stock coupled with possible dividends, leading to an attractive after-tax yield — and all at an acceptable risk. How attractive that after-tax yield must be is purely a comparative matter; if you can quite clearly do better and at least as safely in other instruments, then your investment money must go elsewhere.

The one thing you should not want to do is to become an in-and-out trader, no matter how well other amateurs seem to be doing at that, and no matter how attractive your friendly stockbroker makes such trading seem. As so many millions before us have learned so very painfully, amateurs whose main attention is on other matters — such as their business careers — are in no position to compete with professionals in stock and similar markets.

Start with Your Own Company or Industry

In a long-term way, the first company worth looking at is your own, whether or not you have a chance at stock options, stock appreciation rights, performance bonus stock, or any other kind of price- or tax-advantaged stock. It is, after all, the company you are likely to know most about. Do be aware of insider selling restrictions, though; it is illegal to sell a large body of your stock after you find out that sonething terribly adverse is about to happen to your company, which is bound to drive down the price of its stock. Similarly, it is illegal to buy after learning from inside sources that a corporate raider is about to drive up the price of your company's stock.

In considering your own company for investment purposes, you should bring into play all the standard matters to examine when you are thinking about buying any stock. You will want to know, for example, if the stock is listed on a major exchange, such as the New York or American Stock Exchanges. Any stock that is listed is not so thinly held that a small number of shares traded can seriously affect its price, although institutional block trades may do so. If yours is a substantial company traded actively in the national over-the-counter market — that is, off the exchanges — you may buy anyway. But you must not buy — either in the open market or in the form of stock option exercise — if the stock cannot easily be traded. Option stock that is a substantial portion of your assets, but that cannot readily be sold without depressing the price of that stock, is far less attractive than option stock that can easily be traded once you are free to sell.

Aside from company prospects, which you know well, you will also want to know a series of other things about stock and company. What is the stock's history, in terms of both growth and dividends? How do its earnings compare with other companies in the same industry? In other industries? What is its price/earnings ratio — that is, the relation between its market price per share and its per-share earnings? These, and more, are the kinds of questions and answers to be derived from the kinds of investment information sources we have discussed in Chater 3, or directly from the massive financial and business information databases you may be accessing from the computer terminal on your desk in office, home, or both.

In considering companies other than your own for investment, you must do a good deal more, for then you cannot ultimately fall back on your special knowledge of company and prospects. Then it is necessary to reseach the company as carefully as possible, beginning to follow it in the business and financial press, sending for annual reports (though these all too often hide more than they tell), and seeking to learn all you can about it through others, including your financial advisers. It is far from enough to follow "the market," or even a segment of "the market." The chartist approach may be useful for professionals, who move in and out of specific stocks and groups constantly, but the fundamental approach of following an industry company-by-company is far better for personal long-term financial planning. That is why, after your own company, some of the stocks you will be best able to evaluate are those of companies in your own or related industries. You will then know company and industry, perhaps not as well as you know your own company, but often well enough to bring your special knowledge and insight to bear.

Beyond your own company and related companies and industries, you are very much out in the financial world when considering stock for investment. Then it may very well be a matter of developing interests in groups of companies and industries other than your own, much as a professional may specialize. In that way, you can become able to follow trends and to make at least fairly well-informed decisions. In this, investing in stocks is something like working with collectibles; if all you are doing is collecting or investing in an amorphous mass of possible investments, you are unlikely to be able to do well in the long run. Sure, you may be able to follow a trend, like electronics in the 1960s or biotechnology in the 1980s, but without real knowledge of your own you will always be following — which, in the long run in the stock market, always means losing. But if you take the time and trouble to become knowledgeable in a few companies, and perhaps in one or two industries at any given time, you have a substantial leg up on those who are merely followers, and stand a reasonable chance of making some money in stocks.

Stock Investment Fads and Fancies

A book on effective lifelong financial planning is scarcely a series of short courses on how to make money on stocks, bonds, or any of the other investment vehicles discussed here and in subsequent chapters. It is about how to develop a series of approaches that together will build your assets and secure your financial present and future, using your existing strengths and those you can acquire. That is why managers and other corporate people should, above all, use their existing strengths and knowledge to evaluate first their own companies as investment possibilities, then companies in their own and related industries, and also — using the same skill — companies in one or two other sound, growing industries. You are engaged in the operation and ongoing analysis of your own company's business every day; that kind of engagement can and should be part of your own investment decision-making. Of course you will carefully study what investment professionals have to say about investments you are considering; but *your own special skills are what will make the advice of professionals most useful.* That is also why it is wrong to merely follow the fads, tips, and trends of the time, without real knowledge of your own, in stocks or any other investment vehicle.

With that injunction in mind, a few rather basic cautionary comments may be in order, in this period of "record-breaking" stock averages. Not too basic, though. Even some of the more sophisticated of us can tend to move with the investment fads and styles of the moment, especially when our minds are on other matters and we are encouraged to do so by our brokers and friends, who seem to be making money in whatever they are urging us to do.

It is wise to be wariest of all of the "hot" stocks and groups of stocks of the moment, also often called **aggressive growth stocks,** unless they also happen to be stocks and groups you are already closely monitoring, having led the crowd, rather than followed it. Latecomers and latestayers, following the crowd without any real knowledge of their own, always lose their shirts; that is one of the few iron laws of investing.

Similarly, it is self-preserving to view "special situations" with a skeptical eye. Latterly, these have been called "turn-around" companies and situations — that is, companies that have been "underperforming," but are now about to turn their business and stock performances around and make large profits for those smart enough to "get in on the ground floor." That is all very well, but companies in trouble tend to stay in trouble, especially when the cost of money is so high; the stock you know too little about is far more likely to keep on going down, rather than starting up again. It almost sounds oversimple to have to say that, except that for as long as anyone can remember eager stockbrokers have been touting and putting their not-so-skeptical customers into turnaround situations that didn't turn around. This is never more so than in periods of general rises in stock prices, when optimism runs high.

One of the modern get-rich-in-the-market techniques has been to join in the rush to become somehow involved in takeover situations, often now called **takeover arbitrage.** In essence, that is only a matter of buying while the stock price is being pushed up, first by speculators' hopes that a takeover situation is imminent, and then by acquirers and acquirees, as the situation unfolds. The trouble with that technique is that it is very much a game for professionals watching a series of inside moves by the players, rather than a game for amateur outsiders.

Of course, if you are already holding or seriously considering purchase of stock you consider a good buy at its current price, which has not yet been bid up because of takeover fever, you may make some quick gains. However, then the whole matter should change to a short-term rather than a long-term affair, for these takeover situations can seriously damage a company and its prospects, as when a company pays off a potential raider handsomely and thereby adds greatly to its debt and consequent debt service. If you are already holding the stock of a company that is being raided, seriously consider selling it before the issue is resolved, even though that may mean at a price considerably lower than its anticipated high, should it all work out to push the stock price even higher as the situation develops. Then you do not run the risk of holding such stock when a raider unsucessfully withdraws, for then the price of the stock may plummet. If you have been planning to buy stock even without the takeover situation, seriously consider buying and holding as you would have otherwise. If the takeover attempt does not take place, you will have lost nothing; but if it does take place, you may want to sell sooner rather than later, as described above. The main hazard then is that you may succumb to gambling fever and hold on too long as the stock goes up.

Something new is starting for the main body of American investors. It is the advent of the *24-hour international trading market,* a network that will make it possible to enter the international financial marketplace easily. If all goes as projected, it will soon be possible for an individual investor to make money trading in shares, debt obligations, and many other kinds of investments all over the world.

Or lose money. If you think the financial marketplace in the United States has become complex, with great numbers of eager, not-too-well-informed financial sellers vying for your investing money, take a good look at the international financial marketplace. People tempted to plunge into international investing should do so very carefully indeed, for there are far more hazards than exist at home. Severe currency devaluations, changes of government and even of social system, and enormously magnified opportunities for fraud may all be present. Professionals watch international investments very carefully, and still often miscalculate, as the huge early-1980s currency-related losses of so many American companies clearly attest. You can also be sure that the sharp operators and outright thieves who normally move toward unregulated and lightly regulated investment areas will be drawn to the grand new opportunities presented here as well.

On the other hand, investment in the shares of a highly profitable company headquartered in a stable industrial nation may be quite right for you. That will be especially true if that company is one of your company's well-known and highly respected competitors or suppliers, for you may know very nearly as much about the company as you do your own. But even in that kind of situation you should always be aware of political factors to be carefully taken into account; for example, a worldwide wave of protectionism could harm the performance and profits of many of the now highly profitable and fast-growing Japanese companies.

Investing in Bonds

Usually we say "stocks and bonds" in the same breath. But they do not exactly bear describing that way, for stocks are shares in private companies, while bonds are the debt obligations of both the public and private sectors. We use the term "bonds" here quite generally, as is the usual modern practice, to describe a wide variety of debt obligations, including bills, notes, regular bonds, convertible bonds, and zero-coupon bonds, as well as the less familiar kinds of debt obligations found in the international marketplace. The common element is that all involve the bond issuer's *promise to pay,* rather than the share of profits and growth in stock value that are the stock issuer's promise.

Note that you cannot bring your management skills or other business savvy to bear on the questions surrounding bond purchase in quite the same way you can when considering stocks. Your general business and financial skills come into play when assessing risk and reward, certainly; but here you are not assessing the ability of an entity to grow and prosper while doing so, as you can do with your own and other companies. Rather, your main assessments will relate to the ability of public and private sector organizations to pay their debts, and to the probable future course of interest rates, which greatly affect bond values.

Note also that the question of investing in tax-advantaged bonds simply does not come up when dealing with funds that are going to be growing tax-free in private and public pension plans, such as 401(k), SEP, IRA, annd Keogh plans. Managers and other corporate people now have the ability to put much of their investment money into such plans and in some instances to get that money out, virtually at will. When that is so, there is no reason at all to move your money toward risky debt obligations for tax advantage, as that advantage is already present in your long-term portable pension plans.

Risk Factors

For debt obligations, the risks are a little easier to assess than for stocks. We are talking here of domestic debt obligations, not the kinds of obligations you run into out in the international financial markets, for those involve a whole different set of estimates, particular to each country and issuer. National governments routinely repudiate debts, either outright or piecemeal, often through devaluation of the currency in which the debts are payable. So can foreign companies, especially if they are caught in political situations, as when a nationalized company pays bondholders a few cents on the dollar in settlement of debt obligations. If you are going to invest in debt obligations, by all means do so at home.

Interest rates on debt obligations are largely a matter of risk and potential reward, with the risks being assessed independently by nationally recognized bond rating services. Tax-advantaged state and local bonds — that is, **municipals** — appear on the risk-reward scale with their tax advantage taken into account. Longer-term obligations generally pay more than equivalent shorter-term obligations, as an incentive to buyers; but most longer-term obligations are also **callable,** meaning that their issuers can replace them with lower-paying bonds later on and long before maturity, should the interest rates they have to pay decline.

United States **federal obligations,** backed by the taxing authority and ultimately the sovereignty of the nation, are thought to be the safest of all; they therefore yield the lowest real after-tax rates of interest, and are essentially beyond the rating functions. They are safest, that is, in terms of the ability of the United States to pay its promised debts; you can still lose money if you must sell when interest rates have gone up and the values of the tradable long-term federal bonds you are holding have therefore sharply declined. Then you must decide between holding and collecting too little interest, or selling out at a loss.

That kind of question does not come up around the three- and six-month **Treasury bills** so popular among individual investors in the 1970s and early 1980s, as they are not tradable. But in recent years these have been largely superseded by federally insured, and therefore very safe, bank money market accounts, and only slightly less safe money market mutual funds. These kinds of bank accounts are easier and less expensive to handle, and pay a little more interest than do directly purchased Treasury bills.

Treasury-issued bills, notes, and bonds are all direct federal obligations. Beyond those issues, there are the **federal agency bonds,** such as those of the Government National Mortgage Association (GNMA, or Ginnie Mae), which are also routinely top-rated, since they are in fact also fully backed by the federal government. These pay a little more than the Treasury issues. There are also normally top-rated bonds, indirectly backed by the government but issued by private organizations, like those of the Student National Loan Association (Sallie Mae), also paying a little more than the Treasury issues.

As a matter of course, it is wise to check the main bond rating organizations — Moody's and Standard & Poor's — before investing in any bond. Even the non-Treasury-issued agency bonds are worth checking, for with privatization you may invest in what you think is a government bond, only to find that it is really a private bond, and may for some reason be less safe than you assume. Both Moody's an Standard & Poor's start with top-rated AAA bonds, and move down through AAs and As to BBBs and so on down to their bottom ratings. Until now, AAAs and AAs have generally been rather safe in terms of ability to pay. The As have been relatively safe, too — as long as they stay As. But it is only a step from an A rating down into the Bs, which are not so safe at all; and bond rating organizations routinely change their ratings as circumstances indicate, for their function is to provide an initial evaluation followed by continuous and careful reevaluation of each risk.

That makes it important to consult the bond ratings on initial purchase, and also to reexamine those ratings periodically, for signs of increasing risk. For example, the municipality caught in a massive government securities-firm failure may be in deep trouble, and be forced to declare a moratorium on bond interest payments; that would make some of the municipal bonds you hold instantly worth much less in the marketplace, if you can sell them at all, and cost you a good deal of ongoing interest income. Or an AA-rated corporate bond may slip to A and then down into the Bs as company fortunes wane; unless you are monitoring ratings, those facts may slip right by you as long as its interest payments continue, until you learn too late that you will be forced to take substantial losses on the bankruptcy of the company. By all means watch the financial press regarding all your investments; also periodically revisit the Moody's and Standard & Poor's bond ratings.

Don't, by the way, buy individual **junk bonds** — that is, low-rated bonds paying a good deal more, even up to several points more, than AA and AAA bonds. Some securities houses have made quite a good thing of initiating and selling such bonds, pointing out that on an averaging-out basis the rewards considerably outweigh the risks. Perhaps, perhaps not — there are conflicting studies on that point. But put those studies aside. *For individual investors, this kind of averaging is meaningless.* For most of us, one substantial loss on a junk bond will far outweigh any gains we might make, for we do not have the resources to go into this kind of speculation. Buy junk bonds only as part of risk-spreading mutual funds.

The bond ratings set forth no rigid hierarchy of risks and rewards, but rather a set of general indications. The short-term federal obligations come first, at least risk and least interest, followed by the federal agency and federally related agency bonds. Then come the best of the "blue chip" corporates, side by side with some longer-term federal bonds and a few of the very best municipals, followed by the rest of the corporates and the mass of the municipals, running across a considerable spectrum of risks.

But the bond ratings can tell only part of the story of the risk and potential reward in such a volatile period as this. When interest rates fluctuate rather widely and quite unpredictably, the additional risk is that tradable bonds you are holding — bonds that in other times might fluctuate little if at all — will lose a good deal of their value if the general level of interest rates rises sharply. Bond prices go down when interest rates go up. Conversely, bond prices rise when interest rates go down. When issuers have to pay more for the money they borrow, tradable bonds already in the marketplace become worth only as much as the amount it would take to yield what the current level of interest yields, as somewhat modified by the fixed interest payments due on those bonds.

For example, long-term corporate bonds sold back in the late 1960s and early 1970s, carrying much lower interest rates than those currently being offered, have for years been described as **deeply discounted;** that means that they are worth much less than their face values if they are resold short of maturity. Their unfortunate holders are getting far less for their invested money than they could be getting, and that is a very substantial set of opportunity costs; those who sold their bonds have already taken substantial losses. Purchasing a long-term bond means making a guess on the future course of interest rates.

That is especially true when you are dealing with **zero-coupon bonds,** those usualy long-term bonds from which the interest has been stripped, leaving in place only the long-term promise to pay. They are sold as very safe obligations, to be tucked away and virtually forgotten, until their maturity decades later; in fact, they have been converted into highly speculative securities. Without the interest-payment promise in place, those bonds will during their lifetimes fluctuate in value far more widely than normal bonds. And to add real injury to potential injury, *you will have to pay taxes on imputed interest every year during the life of the bonds, in real dollars.* If interest rates go down, and you want to sell, you may have a bonanza; if interest rates go up, you may have a literally unsalable bond on your hands, on which you are paying taxes every year while you wait for the issuer's promise to mature. You may be able to get around the imputed interest problem by buying the zero-coupon bond through your tax-advantaged pension plan, or in which all interest compounds tax-free; but you are still potentialy locked into a speculative security.

Even though many of these zero-coupon bonds are wholly or largely based on long-term government bonds, it is still wildly imprudent to run the risk of tying yourself up this way for many years and perhaps decades, no matter how good the ultimate payoff seems to be. Zero-coupon bonds seem to safely lock n long-term promises to pay; but in some quite foreseeable circumstances, they may only serve to lock their owners into tax payments and losses that may then be not at all avoidable.

Municipals

Municipals — that is, state and local bonds — are a special case. As already indicated, they have no particular place in long-term tax-advantaged pension plans, although many of their sellers steadfastly claim that they do. There is also considerable reason to suggest that they are to be regarded with very great caution altogether. Many local governments are in grave difficulty in this period, and many special-purpose bond issues pose great potential problems. The Washington Public Power Supply System disaster, which may ultimately cost bond buyers well over half a billion dollars, is only one spectacular recent case in point.

At least equally disquieting is the prospect of state and local debt obligations losing some or all of their tax advantage, as has at least once in recent years been seriously proposed by the national administration. Should that occur, people holding bonds may instantly be holding deeply discounted bonds at great losses, for new issues will then have to come out paying much higher rates of interest to make up for the lost tax deductions. Those new issues would then be even riskier than older municipals, as the higher rates of interest paid would be that much harder for issuers to meet. In those circumstances, it would be reasonable to expect moratoriums and defaults by municipal bond issuers to rise very sharply. Indeed, given current difficulties and the threat of loss of tax advantage, it might be wise to stay away from municipals entirely, in this period. Those big net after-tax yields sellers push so hard can seem very attractive, but consider that the very size of those yields indicates the bond trading professionals generally regard most municipals with great wariness at this time.

There are exceptions, certainly. If your well-situated suburban town issues a high-yielding municipal bond that will be exempt from all federal, state, and local taxes to residents of the town, and you think the bond and the town very sound, buy it, hold it, watch it, and eventually either sell it at a profit or hold it equally profitably until maturity. Then you are doing the equivalent of exercising an excellent stock option in your own sound, growing company; it is the best kind of investment. On the other hand, if your greatly troubled city or county is the issuer, or it is a nuclear power authority bond, stay away from it, no matter how tax-advantaged. *A tax shelter must first of all be a sound investment.*

Mortgage-Backed Securities

The mortgage-backed security is not a single kind of debt obligation, but rather a form that has been created by financial sellers, in which large mortgage debt obligations are used as the collateral backing bonds sold in much smaller — and therefore much more practical — denominations to individual investors and some institutional investors, as well. Putting it a little differently, in creating a mortgage-backed security, the seller repackages large debts into small ones, in the process gaining access to new sources of income from investment banking and securities commissions.

The new securities so created are essentially as good — or bad — as the collateral and guarantees backing them. Some of them, either directly or almost directly guaranteed by the federal government, are AAA-rated. When you buy securities backed by the Government National Mortgage Association (Ginnie Maes), the Federal Home Loan Corporation (Freddie Macs), or whatever other federal or quasifederal agencies are issuing such obligations, you are buying the practical equivalent of a long-term government bond.

Of course, some hazards accompany purchase of such agency bond issues and the mortgage-backed securities derived from them, but these are primarily hazards that come from interest rate increases. Mortgage-backed securities are tradable securities, and interest-sensitive; when interest rates rise, such bond prices decline; and when interest rates fall, such bond prices rise. But these are normal risks, not potential disasters; the federal promises will, short of catastrophe, be met, and the bonds will in all likelihood pay their stated values at maturity.

Without this federal promise to pay, mortgage-backed securities offer a considerable spectrum of risks, and you must carefully consider each offering in terms of those possible risks. Many are insured privately, not federally. As in all private insurance, that kind of guarantee is as good as the insurer, and the reliability of insurers differs widely. In the mid-1980s the Bank of America suffered a loss in the $85 – $100 million range when it found that it was standing behind mortgage-backed securities in which the collateral — the underlying mortgages — were worth far less than stated, and that the insurance company guaranteeing that collateral had far too little money to meet claims. If you find Metropolitan Life, Equitable, Prudential, or a pool of major insurers standing behind privately insured mortgage-backed securities, as when such companies insure a unit trust (a body of relatively low-priced shares in a pool of mortgages) you are seeing a worthwhile guarantee. But if that guarantee is being made by a small company, no matter where located and how well-regulated, you are, in practical terms, seeing little or no insurance at all. Similarly, you will find some mortgage-backed securities that are essentially tax-exempt municipals, being backed by state and local issuers. You should treat these as municipals in terms of risk; they are only as safe as the issuers backing them, and are therefore to be handled with care.

When you buy a mortgage-backed security that is backed neither by federal guarantees nor by major insurers, you are essentially putting your money into a pool of mortgages, and sharing the risks and interest income with the lenders holding those mortgages. In those circumstances, you must look at the risk almost entirely in terms of the safety of the collateral being offered — that is, the quantity and quality of the underlying mortgages. If a bank holding a pool of high-quality home mortgages greatly overcollateralizes — that is, puts behind those securities mortgages worth a lot more than the securities themselves — then if the interest is right, you may be looking at a sound and lucrative use of your money. Then the collateral is good enough and there is enough of it to protect you if, in difficult times, the value of the underlying mortgage portfolio goes down, due to such factors as foreclosures and decreases in real estate values.

On the other hand, the underlying mortgages being offered as collateral may be worth only as much as the securities themselves, or even less, as when values are wrongly appraised, and therefore be entirely vulnerable to swings in real estate value. Or the collateral may be in the form of volatile commercial real estate debt obligations, or even in other kinds of debt obligations, by the time you are reading this work. Then, in the absence of meaningful guarantees, the risks may be high and unacceptable. You may even run into "mortgage-backed" securities that are not really mortgage-backed at all, but in fact are only the general debt obligations of banking institutions. Watch carefully for these, and go into them only if you would buy an uncollateralized bond issued by that bank, for they are only as good as that bank's bare promise to pay.

Investing in Mutual Funds

A mutual fund is a pool into which investment money is poured, and through which investment professionals, for a fee, place the money of others. The terms **mutual fund** and **investment company** are synonyms; when you put money into a mutual fund, you are buying shares in a investment company.

That investment company may be either a **closed-end** or an **open-end** company. The closed-end company, much less used today and with far smaller total assets, sells a fixed number of shares at its start, thereby creating a fixed amount of investment capital; it then works with that capital on behalf of its shareholders, its shares often being freely tradable on the open market. The open-end company, the main form in use today, sells as many new shares to the public as it can throughout its unlimited lifetime, and works with whatever capital it can create on behalf of its shareholders, though some open-end companies do convert themselves into closed-end companies by stopping new sales.

Fees and Commissions

Whether you buy into an open-end or closed-end mutual fund, the basic transaction occurring is that you are hiring professionals to manage some of your investment money. However it is stated in the prospectus, you should expect to pay yearly fees of .025% – 1.5% of your total fund assets each year for management of your money. As a practical matter it is wise to accept a 1% – 1.5% figure as normal; where it is lower, fund management is probably taking the money out in additional cost charges or as part of selling commissions, or can be counted on to raise fees shortly. You will have to pay something for professional management of your money, whether in fees to financial advisers, mutual fund managers, and bankers, or as commissions to bankers and brokers.

What you don't necessarily have to pay, though, is high front-load, back-load, and life-of-commitment selling commissions. Sales charges have absolutely nothing to do with the quality of mutual fund investment management; they can and should be either entirely avoided or kept to the barest minimum.

To avoid such sales charges, you have to understand them. When you buy a mutual fund, you may be paying sales charges of up to 9% — more typically, 8.5% — right off the top of the total transaction. For example, a $10,000 purchase of shares in a mutual fund charging 8.5% means that, as of the moment you bought those shares, your investment became $9,150. If you want to sell your shares the next day, or the next week, at the price you paid, you would have to take an immediate loss of the $850 you paid in sales charges, in this case **front-load** charges. It also means that if you were to hold the fund for a year, and gain $850 on your $9,150 of fund shares — a not-bad 9.29% — you would only be back up to your original $10,000, and would actually have lost ground by whatever the rate of inflation was that year.

Even worse, those huge front-load commissions create a situation in which shareholders are reluctant to sell their fund shares, because of the commission losses they would suffer, even when the market is declining for those shares and they should be selling. There is liquidity, all right, in that you can sell the shares freely enough, but when the front-load commissions mean you can sell only at a considerable loss, the tendency is to hold — in a practical sense, to create your own *illiquidity* — while the mutual funds go down and down, eventually forcing you to sell at an even greater loss. Avoid these heavily front-loaded funds, for they are doubly damaging in volatile markets.

That sort of perception is widely shared today; therefore, **no-load funds** have become increasingly popular in this period. But surprisingly, large numbers of people still listen too hard to selling talk and pay too little attention to the charges when buying into mutual funds. Selling commissions and promotion do cost mutual fund companies a good deal of money, and investors must be careful about paying high sales costs organized in less obvious ways. For example, some mutual funds are charging additional fees of up to 1% per year for selling costs, on top of their management fees. That's a lot. Such fees over a period of years can add up to just as much as a high one-time front-load charge. You are a little freer to sell under those circumstances, but that is all that can be said for the practice, which in fact creates large, hidden charges and victimizes the unwary.

Similarly, many mutual funds are now charging **back-load**

charges — that is, charges that come into play on sales of your fund shares, sometimes more heavily on early than on later sales. A back-load charge of as much as 5% may be levied on sales occurring during the first year of share ownership, and after that less, on a sliding scale. This, too, tends to create a practical illiquidity, although it does allow your money to grow at full value from the start of your fund share ownership, and may do no very great harm if you intend to treat your mutual fund investment as a very long-term matter.

You have no very great need to pay such sales charges, unless you are so impressed by a particular fund's performance and current management that you are willing to accept such charges in order to own shares in that particular fund.

Often, the "hot" fund and set of fund managers turn out to be rather speculative in nature, with the fund declining in adverse markets at least as fast as it went up. Hot funds have to be made up of hot stocks and other hot investment vehicles; and such vehicles are inevitably speculative. "Aggressive growth" funds are composed of "hot" growth vehicles; all that selling language and fevered talk adds up to nothing more than putting money into the fads and fancies of the moment, whether those are electronic stocks in the 1960s or computer software and genetic engineering stocks in the 1980s.

There is a period in the growth of every new industry in which many small companies ride a wave of interest, and their stocks and funds composed of those stocks do extremely well. It is always followed by a shakeout, in which very many companies fail, others merge into larger companies, and the stocks in that field fall into disfavor. There are also periods in which companies dealing in certain main kinds of assets do extremely well, and funds heavily invested in those companies do well, as when stocks of gold mining or strategic metals companies go up very sharply in certain financial and metal market conditions. But in these matters, what goes up must come down, most especially when it is a fund invested heavily in several or perhaps many companies, only some of which — if any — will do well in the long run.

If you want to invest in a new field, or in a certain kind of asset, it is far better to become knowledgeable and make your own judgment call, investing in your own well-chosen companies, rather than in a mutual fund that must, by its very nature, ultimately go down just as it has gone up. Yes, you may buy into a high-flying mutual fund, paying the front-load charges on purchases, or the continuing sales charges, or the back-load charges on sale, and sell just at the right time, at the high. More likely, you will hold too long — intimidated by the charges, entranced by the paper gains, or both.

People who do want to buy into mutual funds without sales charges (the no load funds) can rather easily find soundly managed funds that sell by advertisements and mail; look for advertisements in the financial press, examine lists of no-load funds (which most discount brokers will supply on request), or ask your bank. The prospectus you will get from a no-load fund or low-load fund is just as complete as the one you get from a high-load fund, and will detail fund track record, management, and fee structure just as fully. There is no reason at all to buy into a high-load fund.

Although banks are prohibited by law from setting up mutual funds of their own, many banks are now in the mutual fund business, having effectively entered into partnerships with existing mutual funds. Most of the mutual funds offered by banks are no-load funds, but some do carry load charges. Be careful to examine bank-offered funds very carefully for hidden and higher continuing management charges than those set by the same kinds of funds operating independently. When you buy a no-load mutual fund through a bank, the likelihood is that those additional charges will be there somewhere, although perhaps well hidden, for both bank and mutual fund must make money on the continuing charges, rather than the mutual fund managers alone.

Money managers who, by the size and direction of their massive trades, make markets, have a very difficult time outperforming the markets they have made. One of the oddest features of this whole period, in investment terms, is that highly professional money managers — who are, in some instances, managing scores of billions of dollars — are in most instances performing worse, not better, than the main averages, although those averages have to a great extent been formed by the direction of their own trades. However the speculative — read that "aggressive growth" — mutual funds do outperform the markets, in both directions. On the way up, they do spectacularly well; on the way down, they do extraordinarily badly.

It is important to know what you are paying for when you buy into a mutual fund. If you are buying professional management that cannot be counted on to do better than the main indexes, except for the speculative funds you may not particularly want to buy, you may be far wiser to go ahead in the financial marketplace with the help of a professional financial adviser, forming your own judgments and making your own moves regarding specific investments. On the other hand, some mutual funds can help diversify your holdings; if you do this in a balanced way, it can cut risks, and may be worthwhile.

Different Kinds of Funds

You can place money into mutual funds with many kinds of investment purposes in mind, for these funds really are forms into which investment money is poured, and the forms change as investment styles and interests change.

The one form that has come on with a rush in recent years is the **money market fund,** which is really a short-term debt obligation fund. Some money market funds invest in a whole range of short-term obligations, from overnight loans and very short-term commercial paper to six-month CDs, with average obligations in the 90–120-day range. Others invest only in short-term federal obligations, providing maximum safety but slightly lower yields. Those that do so rely on federal guarantees for ultimate safety; the more widely invested short-term money market funds depend upon the shortness of terms of the obligations and on private insurance arrangements for safety. Either way, these funds tend to be top-rated for safety, are liquid should you want to get your money out quickly, and are excellent repositories for short-term money. When interest rates are moving up quickly, they may pay marginally more than six- to twelve-month bank CDs; when interest rates are stable or moving down, they pay a little less than CDs. Many money market funds also offer free check-drawing privileges, usually for checks of $500 or more.

There are also some long-established forms: balanced funds, stock funds, and bond funds, defined within those broad categories by the main announced goals of their investment managers. The **balanced fund** invests in both stocks and bonds, varying the mix of those investments as its managers perceive market conditions. Some balanced funds reach most for cash yields, whether as bond interest or stock dividends; others reach for a mix of income and appreciation in value of the fund shares. Both are, in practice, tendencies rather than hard-held approaches; and in both kinds of balanced funds, managers move about rather freely, attempting to provide that fully balanced portfolio of stocks and bonds that relatively safely meets fund management goals.

The several kinds of stock and bond funds focus on either stocks or bonds, and within those broad categories on specific kinds of investment objectives. In **stock funds,** you can generally buy **income funds,** stressing yield from dividend income; funds stressing long-term capital appreciation, and therefore called **growth funds; balanced funds** which attempt to balance growth and income; and **aggressive growth funds,** which seek to maximize appreciation, even though that may require speculation. These, too, are very much tendencies; in fact, all but the income funds are quite likely to do some considerable risk-taking in rising stock markets, while holding a good deal of cash when stocks are declining.

In both boom times and speculative times like these, much advertising and investor attention is devoted to how well the several available speculations have done. In mutual funds, that meant in the 1960s heavy speculation in the growth funds. When the stock market put together what seemed to be a longish-term upward movement in the early 1980s, the growth fund was back, now as an "aggressive growth" fund, to suit gambling tastes a little better, in a world that had by then embraced small investor involvement in commodities futures, options, and several other kinds of high-risk speculations.

The two main kinds of **bond funds** available are composed of **federal government bonds,** mostly medium- and long-term; and **high-rated corporate bonds.** Both stress safety and yield, although the government-based funds are clearly somewhat safer than the corporate-bond-based funds, with the corporate bond funds commensurately higher yielding.

A third kind of bond fund is the **"high yield" fund** — also meaning high-risk fund — which seeks to maximize yield by investing in considerably less than top-rated corporate bonds. For people who want to risk some money in junk bonds, this is probably the way to do it, for here spreading the risk may indeed help preserve your investment. Even so, hard times well short of a major depression can create very adverse conditions for the kinds of corporate issuers behind high-risk bonds, and you still invest here at considerable risk.

Another kind of fund is the **municipal bond fund,** which invests solely in municipals. All these obligations are exempt from federal taxes; some may also be exempt from state and local taxes. The widely advertised "triple-tax-exempt" kind of fund is comprised of securities exempt from federal, state, and local taxes for investors residing in the place of issue.

You can buy municipal bond funds that stress the duration of the underlying bonds: short-, medium-, or long-term municipal bond funds. You can also buy into a "high yield" municipal bond fund, though this means a fund comprised of very high-risk bonds indeed, considering the risks involved in buying the vast majority of municipals today. We have already expressed our serious reservations about municipals, but if you do want to invest in municipals other than those you know extremely well, by all means consider doing it through bond fund purchase, for then you will at least spread the risks somewhat.

Beyond these basic kinds of mutual funds, there are in each period several kinds of **special-purpose mutual funds,** usually organized to invest either in a specific kind of stock or other investment vehicle or to take advantage of one or more tax-avoidance devices. As many kinds of special-purpose funds exist as can be sold; in practice, they are limited only by their marketability in a given period. In the 1960s, "hedge funds," "convertible funds," and "funds of funds" were popular—until they lost large amounts of money for their investors. In the 1970s and 1980s, there were energy funds, oil and gas funds, and a number of other kinds of tax-sheltered, often highly speculative funds.

In the mid-1980s, some of the kinds of funds described above are no longer very popular, but they have been replaced—and then some—by a proliferating number of other kinds. Now, you can buy most of the kinds of funds you could buy in earlier years, including the gold-mining funds and whatever other special-purpose funds continue to be attractive. You can also buy a whole new body of mortgage-based-security mutual funds, ranging in safety from quite safe, effectively federally guaranteed funds based on Ginnie Maes (Government National Mortgage Association bonds) to funds heavily invested in second mortgages, which are inevitably much less safe, as the underlying investments are intrinsically less safe. These are essentially bond funds, but they are relatively new mutual fund forms, and to be treated warily. Your main way to evaluate the risks involved is to look for federal government guarantees of the underlying bonds.

There is also a new interest in **international funds,** and the possibility that a large number of new international funds of several kinds will be formed. Handle all these with great care until some years have passed and you have some track records to examine.

In this period, as new speculative instruments have been developed and sold into popularity, a wide range of new speculative mutual funds has also come into being. As of this writing you can buy into an increasing number of funds devoted to such instruments as indexes and commodities. That opportunity — if that is what it is — will grow as more and more new speculative instruments are developed. We will discuss these kinds of speculations more fully in Chapter 8.

When you buy into a mutual fund, all you buy is professional management of your money while it is in the fund; on the way in, everybody connected with the fund will tell you to buy, but on the way out, nobody will want you to sell. You cannot, for example, reasonably expect a mutual fund manager or seller to tell you that it is time to get out of securities altogether and put your money into short-term bank CDs, collectibles, gold, and gemstones. Yet those were the kinds of investments that paid in the early 1970s; and the small investors who left the securities markets for them in many instances did far better than the professional money managers who stayed behind. Because of their focus on securities, and the much higher yields that can come from rising securities than from conservatively held cash, many professionals have been slow to leave declining markets, and their losses in down periods have reflected that slowness.

Retelling that kind of experience certainly underscores the desirability of buying no-load and low-load funds so you can leave quickly as conditions in volatile markets change, and equally underscores the foolishness of locking yourself into high-load mutual funds. It also makes it very clear that a mutual fund investment is no more to be made and then neglected than any other kind of investment. You may buy professional management when you buy a mutual fund, but you still have to watch that investment and make the basic decisions as to when to get in and when to get out. In this, as in all other personal financial matters, you are running your own business.

8
Speculations and Hedges: Options, Futures, Precious Metals, and Collectibles

Gambling games really have no place in long-term personal financial planning; this chapter is therefore more cautionary than it is advisory. But many gambling games are quite useful and very conservative hedges, if played a little differently, and we will in this chapter also discuss how that can be so.

Hundreds of thousands of investors who might reasonably be expected to know better engage in investment gambling games, some of them for rather large proportions of their available investment money, and often in the erroneous belief that what they are doing is investing. Because of this, we must here explain some of the main games being played in this period. We certainly will not be taking up all the kinds of gambling games, partly because new games are being generated at a great rate, often in the guise of new investment instruments made possible by deregulation, and partly because by the time you read this chapter some games now popular will have lost their luster due to the huge losses suffered by many of their investor-players. But some rather basic understandings can help illuminate the nature of both the games now being played and those that are bound to come along, and in so doing can save no end of financial pain.

First among these is the role of leverage, that is, the use of borrowed money, in investment gambling games. Any kind of investment can be turned into a high risk if leverage can be applied to it. That is essentially what happens when you buy futures or options, or stocks on margin. It is also what happens when you buy land with a down payment and borrow mortgage money for the rest of the purchase price. Leverage enhances the possibility of gain or loss; that is its role. It also enhances the risks involved, for small changes in the market values of your leveraged investments therefore greatly affect the value of the money you have actually put in. It is worth reviewing here: $100 in cash put into an investment, on a 10% margin basis, actually buys $1,000 worth of that investment. If the value of the investment goes up 5%, you make $50, minus any associated charges, meaning that you make nearly 50% on your actual $100 investment. But if the value of the investment goes down by 5%, you lose $50, plus any charges, and you lose over 50% of your original investment. The net of it all is that, with leverage, you greatly enhance possible gain, loss, and risk.

You have also stacked the deck against yourself to the extent that you must pay associated charges, for even if the investment itself shows neither gain nor loss, you will lose the amount of the charges. You must therefore gain somewhat just to break even. These charges can be a small matter in some kinds of speculations, but, as we will see, can be truly enormous in some others. Suppose, for example, that you have investments in the kinds of markets and transactions that absolutely require a very large number of trades. Suppose indeed — for this is the way it actually works for commodities futures and options — that in a typical year your brokerage fees are entirely likely to add up to 50% – 100% of your entire cash investment; that means that your $20,000 account is likely to incur $10,000 – $20,000 in brokerage fees every year, on top of any other risks involved.

That is not risk any more; that is an absurd waste of money. The deck is so badly stacked against you that you are far more victim than gambler or investor. If you were to walk into a casino in Las Vegas or Atlantic City and bet against the dice at a craps table, the odds would be better for you. Investors who become involved in these kinds of gambling games are merely lambs being led to their own slaughter; and the professionals leading them are running some of the least ethical games in town.

Speculating in Options

In the financial marketplace, an option is a legally enforceable, tradable right to buy or sell something of value for a stated price at a stated time, as when you pay a dollar for the right to buy a certain share of stock for $100 on a specified future day. The buyer of an option is usually betting that a price will go up, and that the option can then be exercised — that is, the underlying something of value can be bought at the then-low option price and sold at a profit. The seller of an option is usually betting the reverse — that a price will go down or be unchanged, making the option to buy worthless and therefore unexercised.

Some kinds of options, such as employee stock options, have no intrinsic value of their own, because they are not tradable. Others, such as real estate purchase options, may or may not have intrinsic value, depending upon whether they are negotiable and therefore tradable. Still others, though tradable, are not the main kinds of options now popular; they include the right to buy more shares of stock at a set price and time attached to a new issue, called a **right**, and the same kind of option attached to a new bond or preferred stock issue, then called a **warrant**.

The options discussed here are the tradable options to buy and sell a very wide and increasing range of stocks, indexes, financial futures, commodities futures, and whatever else sellers in these markets think will sell. Up to now you could always place a bet with someone, somewhere, on the future price of anything; today, all that is in the process of being institutionalized, with every exchange of any kind in the country rushing to set up trading in options.

Not all option trading is purely speculative, of course. Large institutional investors and some individuals will soberly hedge their risks on other investments with options; in a volatile market, for example, they may hedge against a loss in a common-stock purchase by purchasing an option to sell a similar amount of that stock at a set price. Some managers and other corporate employees investing in options are, at least in part, doing that kind of hedging. But the vast majority, and the vast majority of individual traders in these markets, are gambling here; that is, they are speculating on the future courses of prices with inadequate knowledge of the risks and costs involved. At least one trading exchange has proposed extending the gamble beyond the prices of assets to the prices of services, as well; if and when that happens, you really may be able to gamble on the price of almost anything on an organized exchange.

How to characterize an option transaction, then, depends upon who you are and what you are doing with the option. For individual investors who are gambling, options are very, very high-risk vehicles; they are made even more so because they must depend on the skills and judgments of the brokers who are, in reality, doing the gambling, with investors' money, and are charging tremendously high total fees for doing so.

The price of each option is fixed. This is called its exercise price or striking price; the two terms are synonyms. (Until recent years it had been generally called an option premium.) The expiration date of the option, sometimes called maturity date, is also fixed. Until now, the underlying prices have been called underlying assets, but with the probable use of other kinds of non-asset-based prices, we will here call them underlying prices, rather than underlying assets. Option buyers are called just that; option sellers are called option writers.

The option transaction itself is simple enough. If you are involved in an actual option to buy or sell, you buy a put or a call. The **put** is the right to sell at a fixed price at a specified time. The buyer of a put is betting that the underlying price will go down more than the difference between the current price and the price of the put. Then the buyer of the put will sell at the price fixed by the put, making profit by doing so — a considerable profit if the underlying price has gone down sharply. If, on the other hand, the underlying price does not go down enough, or does not go down at all, then the buyer of the put loses some or all of the price of the put. Where that put was bought as a hedge against a sharp asset price drop, as in the common stock example above, and the price does indeed go down sharply, the price of the put is often thought worthwhile in terms of limitation of risk. Where the price does not drop in such an instance, then the put is often thought to have been a reasonable insurance precaution. But where the put was not a hedge but a gamble, what is gained or lost stands on its own, without insurance rationale, and carries exorbitant brokerage fees besides.

The buyer of a **call** is betting the other way — that the underlying price will rise more than the difference between its current price and that of the call. If that happens, the call buyer will buy at the low specified price, and resell at a profit. If it does not rise enough, or not at all, some or all of the cost of the call will be lost.

Around these rather simple transactions spin a host of speculative strategies, some of them fairly useful for professional traders and none of them particularly good for individual investors, for all require a great deal of very fast in-and-out trading, and often purchase of simultaneous buying and selling positions, with the sum of all this activity resulting in huge brokerage commissions and ultimate investor losses. Options and futures are not investment areas amenable to long-term buying and holding strategies; you have to go in and out, often even to close out your position at the end of each trading day, thereby generating even more transaction fees for your controlling broker. This kind of trading is a case of the house placing large numbers of bets for you, and taking what in the long run is a ruinous share of the sum of those transactions.

Much of the overheated speculation in options trading in this period closely resembles the kind of speculation that so characterized the late 1920s, before the Crash. In fact, the main wave of it, as it has been developing, has been commodity and financial futures trading; that is precisely the kind of trading that was prohibited in the United States in the 1930s, in reaction to the excesses of the 1920s, although such trading did continue in the London trading markets. But in the late 1970s, and with great acceleration during the early and mid-1980s, new futures options markets have developed in the United States. Indeed, the development of new options games, including futures options games, is encouraged in the new deregulated financial marketplace, creating whole new bodies of gain-and-loss possibilities for people who want to gamble on the course of prices. In futures options, you are actually pyramiding leverage upon leverage, for the leverage created by gambling on futures is greatly magnified by the leverage intrinsic to options.

Speculating in Futures

For some kinds of traders, futures are not speculations at all, but rather absolutely essential hedging transactions, aimed at securing vitally needed supplies of commodities at determinable prices, for up to a year in the future. Without such supply and price guarantees, companies, industries, and governments using some kinds of commodities would find it impossible to set their own prices and make reliable promises of delivery to others. That is why a worldwide market in such commodity guarantees has grown up in the last several centuries. That market includes both current sales, called **spot sales,** and contracts to buy fixed amounts of commodities for up to one year ahead, called **futures.**

The established worldwide commodities markets have long been organized into many commodities exchanges, which have traded a wide range of commodities, such as sugar, tea, cocoa, wheat, soybeans, cotton, cattle, pork bellies, gold, silver, and many other agricultural and extractive industry goods. In recent years, futures trading has expanded greatly, to include a very wide range of additional trading vehicles, most of them financial instruments, and the end is nowhere in sight.

The futures being traded are contracts to buy or sell stated quantities of goods at a stated time. All contracts in each group are identical as to terms of trade, quantity, and quality; that is what makes them tradable on commodities and other futures exchanges.

When a company buys or sells commodities on these markets, whether on a spot or futures basis, the transaction is being made for use. For example, a tea or cereal company trades on these exchanges because it must, ultimately taking delivery on large quantities of commodities for use. But an individual investor trading in commodities futures has speculative profit as a sole goal, for no individual has any intention at all of actually taking delivery on thousands of bushels of wheat or whatever other large quantities are the standard minimum tradable units in other commodities. Similarly, although an investor may physically take possession of financial instruments that were the subject of futures transactions, that possession is likely to be merely a formal matter, with those instruments sold immediately thereafter. These are purely speculative investments, in which futures contracts are traded in and out fast by professionals who collect commissions on each and every one of those very large numbers of transactions.

Individuals have been moving away from futures trading to a considerable extent, as more and more of them have lost large amounts of money in these markets. A combination of enormous total brokerage fees and extremely volatile markets has made it very clear that it is extremely difficult to do anything but lose your shirt in futures—and often very quickly. The developing option markets have also beckoned, and will until some of the realities are brought home there as well.

A note on the prevalence of slipshod and fraudulent trading practices is very much in order here. The Commodities Futures Trading Corporation (CFTC) is far easier in its regulatory practices than the Securities and Exchange Commission (SEC), and industry trading practices very much reflect this. There are still a few "bucket shops"—fraudulent telephone selling operations— in the stock and bond end of the securities business, but the SEC has done a great deal to destroy such operations, and has the situation very much under control. But the CFTC has had no such success and has, in fact, not tried very hard in this area. As a result, there are hundreds of fraudulent operations fleecing investors all over the country, often through the device of financial or commodities futures trades off any exchange. If you must trade in futures, do so through the organized exchanges; even then, you may very well run into sharp practices, but at least you will have a reasonable chance of honestly making or losing money.

Gold, Silver, and Similar Stores of Value

Gold is still seen by many people all over the world as the ultimate store of value; and possession of gold is seen as a powerful personal hedge against the personal and financial impacts of war, revolution, currency devaluation, depression, and all manner of ills. Perhaps so. It has been so in enough times and places to make a powerful argument for holding gold. In some places, holding gold and similar stores of hard, valuable goods may still be an excellent idea, for in many countries people have scarcely any opportunity to reach for any other kinds of financial instruments.

But not here; not now. There may again come a time for holding and perhaps even hoarding gold and other such goods in the United States, but our belief is that it is unlikely to become appropriate in the foreseeable future, and therefore has no place in serious lifelong financial planning. There is nothing immutable about that; people who carefully watch their financial affairs can move into valuable hard goods if and as that seems right, as many did with rather lucrative results in the 1970s.

But for Americans, gold is best seen as a commodity, which can be used as an inflationary hedge during a period of runaway inflation, but which, because of its nature and mystique, is far more likely to fluctuate sharply than are most other commodities. It also can be used as a speculation, one influenced by a very wide range of ever-changing economic and political factors. It is certainly watched, traded, and speculated in by professional traders all over the world, making it a particularly difficult speculative tool for investment amateurs.

The simple side of it is that in economically stable, relatively peaceful times, when inflation is low and investor safety fairly well assured, gold tends to lose some of its value, as people move instead into interest-paying and equity-growing investments. When times are difficult, on the other hand, people tend to move into gold and other such goods, both because they are then seen as safe and because that very move brings upward pressure on their prices. The more complex side of this activity is that hoarding, speculating, large-scale trading, and a whole web of national and international economic and political matters much affect the prices of gold and other such goods, making them fluctuate considerably more swiftly than many other commodities and financial instruments.

Gold is particularly vulnerable to political factors. Its supply, and therefore its world price in any given period, can be greatly affected by the withholding of production on the part of South Africa and the Soviet Union, the world's major gold-mining countries. Dumping by these countries or by the United States, the International Monetary Fund, or China can also deeply affect gold prices. The situation of South Africa can especially impact on world gold supplies, as it is by far the world's leading gold producer, and is also a country with deep and potentially disastrous internal and international problems. The South Arican government keeps tight control over gold production and export; if it should feel the need to dump gold on the world's markets, or if a successor government should feel the need to do so, the impact on gold prices could be very great. Any large new supply of gold on the world market tends to drive prices down, with multiplied impact as traders and speculators scramble to get out. On the other hand, political and social unrest in South Africa could disrupt production, producing the opposite effect.

Furthermore, volatile and difficult world conditions accentuate the tendency to hoard gold. That tendency is always there, for the mystique of gold as the ultimate store of value is such that there are always many who will hoard, even though no major country in the world now remains on the gold standard and it is unlikely that any will go back to gold-backed currencies soon. In unstable or inflationary times — and these conditions often occur together — that hoarding tendency is much enhanced. Then gold supplies shrink and prices start up; traders and speculators rush in to attempt to profit from the upward price trend, often with borrowed money, thereby driving gold prices up faster and further than any normal supply-and-demand factors would dictate.

But bubbles always burst. The classic case in this valuable hard goods area was the attempt, in 1980, of Nelson Bunker Hunt and his associates to corner the world silver market. Instead, they managed to drive the world price of silver from $6 to $50 per ounce, using a great deal of their own cash and much borrowed money to do so, and then had to watch their attempt fail, losing hundreds of millions of dollars in the process. What happened was that, quite unexpectedly and largely for internal economic and political reasons, interest rates in the United States tripled, making it first difficult and then impossible for speculators to hold their then terribly overborrowed positions. Lenders terminated loans, brokers liquidated positions when fresh margin calls were unmet, and the price of silver went right back down to $10, and then less.

Gold is, in and of itself, not a particularly good investment. It has had one historic runup, in the years following the United States' abandonment of price fixing in the late 1960s, but if you went in at or near the high, you bought at the range of $700 – $800 per ounce, and then for many years held at half that, in the $300 – $400 range, waiting for gold to up again, while you earned absolutely nothing in interest or dividends on the gold you were holding. Many who bought high became tired of waiting and sold out at large losses. Nor did gold in the fairly short run fulfill its main stated hedging purpose — that of holding its value — for it did not move up against the pace of continuing inflation after runaway inflation had somewhat eased. Gold does tend to hold its own in value, but only in the very, very long run; therefore, the price of holding it in a relatively stable, working society — like that of the United States in this period — is much too high.

But gold does have a certain mystique. In truth, there are some people who are not happy unless they have some tucked away somewhere. If you are of that persuasion, and must have some gold to bury in your back yard, by all means buy it on some sunny spring day in the middle of a very stable — or at least stable-seeming — period, when hardly anybody thinks gold is worth having at all, when the speculators are gambling in options and futures and the price of gold is therefore way, way down. As of this writing, gold has been hovering around $300 per ounce for quite some time, while the market conditions described above pertain. That is always a wonderful time to buy gold for long-term holding, if that is what you are impelled to do. In time of near-panic and great fear, it will cost much more.

Gold, silver, gemstones, platinum, and strategic metals are all hard, valuable commodities that can be held, used, traded, and speculated in. You can buy and physically hold them; you can also invest in companies mining, trading, and selling them, and bet on the future courses of their prices.

As investment vehicles, the values of the stocks of companies engaged in mining, trading, and selling these kinds of commodities are closely related to the prices of the commodities. If the world price of gold goes up, for example, then the stocks of gold-mining companies will tend to go up in direct relationship. And if anyone ever again comes close to cornering the world silver market, driving silver prices up enormously in the process, silver-mining stocks can be expected to move up sharply for a while.

This direct relationship of stock prices to metal prices reflects speculative interest in those companies, rather than a long-term kind of approach to their prospects. Those prospects may be related to such basic matters as the nature and extent of remaining deposits and government stability in mineral-producing countries. That is particularly relevant in the instance of South Africa, the world's leading gold and gemstone producer, and home of many of the world's most invested-in precious-goods mining companies. Entirely aside from any moral questions, given the terribly volatile political situation in and around South Africa and the negative possibilities that exist even short of expropriation of mining properties by any new government, we would have to view any investment in South Africa, including mining company investments, as quite speculative and short-term, and therefore having no real place in any program of lifelong financial planning. If you are going to invest in mining companies, you would be wiser to stay with companies with headquarters and main properties located in North America.

The same thinking applies to investing in special-purpose mutual funds devoted to gold and other mining stocks. The South African exposure in these mutual funds is bound to be great, and should be avoided.

You can also speculate in futures and futures options in these investment areas. But there is nothing in these metals that sets these kinds of futures and options off from any other futures and options, other than a possible subjective urge to be somehow involved in gold, gemstones, or any of the other commodities in this group. In some ways, they may even be riskier than some of the other futures and options, because of the possible international complications, such as those posed by South Africa.

Buying Collectibles

During the 1970s, collectibles of many kinds became popular as speculative investments. In those years many kinds of collectibles did, in fact, considerably outperform the main stock and mutual fund indexes, even when they were purchased and held by people who knew not at all what they were doing. People bought millions of silver plates and other goods made of intrinsically valuable materials, at prices far greater than the intrinsic value of those materials. Then they held on to them and watched their values go up and up and up, as hundreds of thousands of other new "collectors" bought, pushing all prices up in overheated markets. It was similar to the way people bought gemstones of several kinds, and watched their values be bid up in a sharply rising market. The market for gemstones was so hot that one astute group of thieves was able to sell allegedly valuable gemstones in packages that were not to be opened and examined, or the warranty would be breached — and they found many gullible buyers.

Those who bought collectibles they knew nothing about in that period were buying them both in reaction to stock markets that had plunged, leaving them with large losses, and in an attempt to hedge with hard valuable goods against double-digit inflation. When money market funds and federally insured bank accounts began to pay excellent rates of interest, other investment markets began to revive, and the rate of inflation declined; then a lot of those plates, plaques, prints, and the like lost much of their illusory value, and many innocents who were confidently holding them lost a good deal of money. Many people who had been holding collectibles even found that the previously large and ready-to-buy market that had once seemed so permanent had disappeared, and they couldn't sell their collectibles at any price, for there were no buyers. Then they found themselves holding nearly worthless goods that paid no dividends or interest, and were mostly a dead loss.

In this period, collectibles as a kind of speculative investment have understandably lost a good deal of their mass appeal, and are not very likely to soon regain it. At the same time, some kinds of collectibles continue to be excellent long-term investments *for those who take the trouble to learn a good deal about them.* For centuries, there have been well-established worldwide markets for such goods as paintings, sculpture, books, furniture, stamps, coins, and scores of other kinds of collectibles. In the modern period, these have been joined by many much newer kinds of collectibles, all the way from vintage wines and old photographs to automobiles, baseball cards, and early barbed wire. All are perfectly sound kinds of investments — for people who know what they are doing — as long as a core of interested people and commercial traders continue to make definable markets for them, and move through well-established channels into those markets.

You can certainly lose your shirt in "collectibles"; but you are unlikely in the long run to lose and will probably make out rather well if you limit your collecting interests, learn everything you can about one market, and move into that market with long-term collection and trading in mind. In the process of becoming expert and by taking a long-term approach, you can maximize profit and at the same time develop a later-years part-time or full-time business that can go a long way toward generating the cash you will need later in life.

9
Investing in Real Estate

The last major investment vehicle we will discuss is real estate. Like the other main kinds of investments, it can be poured into several forms. You can own and occupy your own home; own and directly rent residential or commercial space; participate as general or limited partner in several kinds of real estate ventures; loan money directly or indirectly to realty buyers, as through second mortgages, second-mortgage participations, and the purchase of mortgage-backed securities; or invest in raw land. You may simultaneously own your own home, a general partnership in a local motel, a limited partnership in office buildings, shopping malls, and condominiums all over the country, a vacation home, and some raw land, either as outright speculation or for your grandchildren.

You may know a good deal about some of your real estate interests, and regrettably little about a good deal more, having purchased them as part of a series of tax-shelter moves over the years. And the odds are that those you have considered and watched carefully as long as you have owned them have done well, perhaps very well in a real estate market that has for decades far outpaced the rate of inflation. The odds also are that you are hurting where you have followed adventurous advisers into speculative real estate deals that were also bad business deals, no matter how tax-sheltered; an empty office building or shopping mall in a city like Houston is not so much a tax shelter as it is a bottomless pit into which your money has been thrown, never to be seen again.

In real estate, as in anything else, the best results are secured by people who have taken the trouble to learn. Not to dutifully follow the advice of their advisers, no matter how well respected, but to know for themselves. Certainly part of their own knowledge will indeed have come from advisers, but the essence of the matter is the development of personal knowledge, however obtained. In local real estate, such knowledge is accessible. Those who want to participate in large, remote, often rather complicated real estate ventures will have to rely largely upon the advice of others.

Managers and other corporate employees, who often spend their working lives at some remove from areas where they live and can reasonably expect to move from time to time, are at a significant disadvantage when it comes to knowing about local real estate. For local real estate is one of the few investment areas in which people can gain real personal knowledge, with that knowledge improving greatly as the years go by and you become better set in an area. People who are really local can accrete that kind of knowledge naturally, as they go through their day-to-day paces; managers have to work a little harder to get it, and may also have to be a little more conservative in their local real estate investing habits than some others. What a local lawyer, accountant, or realty professional knows about local real estate opportunities comes easily and daily; what a commuting manager knows more often comes from working with such local professionals and from print sources.

The extra work can be very much worth it, though. Local realty opportunities — ones that you really have taken the trouble to learn a good deal about — can be some of the best opportunities of an investing lifetime. Similarly, someone local who fully plans to be in an area for many years can take longer-term approaches, like buying a home in an area that is "on its way up," rather than in an area that may be more expensive but has already "arrived." The corporate employee may have to play it somewhat safer, for both job opportunities and job hazards may mandate a shorter-term view. That is why the expensive home in the expensive community may or may not be a conspicuous consumption trap for a manager; it all depends on the specifics of the instance, as we will discuss later.

The use of leverage is central to all real estate transactions in which you are involved as direct or indirect purchaser (not necessarily when you are direct or indirect lender). That is not so much a matter of searching for the possible leverage in a situation, as in some other kinds of investments, but rather that the purchase prices are so large that they must inevitably require the use of borrowed money. The leverage opportunity then is merely a byproduct of the transaction, although it can be and is manipulated in many ways, usually to increase both the risks and possible rewards involved.

Federal taxing policy has also been a central determinant as to the desirability of specific real estate ventures for many years, though a considerable reaction has set in among lawmakers, throwing the whole area of tax advantage in real estate transactions somewhat into question. Should major changes in the way real estate ventures are tax actually come about (an open question as of this writing) many residential and commercial real estate moves will be much less advantageous to investors than they have been for decades. But the long-term impact of such tax changes will be less than it might seem close up, for the long-term trend in residential and comercial real estate values will continue to be up.

The Benefits of Owning Your Own Home

One of the great investment opportunities of every American lifetime is the owner-occupied home. Indeed, there is nothing quite like it for asset development; it is no accident that their homes are by far the most important assets of most homeowners. Managers and other corporate employees well established in their careers often have other major assets as well, for their incomes tend to be considerably higher than national averages. Even so, the manager who bought a $35,000 – $45,000 "starter" house 20 or 25 years ago is quite likely today to be owning and occupying a house in the $250,000 – $350,000 range. In some instances, that has been largely a matter of staying put, making modest improvements from time to time, perhaps "trading up" once or twice, and simply watching values of well-situated homes take off. In others, that has resulted from the need to buy new homes from time to time due to job location changes, with a certain amount of trading up. However it did occur, the main thing that happened was a national suge in the values of well-situated homes, far beyond the pace of inflation, and lasting for decades. When people traded up, they used accreted home equities to provide new down payments; when they stayed put, the values of their homes continued to rise, even if they did little beyond ordinary maintenance.

For many managers, the reach for an affluent lifestyle — so

economically negative when it is merely conspicuous consumption — quite accidentally generated the best possible investments they could have made, truly the investments of a lifetime. The numbers are quite familiar by now, and still tell the story best. Assume that 25 years ago, on a not very large corporate salary, you bought a then-quite-expensive $60,000 house in an affluent suburb and have occupied it every since. That house is quite likely to be worth five times more today, or $300,000; in some particularly well-situated places, it may well be worth more like $400,000.

However, that big jump in value, far outpacing inflation, only begins to tell the story. The actual cash you put into it may bhave been as little as a 10% down payment of $6,000 and closing and moving-in costs amounting to perhaps $4,000 more, for a total of $10,000. The truth is that on a purely cash-in, cash-out basis, the relation between the $300,000 now and your initial $10,000 is about thirty to one, and you have a gain of nearly 3,000% in all. And if you sell that home when you are past 55, you will not even have to pay taxes on a good deal of the gain in it. Had you put the same $10,000 into investments netting and compounding a very respectable 10% yearly for those 25 years, it would have grown to $108,000 plus, almost eleven to one. That is an excellent return, and far better than most individual investors have managed in the last quarter of a century, given the ups and downs of the stock market and several other kinds of investment vehicles. But eleven to one is nowhere near thirty to one.

The fact is that on a cash-in, cash-out basis, the well-situated, owner-occupied home, the kind of home that managers and other comparatively well paid corporate employees have been buying all along, has been an extraordinarily lucrative investment, because the leverage in the transaction has been enormous. It has also been one of the safest possible kinds of investments. Leverage can, of course, be used to make a sound investment over into a very risky one, or a risky one into an even more dangerous one. But the use of the leverage in an intrinsically sound and safe transaction can yield tremendous rewards, and that is what has happened and will happen when people buy and live in well-situated homes.

That has been and will be so, *regardless of the tax and interest rate aspects.* Focus on these factors quite misses the main point about the owner-occupied home, which is also the reason that the cash-in, cash-out comparison is the right way to look at the question: The key point is that you are going to spend the money for housing yourself and your family anyway. That has been the perception of tens of millions of American homeowners for many decades, and it is the simple truth.

It is a truth that can easily be overlooked, when you are worrying about what might happen if real estate tax and mortgage interest deductions were to be discontinued, and how much more expensive it is to carry a mortgage when interest rates are high. But should tax advantages disappear, they will disappear for comparable rental housing as well, and rental rates will reflect that fact. And when interest rates are high, rentals must inevitably reflect that, too. Comparable rentals don't cost less than owner-occupied homes; they cost more. They must, for rental property owners must pay many management and maintenance expenses that owner-occupiers handle for much less, and often largely handle themselves. Comparable rentals must also be higher because most rental property owners seek profit, as well as growth in property values.

Should tax breaks disappear, the cost of housing will increase, for both owners and renters, but *the fact of rapid accretion of value in well-situated properties will not change.* When interest rates are high, the cost of housing goes up, for both owners and renters, and many people have a harder time swinging costs and qualifying for mortgages. But the basic facts of value accretion are unchanged, for there is and will be long-term continuing pent-up demand for good, well-situated housing. At worst, there can be short-term downward fluctuations in well-situated home values; in the long run, such homes will continue to rise in value far more quickly than the pace of inflation, and far faster than any other relatively safe investments, once you calculate their value accretions on a cash-in, cash-out basis.

For managers and other corporate employees, who have been buying these kinds of houses for decades, the foregoing has considerable implications. We are scarcely recommending that you buy the most expensive homes you can dinf, in the most expensive communities you can find, and live it up in the good old corporate affluent way. Far from it. Clearly, conspicuous consumption is the enemy of all personal financial planning, for people who have too little can accrete too little. But for managers and other corporate people, the times do seem to call for holding a safe house, meaning a rather expensive house in a rather expensive community, coupled with a far-from-expensive lifestyle. The rather expensive house with some land, heated mainly by wood stoves, and one which you do most of the maintenance yourself, while driving one or two not very new and originally not very expensive cars, just about does it.

The Potential Hazards of Real Estate

Managers do have to be more careful than most others about the house being a safe investment, though. Job changes can mean considerable home-selling hazards, for they may occur inopportunely. Your own company probably has many fewer involuntary corporate moves than even a decade ago, but you may still face the promotion, the move to a more desired location, the voluntary but quite pressured transfer, or the intercompany move. In all these situations, you may well be able to negotiate excellent downside risk protection, in the form of guaranteed minimum home price arrangements to protect you in a temporarily sagging housing market. You may also be able to negotiate such valuable protections as mortgage interest rate guarantees, and rental payment subsidies while you are looking for a new home. You may even be able to negotiate a "fair market value" guarantee, in which your company agrees to pay you fair market value as of a certain date, if you have not sold your house by then for at least that stated price. But these arrangements are rather unusual, and you cannot count on having them available when you make your move, although they are very much the stuff of job-moving negotiation, and are well worth pushing hard to accomplish.

However, in the very uncertain modern American business world, you may also find yourself out of a job inopportunely, and be forced to sell your home for economic reasons. Or you may be out of a job, find a job elsewhere, and not be able to negotiate any significant downside risk guarantees at all. For that matter, you may leave employed status of your own accord, as when you decide to strike out in business or the professions on your own, in a different location. In such events, it becomes very important to have chosen your house and its location well, for although the long-term value trend in housing is up, the short-term housing market can be counted upon to fluctuate, which in some cases can cause you catastrophic losses.

After all, leverage works both ways. You can find yourself in a housing market that is down enough to cause you to lose whatever modest equity you have in a home bought recently with a large mortgage. That, in turn, can very easily cause grave difficulties in securing a new home elsewhere, for without that basic down-payment capital, you may have to pile mortgage on mortgage right from the start, with consequent heavy strains on your family economy. That's leverage, too — high-risk, hard-to-handle leverage. For managers, it is vital to play the home-selection game very carefully and, where downside risks are involved, very conservatively.

The above injunction also applies to the two-income family, which often seems entirely solvent while both incomes are coming in but turns out to have ben far from economically healthy when one of the two incomes is lost. The truth is that in America today many high-priced homes and accompanying affluent lifestyles are being swung only with two corporate and professional incomes, with woefully small reserves. In such instances, safety still demands careful choice of home location; it also very often demands choice of a home in the medium to medium-low end of the price range in the location chosen. Clearly, the well-situated home that can be carried, though perhaps with some strain, on one income is far safer than one that requires two. Just as clearly, the "executive" lifestyle that impresses hardly anyone worth impressing, and merely builds up debts, is a foolish gamble.

People like managers, who by the nature of their work may have to change locations smewhat unexpectedly, take greater risks than do more firmly rooted people when they seek leverage by moving into "coming" areas and neighborhoods. Honeybuyers whose work allows them to stay put can make not-quite-right estimates as to the pace of change, hold on a little longer, and see their expectations come true; but that leeway may not exist for mobile families. That is so in suburban areas, but is particularly so in rundown city areas that are in the process of "gentrification" — the wholesale renovation of structures in a neighborhood, accompanied by the influx of substantial numbers of new, relatively affluent people. The early move into that kind of situation is speculative; it can indeed be a very lucrative speculation, if all works out well. If you do it, though, understand that it is a speculation in which the risks may be magnified by your personal situation. You may make what turns out to be an error and move into a less-than-prime location that costs you a good deal if you must move quickly.

Potential Location Problems

Many kinds of location hazards are easy to perceive. No matter how attractive a buy, a home too near a functioning industrial plant must be suspect; a home near a chemical plant is an especially poor idea. Even if it is safe, the possibility of a contamination scare anywhere in the area may dramatically cut resale value just when you need to sell. Similarly, a home located near an electrical installation or major power line may or may not be safe, but in investment terms that scarcely matters. All you need is a major study indicating that such homesites are unsafe to destroy your resale value.

There are no good buys where potential environmental contamination questions exist. As it becomes increasingly apparent that we have much underestimated the extent of these kinds of problems, sensitivity to them grows. With that sensitivity comes increasing reluctance to take a chance on being poisoned, and on buying homes that can lose much of their value as soon as contamination possibilities are even raised, much less proved.

Some other not-so-obvious major hazards are worth mentioning, for they can sink your home investment just as surely as that chemical plant. One of them can quite literally sink your home. As homes and the land they stand upon have grown more and more expensive and harder and harder to acquire and carry, many structures have been built on substandard land. In community after community, the land in the swamp at the bottom of the hill, land that in earlier periods was seen as unbuildable, has been built upon. So, too, the low-lying bottom land on the riverbank, the land on the steep hillside that has always washed away in wet years, and the now hugely expensive land on the oceanfront. Some new factors have come into play, as well; for example, Houston sinks a little every year, as building proceeds and the underlying land is drained, and northern New Jersey floods a little more every year, as continuing laying of pavement diminishes the areas of natural drainage.

Another of the major hazards here is part of the price we are all paying for having allowed substantial portions of our environment to be poisoned. Where the ground and water are known to have ben poisoned, as from industrial plants, chemical warehousing, or dumping — some of it quite legal and terribly lethal in its day — home resale prices can scarcely be said to exist at all, nobody will buy, and the investment questions do not come up. But where that has happened *and the facts are not yet known,* an enormous hazard exists. The new and expensive condominium that turns out to have been build on a contaminated landfill may become a dead loss to its unfortunate owners. The lovely community on the land near the river in the old part of town, full of converted factory and warehouse buildings, may run into deep trouble if those warehouses and factories dumped the wrong kinds of material there before anyone really understood the long-term effects, or if some homes are built over capped oil wells that build up explosive methane gas concentrations, as has hapened in Los Angeles.

There are no easy answers to any of these situations, especially to the problem of earlier, unknown contamination. You have to ask around, talking to realtors and local residents at length before buying. You also have to research in the local library, in back issues of the local newspapers and in any local histories available, to try to understand what kind of area you are moving into and what the extraordinary hazards may be. That is often difficult, especially when you are moving into a wholly new area; it is also indispensable, once you properly perceive the possible hazards.

Understanding Today's Mortgages

Not so long ago, a residential mortgage was for the vast majority of transactions a single kind of instrument. It was a **fixed-rate**

mortgage loan, payable in equal installments, usually for 25 or 30 years. For most of the quarter-century between the end of World War II and the end of the 1960s boom, it was a low-cost mortgage, too. In fact, that mortgage, accompanied by low down payments, did a great deal to fuel the huge housing boom of that period, simultaneously providing tens of millions of Americans with the best investment opportunities of their lifetimes.

But the boom ended, interest rates soared and remained high, mortgage money was often scarce, and even quite well-paid people began to find it hard to swing mortgages. In those circumstances, a considerable body of alternative mortgage arrangements emerged, as, out of sheer necessity, realty sellers and financial institutions began to develop the body of financing arrangements collectively called "creative financing." Though there are really just a few basic arrangements, there are so many variations on these few themes that the best way to handle the available alternatives is with a computer program, in which you can change individual variables to come up with the least expensive and most feasible alternatives.

One of the net effects of that quarter-century of low rates was the bankrupting of large numbers of lending institutions, when interest rates went up and stayed up. Even now, years later, banks caught in that interest-rate trap continue to go under. The understandable result was that lenders became very wary of the fixed-rate mortgage loan; instead they developed the **adjustable-rate loan,** selling it hard and charging lower interest rates for it. The reverse side of that coin was that homebuyers resisted — and continue to resist — variable-rate mortgages, correctly reasoning that even small percentage increases in their mortgage rates could increase monthly payments a great deal.

That is the basic situation as of this writing. The two main kinds of mortgages available are the fixed and the adjustable or flexible-rate mortgage. Lenders push adjustable rates; homebuyers want fixed rates. So far, the fixed rate is still the main mode, although for a little while it seemed that the adjustable rate would supplant it. But what happened and continues to happen is an entirely justified case of mass consumer resistance. Most homebuyers continue — rightly — to be willing to pay more for the certainty in fixed-rate mortgages.

Some people do choose to go for an adjustable-rate mortgage, however, often because the lower mortgage interest makes it possible to qualify for a mortgage of the size needed, given the income of the applicants. That can be a perfectly sound reason in a tight housing market, but you certainly should not take an adjustable-rate mortgage because you think it is a bargain.

If you do choose to go that way, be sure that you have a cap — a maximum amount the mortgage interest may be raised, in any given year and for the life of the mortgage. Such caps normally run 1%–2% per year, and 4%–7% for the life of the mortgage. Negotiate hard for the lower figures, remembering that a single percent on a 12% adjustable-rate mortgage can increase your monthly payments by 8.5%, as from $1,200 per month to $1,302. Also be very sure to know that the index on which the mortgage is based is a reasonably stable one, such as a short-term federal debt obligation or a national mortgage loan index, rather than something you and your lawyer know nothing about. Also be careful that the yearly mortgage cap is a real cap, *rather than merely a cap on payments;* otherwise you may be charged on the whole mortgage at higher rates, and pay those higher rates in the long run, with unpaid interest being added to the principal owed. Finally, be sure that what you have secured is for the whole term specified, rather than a short-term mortgage that can be renegotiated upward on all or many of its main terms after a few years; some adjustable-rate mortgages are terribly deceptive in this regard.

The **balloon mortgage** is not at all deceptive in this regard; it clearly states that you are taking a short-term mortgage on which you will pay only the interest as it comes due, with the whole principal coming due all at once at a stated time. Such arrangements do seem to cut mortgage payments nicely; they are also extremely dangerous to your economic health. This balloon mortgage technique was the main home financing instrument of the 1920s, and banks routinely "rolled over" mortgages, providing homeowners with new mortgages, as long as interest payments were kept up. But when the Great Depression hit, and people could not find mortgage money when the balloon payment fell due, even those who could have maintained fixed-payment mortgages often lost their homes and farms.

Well short of another major depression, the balloon mortgage is still extraordinarily dangerous, for these are volatile times, our whole financial system is in trouble, and the home financing end of the financial industry is in the deepest trouble of all. Even when your company offers you downside risk protection on your home purchase, as on a transfer the company wants you to make, *do not take out a balloon mortgage loan on your home.* Company promises can change and disappear over the years; in these times, so can whole companies.

There is a small variation on this, applicable to managers and other corporate employees. On transfer, some companies will also provide down-payment assistance, but that assistance must often be repaid in a lump sum should you leave the company. Then the down-payment loan functions as a sort of reverse, or front-end, balloon loan. Do take that kind of down-payment assistance, if you need it, but be aware of the reverse balloon possibilities.

The fixed-rate, adjustable, and balloon mortgages are all now in use; there are many subsidiary forms and arrangements, as well. An owner who must sell in difficult times may offer some kind of **takeback,** essentially becoming the mortgage lender for all or part of the selling price. A lender may offer a **graduated rate mortgage,** in which payments are fixed, but lower in the early years and higher in the later years of the mortgage. There are also **buydowns,** in which builders offer short-term cut rates on mortgage payments as an inducement to buy now. Occasionally, there is even an assumable lower-rate mortgage from many years ago, although most mortgage lenders have for quite some time made their loans nontransferable to new owners on sale of a home. The variations are considerable, and continue to proliferate, especially in difficult periods. But the advantages and disadvantages of the several basic mortgage forms do not change; the conventional fixed-rate mortgage is still both the most common and the most desirable of the mortgage forms.

A side note: Mortgage life and disability insurance is often available from banks and insurance companies. It is right to buy such insurances, for they are certainly valuable kinds of catastrophe protections. When you do this, be sure to coordinate these policies with your other life and disability coverages. As your mortgage decreases, so will the life insurance you have bought. But the disability coverage remains level, so you must take the initiative to decrease coverage as the mortgage decreases.

Second Homes, Managing Properties, Partnerships

Beyond the unique opportunity that comes with owning your own home, there are several other ways to own and participate in the ownership of real estate. You can own a second home, invest in and perhaps manage other pieces of property, join with others as a general partner in real estate investment, or become a limited partner — that is, limited in liability and rewards — in real estate ownerships.

Throughout the period since the World War II, all these forms of ownership have, in the United States, depended heavily upon the tax-avoidance opportunities built into the Internal Revenue Code. The twin devices of interest deduction and accelerated depreciation (most recently called accelerated cost recovery) have seen to that. The interest deduction has enhanced leverage, for necessary borrowings to finance purchase and construction have generated large tax deductions. The accelerated depreciation device has generated large depreciation deductions in the early years of ownership. The two together have generated large tax losses in the early years of ownership, losses that have much enhanced the net after-tax yields enjoyed by real estate investors. As a byproduct, they have also generated high velocity in the real estate marketplace, for it has generally paid far better to hold real estate for a short time, take maximum tax advantage, resell, and start the tax-advantage process all over again with a different piece of property.

We are, however, at what may prove to be a historic juncture in the area of real estate investment and its accompanying tax advantages. As of this writing, there is very substantial attack on those advantages, by both the national administration and substantial numbers of both Republican and Democratic legislators. The particular set of attacks on these tax advantages may not result in meaningful changes now, but bipartisan sentiment seems so strong that the only tax advantages that seem sure to remain are interest deductions on owner-occupied homes and some kind of depreciation, though not necessarily accelerated, on business property. Should even a substantial portion of the changes that are now being discussed actually occur — and they may — the entire real estate investment picture in the United States will greatly alter.

Whether those major tax law changes occur or not, their discussion and the probable passage of at least some of them have already changed the real estate investment scene. Until the situation has settled — and that may take years — it is most prudent to view new real estate ownership investments as if they were effectively *without* their extraordinary tax-shelter aspects, and to see the tax advantages accompanying them as bonuses, for as long as they continue.

Second Homes

Tax shelter or not, a second home can sometimes be an excellent long-term asset-building opportunity, as well as a source of pleasure. The two-home family has become a feature of the American scene in the last few decades, with tax advantage helping fuel the trend. But even without that tax advantage, some of the same factors that so favor the owner-occupier of a home are at work here. If it is a well-situated home, in terms of properly anticipated value growth, leverage can work as favorably here as in the main home-ownership situation. Sometimes, it can even work better; a holiday home in an area outside of but accessible to an expanding major metropolitan area can also involve land purchase as well. In such locations, and if you are planning to hold it indefinitely for personal use, an old farm and accompanying farmland, for example, can become a major asset. When the value of the asset will actually grow is often a matter of rather faulty conjecture. In this respect, buying a vacation home is in investment terms a good deal like buying raw land. You have to be prepared to pay taxes on it, get nothing back in current income, and hold it for the long haul. If you buy with current use and possible long-term appreciation in mind, you have little to lose, for you will have spent the money on vacations anyway.

But most second homes are bought at some remove from main living and operational bases, and therefore usually with less knowledge of property values and trends than is desirable; in that case, speculation in them is likely to be a very poor idea. Speculation in country land is, by the nature of the knowledge needed, best done by local people and by professionals ready to enter an area and learn enough to make informed buying decisions, rather than by outside amateurs.

In your home community, of course, it is you who are local, and thereby potentially rather better able to identify real estate opportunities than outsiders. But that is sometimes not true for managers, who may live in a bedroom community for a few years, in those years spending their customary 60–70 hours a week commuting and working in their offices and homes on company matters, and then move on. Then the hazard of possibly having to make an inopportune career-connected move, along with necessary focus on corporate work, make it difficult to see and properly take advantage of local real estate opportunities on your own.

However, it is still possible, from a local position, to become an investing partner or lender in local real estate, often working with local real estate professionals, lawyers, and accountants. The opportunities always exist, and so do people who are seeking them professionally — and who almost always are also seeking financial partners. If you want to cultivate this kind of investment opportunity — and in many of the kinds of communities managers move into this can be quite worthwhile — you will want to reach into the community to find the kinds of people you want to work with.

That is not very hard to accomplish, especially in smallish communities, though somewhat harder in larger ones. You need only ask around a little, in religious, fraternal, and social organizations, or for that matter just listen a little at social gatherings. Once you make it known that you are interested in doing a little local real estate investing, lots of people will turn up who will be happy to help you invest. You will most want to work with seasoned people who have been in the community and area for many years; newcomers, however bright, will seldom be working from an "inside" position, and it is that inside positioning that is most valuable.

General and Limited Partnerships

In real estate, the classic forms of ownership have been sole ownership, as of your own home, and general or limited partnership. **General partnership** is the main form for people who are major investing or operating owners; **limited partnership** is the main form for people who are less substantial, passive investors.

Note that these forms of ownership have in recent years also

extended far beyond real estate, into such areas as cable televi-
sion, equipment leasing, and oil and gas drilling, and that the
following discussion applies to the several kinds of enterprises in
which limited partnerships have been formed in his period. Those
partnership forms, rather than the corporate forms of ownership,
have developed primarily because of the tax laws, which made
extraordinary tax advantages available to partnerships but not to
corporations. Should very substantial tax law changes occur in
this area, the whole question of the forms of ownership and investment in real estate and other tax shelters wll need reevaluation, and new forms will undoubtedly emerge.

General partners jointly owning real estate share both unlimited liability and unlimited possibility of gain, as do general
partners in any kind of business. Limited partners in real estate
and other businesses share only the liabilities and gains specified
by the terms of the ownership share purchase. The corporate
form of ownership would also carry limited liability, but not the
tax advantage. When going into a venture in your home area as
owner-operator, you are likely to be going in as sole owner or
general partner. When going in as a passive investor, wherever
the physical location of the property or business, you are likely to
be going in as a limited partner. And where you are in an unfamil-
iar area, prudence demands the limited partnership form.

A safely constructed limited partnership assures both limited
liability and tax advantage for the limited partners. It passes
profits and losses through to limited partners in such fashion as to
allow the usual depreciation and interest-related losses in the
early years of ownership. These become desirable tax losses for
investors, and that has, for most high-income investors, been the
main value of such limited partnerships. It also allows any profits
made in the later years of ownership to come through to investors
taxed only once, rather than twice; in the corporate form of ownership, first company profits are taxed, and then shareholders'
earnings are taxed again. In recent years, the extent of the tax
deduction generated by limited partnerships has been somewhat
limited by changes in the previous law, but they have continued to
be very substantial, and for many the main reason for investing.
The net effect of it all has been to produce enormous, quite safe
tax advantage for high-income investors, *as long as the real estate*

or other limited partnership was safely constructed as to limited liability.

That question of safe construction in each venture is extremely important, as there are some circumstances in which liability can extend far beyond the actual cash investment. It is vitally important to read every limited partnership prospectus very carefully, as you should any kind of prospectus. The prospectus is most emphatically *not* a selling document, to be discounted or ignored. Quite the opposite; the prospectus is a disclosure document, forced upon offerors by government regulators, and is often full of highlighted warnings to potential investors, warnings that should be taken very seriously indeed.

That is particularly so in many limited partnerships offerings, which have greatly relied on tax-advantage aspects, and have all too often been substandard business risks, the tax aspects aside. In limited partnership investments, it is really quite important to go beyond careful reading of the prospectus. These limited partnership offerings, in real estate and other areas, are so complex that it is wise to seek advice from both your accountant and your attorney before going into them.

10
Making the Future Work for You

Much of this book has dealt with accumulation — building savings and investments to meet such major lifetime wants and needs as homes and educations — and with trying to create the kind of financial independence that is the basis for a significant portion of personal freedom. That accumulation can be used to meet the needs of the later years as well, for the needs created by long life will be great, and we cannot reasonably expect to live comfortably on what pension incomes and society will provide in our later years.

Long life is wonderful; long life also creates major problems. It is odd that it has worked out this way, but it has; the longevity we have so long sought now causes enormous worldwide problems, for none of us is so rich as we thought we might become, even in the United States, still the richest country of all. That is so in the large, for the world and for countries; it is also so in the small, for each of us, trying to provide for ourselves and those close to us for the duration of lives that will be considerably longer than we had any real reason to expect.

For individual planning purposes, the long run has to be seen as very long indeed. It is as simple as this: So many millions of us will be living into our eighties and nineties that it has already become terribly imprudent to plan for less than a life in which you will celebrate your ninetieth birthday — perhaps your ninety-fifth, if you are now only in your twenties or thirties.

If American industry could be counted on to grow boundlessly, and if the United States were the golden cornucopia some once thought it was, long life would pose no problems. The American dream would be in place, and we would all go into our golden years and then off into the sunset in grand style. But it is not so — it never was, it will not be. We are already seeing a massive assault on government-funded pension and health care plans, and a mass withdrawal from pension plan and health care promises on the part of American companies. Perhaps with other national priorities this would not be so; perhaps all will change for the better in years to come. But we must live with, rather than on, our hopes. What is, is. In late twentieth-century America, you must plan essentially to take care of yourself into your early nineties, counting on only a little help from government and former employers' pension plans, and relying for most of your income on your own resources.

Understanding the Impact of Inflation

One of the greatest of all the financial impacts connected with long life is that of inflation. Not necessarily the kind of runaway inflation we experienced in the 1970s; but certainly the kind of long-term inflation that has been literally built into the world economic system for at least the last two centuries.

In this period, most people still retire from their corporate jobs at age 65; that is when federal Social Security and most corporate pension plans begin full-scale payments. That is beginning to change now, as more corporate people begin to stay on their jobs past 65, but change here will continue to be slow, until the Social Security retirement age is set later into the sixties, then to be followed by later pension plan activation dates. Even so, a national retirement age of 67 or 68 will make little difference for long-term financial planning purposes, for by the time it comes, life expectancies will be even longer. People who are corporate employees should expect to live a quarter of a century beyond "retirement," and that makes it necessary to estimate the probable impact of long-term inflation.

At a modest 6% average inflation rate for the next 25 years, the Consumer Price Index will become 429, using this year as a base year at 100. If that average inflation rate were a not unlikely 8% for that 25 years, the index would become 685 to this year's 100; and if the average rate were a high, but still not unlikely, 10%, the index would become 1,083 to this year's 100. Translated into the practical facts of retirement incomes, those numbers mean that a fixed pension income of $20,000 this year, which is not bad as pension incomes go, is likely in 25 years to buy 10% – 25% of what it will buy today. In real dollars, then, figuring from today, the $20,000 you can live on today becomes worth $2,000 – $5,000 then, which you can't live on at all.

In the longest sense, it matters little whether the reality is in the higher or lower portion of this range of inflation rate possibilities, for the net effect will be the same. There will be some continuing, but increasingly inadequate, adjustments of Social Security payments to inflation, but fixed-rate corporate pensions will not be adjusted. Besides, the truth is that you cannot expect to live on any such combination of pension payments.

It is prudent, by the way, to expect long-term inflation to be in the higher end of this range, perhaps much higher. Governments always repudiate their debts in the long run, whether all at once, as after a revolution; in a series of dramatic devaluations of their currencies; or piecemeal by paying back in currencies that are worth less year by year because of inflation. The United States is mostly likely to do it in the last of these ways; a totally unmanageable $3 trillion national debt, if held at that level, becomes in fact a reasonably manageable $300 billion national debt if paid off in 10% inflation dollars.

These inflation projections should not be seen as particularly unusual or startling, by the way. Even without the impact of hidden inflation, the average rate of inflation during the 25 years prior to 1985 was in the range of 5% – 6% per year, and that period included the extremely low-inflation years of the early and mid-1960s. In this whole century, except for a few years of the Great Depression, inflation has been normal, and older people on fixed incomes have suffered because of it, the oldest suffering the most. What has been new in the last two decades is the indexing of federal Social Security and other federal pension payments to the rate of inflation; and it is that new practice that is now under heavy and continuing attack.

What causes and will cause an enormous magnification of the problem is that so many people are living so much longer. To plan for 10 or even 15 golden years after retirement from your corporate job may be doable for some, though even that can be quite difficult for most of us in periods of high inflation rates. But to plan for 25 or 30 years, while soberly taking the probable impact of inflation into account, is for almost all of us really impossible, unless we plan both to develop growing later-years funds of our own and to continue to produce income dollars from current gainful occupations during most of the rest of our lives. That's the bedrock, unvarnished, and not terribly palatable truth of the situation for older people today and tomorrow, including managers and other corporate employees. The corporate years must also be personal accumulation years; the golden retirement years one way or another must continue to be working and earning years.

Individual Retirement Accounts

Beyond company plans, managers and other corporate people have a superb personal investment instrument available, through which to develop a greatly tax-advantaged later-years fund. It is, as we all by now know, the Individual Retirement Account (IRA). What we don't necessarily all know so well, however, is that an IRA, if handled carefully, can become a very large, sure, stable source of much-needed later-years money, and therefore should be regarded as one of the key ways in which the golden years really can be made golden.

The operative phrases in the previous paragraph are "tax-advantaged" and "if handled carefully." For the IRA is a very long-term investment instrument into which many kinds of investments may be poured. If handled well, an IRA can grow as only a tax-advantaged fund can grow; if handled badly, all can be negated, for bad investments will not grow, however tax-advantaged.

The money you put into an IRA, up to yearly legal limits, is a direct subtraction from taxable income. The fund created, saved and invested within the limits set by law, accretes tax-free until you reach an age specified by law, at which time you must begin taking it out over a specified period. During that period, you will pay taxes on the money you take out of your IRA, with that money then being treated as ordinary income for tax purposes.

The specifics relating to IRAs change, as amending legislation continues to be passed almost every year. The amounts of money you can put in yearly, what an IRA can invest in, and a good many other specifics have all changed in recent years, and will change again and again. But the principle of providing a means by which individuals can build up their own tax-advantaged later-years funds seems well established. That, too, may change as hard-pressed governments seeking new sources of tax income attempt to tap what will soon be hundreds of billions of dollars in IRA funds; that is all the more reason to set up an IRA now, contribute as much as possible to it in these years, and get whatever tax advantage you can now.

At the time this chapter is being written, in the early spring of 1985, you can put up to $2,000 per year of your earned income into an IRA. If your spouse is not working, you can together put in up to $2,250 per year. If you and your spouse are both working, you can each put in up to $2,000 per year of your earned income, for a total of $4,000 per year — as long as each of you is earning that much. IRA contributions must come from that year's individually earned income, and no other kind of income counts for this purpose. You need not put any minimum amount in an IRA, except as specified by banks and other institutions in which you want to place IRA funds. Nor do you need to put in money every year, once the IRA has been started.

For tax-avoidance purposes, you can put money into an IRA up to April 16 of the following year and still claim it on your tax return. For example, you can put money into an IRA up to April 16, 1987, and take a dollar-for-dollar deduction on your 1986 tax return. You can also put money into an IRA several times a year, or into several IRAs for that matter, as long as the total amount contributed in any year does not exceed the statutory limits. You can, for example, put your IRA money each year into three different accounts, each set up for different investment purposes, though that will also create three sets of administration charges or brokerage fees when only one account and one set of charges might serve your investment objectives just as well.

Once the money is in your IRA account, it grows tax-free until withdrawal. There is no need to worry about short- or long-term capital gains, dividend exclusions, the taxability of interest, imputed interest on zero-coupon bonds, or any of the other tax and tax-avoidance matters that so greatly affect other investment decisions. Nor, for IRA money, need you use other tax-avoidance devices and instruments. For example, the tax avoidance and consequent net after-tax yield that may make a relatively safe municipal bond attractive is of no consequence at all for IRA money; the municipal must be compared to other investments without reference to tax advantage, almost always then becoming not attractive enough to buy.

You can continue to contribute money to your IRA until you are 70½ years old, although you can start taking money out without penalty when you reach 59½. If you withdraw money before that, you will have to pay a 10% tax surcharge on the funds withdrawn, as well as ordinary income taxes on the withdrawn funds. Don't be afraid of that, though; because of the tax-avoidance opportunity, money builds up so fast in an IRA account that within only a few years you come out ahead, even if you are forced to withdraw money and pay the penalty.

At 70½, you must start taking the money out of your IRA account or accounts; the amount withdrawn depends on what the then-effective actuarial tables indicate your life expectancy to be. For example, if your life expectancy at that time is 20 years and your IRA funds total $500,000, you must take out at least one-twentieth, or 5% of that sum — that is, $25,000 — in that first year of withdrawals. You can take out more, but since the withdrawn money is taxed as ordinary income, you will probably want to minimize taxes and take out only what you must. In the second year, with a life expectancy then of 19 years, you will have to take out at least one-nineteenth of the IRA sum, and so on over the years. *If you fail to take out at least the statutory minimums, you will forfeit half of what you should have taken out that year.*

For those who anticipate outliving the actuarial life expectancy tables or who wish to use these funds for their dependents as well, a recent modification of the law allows an individual to defer withdrawal of IRA funds, beyond your own individual life expectancy period.

This is accomplished by designating a beneficiary of your plan who is younger than you, and electing a joint-survivor withdrawal schedule. Then, for example, if when you're age 70½ your spouse is 60½ and is chosen as your beneficiary, your joint survivor life expectancy is extended 3.2 years.

Combining Your IRA with
Your Corporate Retirement Package

IRAs are particularly useful for people who are leaving or being left by corporate pension, profit-sharing, or Keogh plans, and who therefore have money on which they would otherwise have to take distributions and pay taxes. Such monies are often very large and come in lump sums, sometimes creating large tax liabilities. When they also come during maximum earning years, the total taxes resulting can wipe out much of the tax-avoidance gains built up over the years.

If you have such a plan, and your company terminates it, you leave the company, or you retire, you can do an Individual Retirement Account rollover, moving the entire amount in the plan into a special IRA set up for that purpose alone, and not affecting any other IRAs you may have or any other IRA contributions you may make. The rollover IRA so created is then handled like any other IRA as to tax advantage and withdrawals, but you cannot put any more money into it, except for any other such company lump-sum distributions. When withdrawals start, they are treated on the same life-expectancy basis as other IRA withdrawals. You have then converted a very expensive lump-sum corporate plan distribution into a staged, much less expensive set of withdrawals, and in most instances also locked in all or most of the tax advantage for years beyond your corporate retirement age.

This is an extremely important set of advantages for managers and other corporate employees in these times. It means that when you leave a job with a substantial lump sum due you from a pension or profit-sharing plan, you need not be forced to pay heavy taxes, but can instead create a large personal long-term investment fund under your own control. Similarly, it means that when a company abandons its pension plan, as some are now doing, you may be able to convert your money in the plan into your own IRA. There will be more legislation along these lines in future years; the vitally necessary principle of the portable personal pension plan has now been established, and its applications will grow as the need for such plans becomes increasingly apparent.

Kinds of IRAs

Everybody in the financial marketplace wants to sell you an IRA. Small wonder — there are already between $100 billion and $200 billion in IRAs, and the total grows rapidly, as people contribute to existing IRAs and open new ones, and as IRA earnings rapidly accrete tax-free. This is a time of extraordinarily high real interest rates, and institutions that can pay you 8% – 12% on your money, while relending it for 16% – 20%, are extremely eager to get your IRA deposits. Similarly, IRAs invested in securities may generate large brokerage commissions as the funds grow.

That is why it is so very easy to open an IRA. You need only fill out a very simple form, which legally sets up and registers the account with the organization that will become trustee of your IRA funds, and make a minimal kind of deposit. Often that deposit is as low as $50, though sometimes a few hundred dollars may be required.

If your firm offers one, you can open a company-sponsored and -administered IRA. Or you can open an IRA with a banking institution, mutual fund, or insurance company, all of which will administer and direct the investment policies of your IRA. Or you can open a self-directed IRA, in which you make all the investment decisions.

On balance, the disadvantages of a company-sponsored IRA seem to outweigh the advantages. You do get professional investment management of your IRA, usually free, but most IRA charges from banks or no-load mutual funds are minimal. With your own IRA, you can include a nonworking spouse and increase the maximum yearly contribution allowable, currently by $250 per year, and you can make contributions up to April 16 of the next year. Company plans do not provide either of these advantages.

Bank IRAs cost little or nothing to set up, and *carry the very great advantage of being federally insured, for they are recognized as bank accounts.* They are usually invested in certificates of deposit (CDs) of your choice, but can be invested in variable-rate money market bank accounts as well. Be careful here: Although you can shift your money from IRA to IRA at will, usually for a small transaction charge, there are substantial interest penalties for early withdrawals from CDs. In this period of volatile interest rates, it is best not to try to "lock in" seemingly high interest rates by buying long-term CDs to fund your bank IRA; it is far better to stay short-term — with CDs maturing in one year or less — even though the longer-term CDs seem to be paying more. Be careful, too, about the federal insurance ceilings on bank accounts as they change over the years, to be sure no single IRA exceeds the insured amount.

A major potential problem with bank-administered IRAs is that many banks will not automatically roll your CDs over, unless you specifically tell them in writing to do so when the CDs mature. If you do not, then your funds can languish in a 5% – 5.5% savings account for many months. Keep a careful record of the maturity dates of all your CDs, making sure to roll them over or move the funds in a timely way.

Some mutual funds, including the money market funds, charge no front-load commissions. These provide a way to move your IRA into equities and debt obligations with small setup and continuing administrative costs, and to move your IRA money when and as you wish. But IRAs funded with front-loaded mutual funds encounter very stiff startup charges; therefore they start earning from a considerably impaired position, and make it difficult for you to make the right money-moving decisions in timely ways. Many mutual funds, both no-load and front-load, are sold in "families of funds," making it possible to move your money without additional sales commissions or transaction charges once in the "family," but it is best to seek funds charging no sales commissions at all for your IRA money. They are certainly there to be found; the newspapers are full of their advertisements.

Managing Your IRA for Real Growth

You should not want to lock your IRA money into savings and investment vehicles that make it hard to move that money to seek new advantage. The IRA funds you are creating are long-term funds; that means you are holding and growing them, while watching and moving them about as much as you believe necessary. It most emphatically does not mean putting them away, leaving them alone, and forgetting about them, any more than it does for any other kind of investment. For example, those who advise you to buy zero-coupon securities funded by federal bonds with your IRA money and then just forget about it all because the bonds are so safe and sure, are offering very bad advice. Aside from the obvious imprudence of trusting the long-term payment promises of any government, including our own, those zero-coupon bonds are, by their nature, highly volatile and will fluctuate much more sharply than other bonds during their lifetimes. That is because the interest payments, which tend to limit fluctuations, have been removed in advance. If the law remains as is, you will not have to pay yearly taxes on imputed zero-coupon bond interest during the lifetime of the bond, as you would if the bond were not in an IRA. But if the general interest-rate level should rise, you may find yourself holding zero-coupon bonds worth much less than what you paid for them in your IRA. Then you must keep on collecting far less interest than your money would have earned, or sell the bonds at a big loss. That is the standard long-term dilemma faced by all who are locked into losing bonds.

That, of course, is only one of the many kinds of problems you can run into if you choose to use a self-directed IRA as a speculative investment fund, rather than as a very long-term later-years fund. There is nothing particularly wrong about taking off on your own with your IRA money; what can go wrong is the way you handle that money. Because of its great tax advantage and its long-term purposes, IRA money should be handled very conservatively. It is not money that should be generating large commissions for eager brokers, in a series of little odd-lot stock trades (under 100 shares) that cost much more than normal 100-share trades. Most of all, it is not speculating money. Your later-years fund is far, far more important than that; and because of its tax advantage, it will grow very quickly if you handle it prudently.

The law makes some kinds of otherwise entirely legal speculative practices, and even some not very speculative investments, out of bounds for IRAs. You cannot borrow money in connection with an IRA investment and therefore, for example, cannot use IRA money in a margin account, in a real estate investment in which mortgage money is borrowed, sell stock short, or use it in any other "leveraged" transactions — that is, any transactions in which borrowed money is used to try to make money. You can certainly invest in securities and real estate purchased at full price, or in mutual funds and limited partnerships, or most other speculations you wish to engage in, as long as no borrowed money is used. Nor can you use IRA money to purchase gold, silver, collectibles, or gemstones, though you can put it into the stocks of companies extracting or trading in those kinds of goods. You cannot buy life insurance with an IRA fund, but you can buy annuities.

Common sense also indicates that there is no point in putting IRA money into tax-sheltered investments, as the tax shelter is already in effect, and such investments cannot be expected to be as good as other investments that in no way depend upon their tax-shelter aspects for their appeal. Common sense should also indicate that the stocks of "hot" little companies and the shares of very "aggressive" mutual funds specializing in such stocks are not good places for IRA money, though tens of thousands of people with self-directed IRAs are foolishly making just those kinds of investments every day. It can be great fun to take your IRA funds and roll them around, investing here, speculating there, never having to worry about tax aspects, short-term gains, and all that. But, frankly, we would rather you survived than just had fun.

The enormously hopeful thing about the IRA, and about the whole personal portable pension plan idea, is that the tax advantage gives you an even break against the pace of inflation. Without that even break, the accumulation game is very much stacked against you. Even taking into account the possibility of lower top taxes in some sort of flat-tax arrangement, for the foreseeable future the combined federal, state, and local taxes on personal incomes will take huge bites out of unsheltered yields, no matter how good they are. If you can get a safe, unsheltered 10% on your money, and are in a top combined tax bracket even as low as 40%, that 10% is really worth 6%. If inflation is 6% that year, your earnings in real dollars are nil. If you earn a higher and probably not-so-safe 14% on your money, that 40% bracket makes your after-tax yield still only 8.4%, for a real yield after inflation of only 2.4%. If either the real tax figures or inflation are higher — and they well may be — your real gain may even be a minus figure.

But if you can get the same safe 10% on tax-sheltered IRA money, you will make a real 4% on that money, as against inflation, and the difference will compound and therefore grow as the years go by. Taking that 4% growth figure alone, $2,000 put into an IRA this year will become a real $6,487 30 years out, and a steady contribution of $1,000 – $2,000 every year will result in a real dollar personal retirement fund of well over $100,000. That's in today's real dollars; double that for two wage-earners, allow for the probability that you will legally become able to put in more over the years, and it is easy to see how a real-dollar fund aggregating several hundred thousand dollars can be built.

With that kind of personal fund, you have the basis for some quite golden years indeed — if you handle it well, and also if you earn for as long as you can. Sure, all that nonsense about how you will build up millions of dollars in IRAs is only selling talk that carefully omits the fact of inflation. But even after disinflating the selling talk, your IRAs can become extremely valuable lifetime stores of value; and they are wholly yours, not pension promises that can be repudiated by companies and governments.

Keogh Plans

Many corporate employees can and do set up Keogh plans as well as IRAs. Although Keogh plans are primarily intended as personal pension plans for the self-employed, managers and other corporate people who have earnings, as from part-time businesses, can substantially supplement their personal portable pension plans by setting up Keoghs. Not all will want to do so, even if the income is there, for in some instances, and depending upon current tax laws, existing company plans may function much as Keoghs function for the self-employed. But if you have no such company plan available, or if, by the time you are reading this, such company plans are not longer legally possible, a Keogh may very well be for you.

As of this writing, you can put up to 20% of your net business income, up to a top of $30,000 per year, into a Keogh plan. The money must entirely come out of business earnings, meaning that you are unlikely to have to worry about reaching top contribution limits out of part-time business activities. As with IRAs, the money you put in is a straight tax deduction. You can start a Keogh plan with the same kinds of financial organizations that offer

IRAs. There is a little more paperwork involved than with IRAs, so yearly administrative charges run a little higher. The penalty for premature withdrawal of funds is the same 10%, but you will not be able to make further contributions for five years after the withdrawal, so this money should be regarded as untouchable, except in the direst emergencies.

You can use up to 50% of your yearly Keogh contribution to buy life insurance, which you cannot do with an IRA. And you can take a lump-sum distribution at 59½ and thereafter, if you wish, as ten-year-forward income averaging is available on such lump-sum distributions, much easing the tax pain.

There will be legislative changes in both IRAs and Keogh plans. Both are plans developed to meet the growing later-years needs of an aging population; as need grows, Congress will continue to amend these plans, probably adding new plans as well. The principle of the tax-advantaged personal portable pension plan is changing the way we look at the question of later-years money matters, and placing much-needed new emphasis upon growing our funds ourselves, as it becomes apparent that governments and companies will do less than it seemed they would do. In our later years, then, we can reasonably expect to be living on modest Social Security payments, probably some corporate pensions, profit-sharing, and deferred compensation plan payments, the yields from whatever nonplan assets we have accumulated, and our IRA and Keogh plan distributions and yields.

But we can also reasonably expect that all that will, for most of us, still not be enough. Not with the facts of long life and inflation; our needs will require the addition of one more income-producing element.

Continuing to Earn in Your Later Years

That additional element is the pay that comes from continuing work. High-paying work, that is. The highly skilled, previously highly paid, former manager or other corporate employee will get no satisfaction and not nearly enough income from boring entry-level work as a clerk, security guard, or babysitter.

The key to it all surely is to put aside once and for all the outmoded concept of retirement, and to recognize the later years as career-continuation or second-career years, whichever way you choose to use them. To see that clearly early enough is indispensable, for then you can choose between available later-years career alternatives, prepare properly for the kind of work you plan to do in your later years, and be able to work your plan. It is not really very hard to stay on in a job you like after "retirement" age is reached, and then move in a long-planned way into your later-years working stance. But it is extraordinarily difficult to do any of that if you commit the grave error of retiring, putting yourself on the shelf, and worst of all moving far away, especially into the kind of constricting retirement community that has entrapped so many in recent decades. At 65, 66, or 67, you can very effectively move from your corporate job into highly remunerative continuation or alternative work, with skills, networks, and capital intact and ready to go. At 70 or 75, with skills and networks out of date and capital impaired, it is at least extraordinarily difficult and often impossible to accomplish that kind of transition.

The problem — and the opportunity — lies in the fact that the American system favors the owner, rather than the employee, and never more than in the later years of life. The employee, including many a highly skilled, highly paid corporate manager, must retire in what for many is the prime of life and skill. Age 65 is no longer old; neither is 70, for that matter. But even with anti-age-discrimination laws in place, the fact is that the overwhelming majority of corporate managers move out of their jobs in their mid-sixties; only a few can and do resist the pressure to "retire" and make way for younger managers, who have been less than patiently waiting their turns. That is beginning to change a little, but for the foreseeable future you can still expect to have to "retire" from your corporate employment no later than your seventieth birthday, long before you really need to — and probably long before you will be able to afford to — stop work.

Meanwhile, you will be watching other people, often less skilled and youthful than you, continue to pursue their careers actively and very lucratively as independent professionals and business owners. These owners call their own shots, can stay on as long as they can keep their businesses economically viable, and are often far more skilled than their younger competitors. Owners can also bring in younger people, when necessary and affordable, to do some of the things they no longer want to or can do. Employees . . . well, when you come right down to it, employees do not call any of their own main shots, and must leave when others think it is time for them to do so, whoever they are and no matter how powerful they may have been.

Seen clearly, the main later-years opportunity is in business ownership and independent professional practice. In reality, separating out independent professional status that way is a little misleading, for in this frame of reference the independent professional is in essence a small-business owner, in economic function no different from the independent seller, store owner, or manufacturer. The main working difference between independent professionals and all other business owners is that you will have to spend more time preparing if you want to move into a later-years occupation that requires years of schooling followed by some sort of certification.

The later-years business or independent professional practice can be a big financial opportunity, often bigger than the whole bundle of pensions and income from personal accumulations. As we have seen, the money you get from pensions and accumulations may seem quite adequate in the early years of retirement, but over the years turn out to have become pathetically inadequate, as inflation first erodes real-dollar incomes, then forces invasion of capital, and ultimately brings about effective poverty. But if you move into reasonably remunerative work, rather than "retiring," you may be able to add to real capital substantially rather than invading it during the early years of retirement, and then hold capital at a stable or only slightly eroding real-dollar figure later on.

The most important aspect of such earnings is that, if they are derived from business or professional work, they tend to move up with inflation, while fixed retirement incomes do not. You may have $20,000 a year coming in from pensions and assets in your sixty-sixth year, and only $15,000 more from part-time but lucrative work. But 15 years later, in your eighty-first year, that $20,000 may be worth only $8,000–$10,000 in real dollars, while that $15,000 in earnings may still be worth $15,000, and the total of the two quite enough to live on decently. The dollar amounts will look different then, with the $20,000 still looking like and numbered $20,000 and the $15,000 in earnings numbered at perhaps $30,000. In this example, what will have happened is that what you earn from your business or profession will have kept up with inflation, while your fixed pension and asset income will not. Inevitably, fixed incomes must greatly erode as we live longer; business and professional earnings need not.

Putting it a little differently, if you are getting a pretty good yield of 10% on your invested money, then $15,000 in business or professional earnings is worth $150,000 in capital. In not very many years, when the dollar is worth half its present value, and assuming that such earnings have kept up with the pace of inflation, the $15,000 yearly will have become $30,000, and equivalent to $300,000 in capital. The figures are oversimplified, but the comparisons are entirely valid.

In the later years, some people will continue and expand existing part-time interests, others will make major career skills changes, and most will move from existing strength to new strength, using the skills built up over a lifetime in the business world. Those who are collectors, for example, can and rather often do "retire," and further develop the part-time businesses their collecting interests have become over the years. Indeed, these are often some of the few who can, in their later years, fairly easily move away from their established home bases, especially when their collectibles, such as stamps and coins, are portable and lend themselves to the development of a mail-order business. Similarly, people whose assets and interests have caused them to become skilled in-and-out securities traders can pursue that kind of part-time career through any brokerage office or for that matter through computer terminals in their own homes.

People who want to make major skills changes usually are either seeking to become certified independent professionals or to pursue a long-held dream; both need considerable time and preparation. The manager who wants to become a lawyer, for example, is well-advised to take some law courses during the corporate years, perhaps even going to law school at night. The manager who wants to become a writer or farmer — common long-held dreams — will do well to prepare long before.

The aspiring writer must start to *write*, must begin to practice the trade and see whether there is really any talent, rather than waiting until "retirement." Many have wanted to write; some who have not, can, and very well; more cannot; and even more cannot make any kind of money at it. You should not spend the sixty-sixth to seventieth years of your life finding out that you cannot make any money at writing, or that you cannot learn how to write what you want to write, regardless of money. It is far better to try it earlier, learn what you can about yourself and your possibilities, and move as you must into the later years. Similarly, the farmer, or anyone else who wishes to make a long-cherished occupational move, must prepare. This is not usually a matter of ability, but rather of adequate preparation.

As we have been learning throughout the American business world in recent years, the old idea of "manager qua manager" — that a good manager can manage any enterprise, no matter what it is — must be amended in light of current realities. Yes, a good manager can ultimately manage any enterprise well, but it is also absolutely indispensable to learn the specific business. No matter how good you are, you cannot expect to become the general manager of your own business without knowing a great deal about that kind of business, and as much as possible from the ground up. In the restaurant business, for example, beyond food preparation, much of the heart of the matter is in the face-to-face selling, and the tendency is to focus on that aspect. But the heart of the restaurant business is also in the buying; the restaurant owner-manager who does not know how to buy going in will either learn fast or go out of business. In the farm business, to choose a different kind of example, beyond basic competence, the central issue in these years is keeping the investment, interest level, land value, and commodity price factors in balance — as some hundreds of thousands of extraordinarily skilled farmers have found to their dismay. In that business, apprenticeship is vital; and it must be a dual apprenticeship, at that — farming and farm finance.

Most of those who understand the need to continue to earn in their later years will go from established strength to strength. For example, the skilled seller will, in all probability, go right on selling, if at all possible going over into lucrative independent representation or distribution in the same or a related industry. In many industries, skilled and experienced independent representatives can do far better on their own than while working for others. And skilled people selling formerly competitive lines to their own established customers of many years' standing can do extremely well, even when much of the work in their later years is done by telephone, rather than out of an automobile. In selling and marketing, as in some other business areas, it can work out best of all if the move into an independent business of your own comes years before the "retirement" age is reached. Then the transition is made at the fullest possible physical strength; there is also considerable room for error and even failure. A failure at business in your forties or fifties is greatly preferable to a failure in your late sixties.

Strength to strength; skill to skill. The financial manager may go into the financial marketplace in the later years, as independent accountant, tax preparer, insurance representative, securities seller, financial planner, lending-office manager, or in any of the other occupations that continue to emerge, as everyone in the financial world begins to sell every financial instrument in sight. The general manager of a big division may buy an interest in a much smaller company, perhaps in a related business, and run it well.

Actually, many of the tens of thousands of managers who have been dispossessed as middle management has shrunk in recent years have become entrepreneurs; their skills and drive have helped fuel the considerable new business movement in the United States in the early 1980s. Of necessity, they have done early what others will do later in their working lives: make the transition from employment to ownership. Many have failed, as well. Let us not inadvertently convey the idea that making that transition is easy, just because we think it essential. Most new small businesses fail, including those run by skilled former corporate managers. Great attention must be paid to financing, apprenticeship, and development of all the success skills relating to the kind of business or profession you wish to enter.

In the later years, particular attention must also be paid to the question of capital use. At 45, you can impair capital, recover, and try again, if you will. At 65, the stakes may be much higher, with business failure and capital impairment bringing with them many bad later years. For this reason, too, there is considerable value in starting the transition to ownership early; and also much virtue in using as little capital as possible if you enter into ownership later. At 65, the ideal new business is labor-intensive, with your labor the chief factor in its development. The seller turned independent representative, the executive turned consultant, the comptroller turned tax preparer and independent accountant, and the editor turned freelance editor-writer spend little but their own time. The seller turned dealer or distributor, the executive turned small manufacturer, the comptroller turned franchisee, and the editor turned small publisher all run much greater risks, and not always for greater potential reward. Always limit the risks as best you can. In the later years, go even further out of your way to limit the risks; and take little or no risks at all with your basic nut of needed retirement capital.

Financial and career independence in the later years brings with it some nonfinancial rewards as well. These are most notably very large measures of freedom and self-respect. There is no need to anticipate taking up the role of the aging pensioner nodding in the sun, who goes home to poverty. The later years can be better than that, much better.

Planning Your Estate

During the last decade, major changes in federal estate and gift tax law have occurred. The main net financial-planning effect has been to reduce greatly the numbers of those needing to do complex estate planning and avoidance of estate and gift taxes. People who still need to pay close attention to these matters now are likely to have estates of such sizes that they need the ministrations of highly skilled — and highly paid — professional advisers. Most of the rest of us, even if we are modestly affluent in our later years, are likely to do very well with a competently drawn will, the provision of such liquid funds as our spouses or other loved ones may need to settle up our affairs and during probate, and some previous effort aimed at taking some of our taxables out of our estates.

In planning to achieve those modest goals, and to minimize

any taxes that might be levied on your estate, it is wise to bear in mind that you are likely to live a good deal longer than you had earlier supposed you might, that inflation is inexorable and may in any period accelerate again, and that it is therefore vital to grow your assets safely as fast as possible and control them as long as possible. Unless you are very affluent indeed, you will probably need everything you have if you live out what has in our time become a very long normal lifespan. You will certainly want to minimize death taxes, and especially will want to guard against forced sale of such assets as real estate because you have failed to provide your heirs with enough liquid funds. But you can arrange for all that rather easily.

As the federal estate tax and gift tax laws now stand, a surviving spouse has, except for some kinds of trust-related assets and income, an unlimited marital deduction, meaning essentially that everything one spouse has can pass to the other on the death of either one, without federal death taxes being levied. On the death of the surviving spouse, all will be taxable, except that there is a lifetime "unified estate and gift tax deduction" then applying. In 1985, that unified deduction is $155,000; in 1986 and thereafter, it will be $192,800. Those figures are direct deductions from federal death taxes that might have been levied, rather than deductions from taxables, and are roughly equivalent to $500,000 and $600,000 deductions from taxables, respectively. Any gifts given during your lifetime should be deducted from this unified lifetime deductible amount; for all but a very few of us, however, that will not appreciably alter the size of the deductions available.

Estate matters should be taken up quite early with your lawyer, who will draw the necessary documents; and with your financial adviser and accountant, who with your lawyer will help you develop plans and instruments to meet your goals. These are really not matters to take up on your own, for the documents needed are very precise and must allow for the possibility of many alternatives and contingencies. You absolutely *must* have a will, and may also need insurance and trust documents, all aimed at helping your survivors past probate and taxing authorities, and at avoiding needless disagreement among themselves. State death taxes and differing state laws must also be taken into account.

Astonishingly, many people do not even have a will. If you are one such, do remedy the error immediately; call your lawyer tomorrow, as well as your financial advisers, and start the process of getting a will done. You may revise that will a dozen times in the next 30 years, as goals and relationships change, but get a will done now, for without one your loved ones may be seriously harmed by your failure to act.

To achieve liquidity, there is life insurance when you are young and not so very liquid. Later on in life, though, you may need much less life insurance, as other funds grow. In these times, estate matters are for most of us rather peripheral concerns. Our central concern now is to develop the kinds of assets and skills we will need to survive long and well, and to see to it that our surviving spouses do so, too. Beyond that, current estate and gift tax laws have for most of us greatly simplified estate-planning matters.

Appendix A
Financial Programs
for the Future

Eight Personal Planning Situations

Here are several financial planning examples, drawn from the joint experience of the authors. They are fictional, in the sense that the names used in all instances are fictitious and that any resemblance to living persons is entirely accidental. But they are also very real, in that they are prototypes, occurring over and over again in real life. You will recognize the situations; our hope is that you will be able to relate some significant aspects of at least one of these situations to your own life, making all that has gone before in this book even more practical, tangible, and therefore meaningful.

As throughout the rest of this work, we have dealt with tax aspects and other relevant legal matters as they are at the time of writing, though the pace of change in some such areas makes it almost certain that some of our recommendations would be different had they been written at the moment you are reading the book. That is inevitable; it is your basic approach to these matters that is the subject of this book. It does undescore the need to watch your savings and investments constantly, though; circumstances can change for all kinds of matters the moment you look the other way. In this, personal financial matters are no different from the main matters you deal with in your business career.

Samantha Wentworth

Everybody had always called her Sam, even her two quite unlamented husbands, one of whom had himself been named Sam. Cynthia didn't; at ten, Cynthia still called her Mom. Later on, her daughter would call her Sam, just like all the others. Later on, exactly eight years later on, Sam would have to get up the money to put Cynthia through college. All by herself, too. At 40, after two bad marriages, she was absolutely determined to go the rest of the way on her own. There would be more men perhaps, but no merging of fortunes and responsibilities; it had taken five long years to pay off the debts left over from the last marriage, after good old George had taken off into the wild blue yonder.

She's done it, though, through the exercise of her considerable selling and management skills. Now, 18 years into a successful business career, and with some skill and luck in finding good live-in household help, she is a regional sales manager of a major computer company, and is making a little more than enough money to meet her responsibilities, including payments on the heavily mortgaged house that was the sole asset left over from her second marriage. There are good benefits, too; without the dental benefits, she would have had to borrow the money for Cynthia's very expensive orthodonture, started two years ago. And there is a pension plan, a good one, which by now has vested. There are merit increases, performance bonuses, and several rather nice executive perks, as well. She has a good job, excellent skills, and can reasonably look forward to a lot of good years up ahead. With all that, Samantha still feels terribly vulnerable. And she is. She has been around long enough to know that company fortunes can change rather quickly, and that good jobs can disappear right out from under you, through no fault of your own.

The problem is that, with all those debts and expenses, there has been very little chance to do any meaningful saving, until quite recently. She has built up some equity in her home, has managed to put $6,000 into her savings account, and has bought $3,000 in government savings bonds, as a start on Cynthia's education fund, but that's it. Actually, that's better than most of her friends have done, especially those mired in the high-consumption lifestyle. But she knows that comparisons mean nothing here; her problem is how to go about building a stake that can, if necessary, take her through difficult times, and at the same time assure Cynthia's college education. She figures that, with careful management, she can save about $3,000 – $4,000 a year out of her current salary, with any bonuses and future raises making it possible to put away more.

She also feels that it is time to get some professional financial planning advice. She started with her accountant, who knows her financial situation and prospects better than anyone else. He in turn referred her to a Certified Financial Planner, a woman he has worked with for years. The adviser listened to the whole story — looking pained when Samantha told her about money being kept in low-paying savings accounts and government bonds, and looking very pleased indeed when it became clear that Samantha really could put away $3,000 – $4,000 a year and more later — and proceeded to make some recommendations.

The "good" pension plan had to be discounted, right at the start. Samantha is only 40, and unfortunately the plan has no lump-sum distribution arrangements, should she leave company employment. If the plan is still there, and hasn't been converted into possibly worthless company stock or seriously underfunded in the next quarter-century, she will get a modest fixed monthly payout much later in her life. How much that payout might really be worth, even at the full amount promised, will depend upon the course of inflation in the next 25 years. There is some talk that the plan is to be supplemented or replaced by some sort of meaningful deferred-compensation plan, providing for substantial accumulation and payout of funds imediately upon termination of employment. That would be wonderful, but until then Samantha must plan to accumulate quite on her own.

The first move is to create a conservatively funded IRA, one in which Samantha plans to put as much as the law allows every year, starting with the $2,000 allowed as of this writing. AT the beginning, she is funding it with a GNMA mutual fund. Even if all else proves inadequate to fund Cynthia's education, the tax-advantaged buildup in the IRA is so quick that Samantha will be way ahead if she must withdraw some of her IRA money to help pay for Cynthia's education, even if there are tax penalties to pay for withdrawals before she becomes 59½.

She shouldn't have to do that, though. Her failsafe there will be the developing accretion of value in her home, which is in the process of becoming the best single investment of her lifetime. If necessary, and without touching her IRA money (which is intended to provide lifetime security for Samantha, rather than becoming a college fund), she can take an equity loan — a second mortgage — on her home. That can be expensive, but it can be done, as it has by millions of others faced with similar needs.

Even that should not be necessary, though, if she keeps cn working and saving. Oh, it may be, if Cynthia goes to a hugely expensive private college, but both her accountant and her financial adviser have gone far beyond their straightforward money advice roles, and strongly suggested that Samantha and Cynthia should be thinking of an excellent public college, rather than a private one. There is a fine state university, with several campuses around the state, which is by every measure as good as any private college in the country. Samantha could very nearly support Cynthia in a public college out of current income; a private college would require borrowing tens of thousands of dollars for undergraduate education alone.

Samantha has also reviewed her insurance, and taken both a $50,000 term insurance policy, beyond company coverage, and the highest-deductible, least expensive major medical insurance she could find, in her case through a fraternal association. She and Cynthia are not going to be caught by coverage breaks, should she leave her job.

With IRA, home, and insurance coverage in place, there is still some room for saving and investment in Samantha's personal economy. She is keeping a convenience bank account, but one that sweeps her savings into a higher-paying liquid money market account periodically. The savings bonds have been cashed in, and the money put into CDs and the purchase of a small amount of stock in her own company, which she thinks is about to take off.

She is ready to learn a good deal, and to move her money about quite actively as her knowledge grows, for now she sees that so far she has not treated the financial side of life in a skilled and serious way. Safely, though; she is not about to use her slim resources for high-rick speculation. And not alone, either; she sees the value of securing good professional help. Once a year, she and her financial adviser will sit down to review Samantha's total financial situation and perhaps make some new moves; all during the year, Samantha will watch her savings and investments, develop her own insights and skills, and make her own moves.

Will Rivera

Two months ago, with his broker's help, Will made a small killing in bullion futures. Last month, he put the profits back in, added some, and made a much more substantial killing in T-bill futures. Yesterday, in hog bellies he achieved an even bigger killing — his own.

His broker was sorry that he had been forced to sell Will out, but Will had been on the road when the margin call came, and there was no point in putting more money in that day, anyway, because of the anticipated movement of the market. His broker assured him that all brokerage commissions had been deducted, and that no more money was owed in the account. He suggested that Will might seriously consider putting some money into soybeans, which were coming on strong. The broker had just put his own mother-in-law into soybeans, and he would never have done that if soybeans weren't going to be a bonanza.

Will came away, shorn and saddened — but not necessarily wiser, for Will is not, as you might have supposed, a young innocent. Far from it. He is 38, and has 15 years of progressively more responsible management jobs behind him and two children headed for college. He is not a compulsive gambler, either, drawn to Las Vegas and Atlantic City like a moth to a flame. He does take some very foolish risks, though, on the theory that some portion of his "portfolio" should be in high-risk, high-reward investments. In this he has, over the years, been encouraged by a series of friendly brokers and unsuccessfully discouraged by his accountant.

This time, Will's most recent suicide in the market happened to coincide with a visit to that accountant, who deplored his judgement once again, and finally convinced Will to have a serious discussion with himself and a financial planner. Will had always resisted that, reasoning that his excellent salary would more than take care of such mundane matters as groceries, vehicles, homes, and educations, while whatever company he worked for could be counted on for insurance and retirement needs. He never put it quite that baldly, knowing how silly it would sound to others, but that was really the way he felt about all that planning stuff.

Will was at least momentarily sobered by talk about such matters as impending huge college costs, insurance coverage gaps and consequent traps, the hazards of modern corporate employment, and the like. He readily agreed to take a new and very close look at IRAs, place much more of his income into his company's excellent deferred-compensation plan, supplement insurance coverages, and consider Clifford Trusts for college fund-building purposes. He also very readily agreed that he had to change his investing — and for that matter his spending — ways, if he was to meet his coming responsibilities and simultaneously build some future security.

That is all very well; he's had good advice and will do a great deal better if he takes it. The planners, vehicles, and techniques are there, and these days are fairly easily found. The will to do it all is the essence of the matter.

Jane Harris Carter and Joseph Carter

Success piled on success, during the long golden autumn days when work was done. That was how life was going to be for them — and it was, in every major personal way. Except that it now begins to look as if they may come up short, farther on, and they need to take steps to remedy that. The last thing they want is to become a burden on their children. Not that the children would begrudge them help or be unable to give it, but times are harder, college costs are enormous, and clearly their children are all harder pressed than Jane and Joe were at a similar time of life.

Joe has had quite a successful career, by any standard. At 61, he has worked for only three companies since finishing college in the late 1940s. In his second company, he rose to a divisional vice presidency, and might even have gone all the way to the top spot there, but the whole thing was merged right out from under him in the late 1970s. Now, unless that kind of unforeseeable event occurs again, he is safely slotted into divisional general management in a major and healthy company in his field, and will retire from the company in four years, at 65.

Jane hasn't really had a business career of any kind. There were five children to raise and educate, and then there was Joe's father, who needed a great deal of care these last ten years, until he died six months ago. She has always thought that she might go back to work when all the other responsibilities were done, but like so many others has not prepared to do so, up until now.

It was after Joe's father died, a few months ago, that Jane and Joe began to think seriously about their own later years, and to realize that, with what inflation had done and probably would do in the future, they were going to need more than they could expect to have if they just went on as before. Joe's pay had been good over the years, and they were not exactly high livers, but it had been very expensive to put five children through college, three of them through graduate school. And it had been extremely expensive to take care of Joe's father in his declining years.

A large part of the problem is that Joe's pension plans are going to yield far less than it had seemed when they had last seriously looked at their situation, after Joe's previous job had disappeared in the merger. His first company, long ago, had had no meaningful pension arrangements. In his second, the pension plan had looked wonderful, but it is now clear that its combination of Social Security and pension payout will, in real dollars, be quite small when Joe retires. And in his current job, he has another fixed-dollar pension plan, which will yield little because he has too few years in, although the company last year put in a good deferred-compensation plan, to which the company will also contribute. There is the house, now worth about $250,000, up from the $48,000 they paid for it 20 years ago. There are some savings and investments, and Jane's coin collections, worth about $100,000 in all.

Jane and Joe are scarcely paupers. But as it now stands, their yearly income from all sources on retirement is likely to be about $20,000 a year, which is rather nice, but scarcely enough for them to spend those golden autumn days in the Florida sun, as they had planned. Well, not planned, but anticipated. They have both begun to question the whole retirement-community thing in recent years, as they have seen friends grow old far too quickly with not enough to do. Even more recently they have been seeing retired older friends forced to spend beyond their income, going through their savings, and winding up in their seventies and eighties without enough money to support themselves.

This is what they have decided to do, with the help of an astute investment adviser. First, they are going to take the gain on their home, and put a down payment into a much smaller house or condominium in a neighboring community, one with less desirable schools, lower taxes, and lower property values. By doing that, they can reasonably expect to net $200,000 in additional, investable capital, without substantially raising their current level of housing expenditure, and perhaps even lowering it. They might instead have held on to their expensive, now-unmortgaged home, reasoning that real estate values would continue to rise, but then too many of their eggs would have continued to be in one basket, and a short-term dip in home prices accompanied by a job loss or a possible need to move due to transfer might be very costly. The $200,000 they net will be put into a diversified combination of IRAs, short-term CDs, medium-range government bonds, the tax-advantaged bonds of their own stable municipality, the stocks of two companies Joe knows well in his own industry, and perhaps a tax-deferred variable annuity.

Some of it will also go into an expansion of Jane's coin collection, for although Jane has not directly had a business career, she has over the years become a skilled amateur collector. Now she is going to go into coin trading far more seriously, properly viewing it as a potentially very lucrative and satisfying later-years occupation. Indeed, it is her business that may ultimately enable them to live wherever they please, for it can be pursued from any location.

They will live carefully, too, during Joe's last four corporate years. Joe plans to put everything he can into that tax-advantaged deferred-compensation plan, right up to allowed limits. By doing so, he figures that he will be able to build up their capital by at least another $50,000, and probably more, in just four years.

Joe plans to keep on working, too, though he doesn't yet know at what, for he has just started seriously thinking about the whole matter. His current thinking is that he will try to stay on at his own company as long as possible, even perhaps in some less demanding and lower-paying job. He is beginning to explore consulting possibilities in his industry. In addition, he is loking into small-business opportunities in his own community, limiting his exploration to the kinds of businesses requiring little capital investment. He has enough time to explore properly, and enough capital to make a business go, although he doesn't want to run too many risks with what he has.

Having begun to think and prepare while there was still enough time to do it all right, Jane and Joe will do well. They may still need help from their children if physical problems should make their continuing work plans impossible to pursue, and especially if they are hit with a combination of incapacity and high inflation. But the likelihood is that they will be able to take care of themselves and live as they would like for decades.

Jim Stone

Somehow, he had never thought it would happen to him — not with his skills and track record. He knew all the reasons, of course: the international competition, the move to lighter vehicles, and all that. But he had been sure that top management, with the whole financial and political power of the steel industry behind it, would find a way out, or at least be able to move resources into other areas in a timely way. But the bottom line, as the kids say, was that he was out on his ear, and nobody seemed eager to hire a 58-year-old top steel marketing professional, even for jobs that in other times he would not even have considered.

He had done some saving and investing, back in the good years. Not much, really, with the college costs, the scale of living he and Elizabeth had once aspired to, and then the alimony and child support payments after the divorce. At least the college costs and child support payments were done with, though the alimony remained. After the severance pay and the lump-sum pension-plan distribution, and with what he already had, he would have about $150,000 in all, plus about $40,000 in equity built up in the small house he had bought after the divorce. And no job, no prospects, no more company pension-plan payouts, and seven years before even Social Security payments started.

His first need is, of course, to find a job; after the initial shock, he is working hard at that. A good marketing professional is very often also a good salesman, and that indeed is how he started out, almost 40 years ago. He is exploring sales and marketing possibilities in imported steels and metal products, as well as crossover possibilities into other industries. And he will probably come up with something — but it will take time.

Meanwhile, he has taken a sober look at his financial situation, with the help of his accountant and a financial planner, knowing that how he negotiates the terms of his termination and moves his company-derived money into other financial vehicles can have considerable effects on the state of his financial health.

One of the most important things he accomplished going away from his company was to negotiate a full-year extension of his medical coverage, including his major medical coverage. He has immediately applied for new, duplicative coverage through a fraternal organization, to avoid the preexisting conditions trap.

He has also avoided a tax trap, by rolling his lump-sum distribution over into an IRA. He may need some of that money to live on, if his unemployed status lasts too long, but even in adverse circumstances should be able to leave that IRA money alone until he is 59½; then he will be able to begin withdrawing it, if he must, without tax penalty. He would have liked to do some tax avoidance with his severance pay, but he needs that to live on right now.

Jim is holding some company stock, optioned quite favorably long ago. He has held it more out of loyalty than anything else, but will now follow his financial planner's advice and sell it, moving the money into one-year CDs, for he must stay safe and liquid, at least until his job situation changes.

Luckily, there is no need to sell his home, unless he must relocate, and even then he may decide to hold on to it as a good investment, for it continues to accrete value far more quickly han anything else he owns. It probably will continue to do so, too, for it is locatedin one of the prosperous suburbs of a major city. Had he been in operating management, perhaps terminated because of the closing of the main industrial plant of a one-industry plant, he might have been trapped in a home that had suddenly lost almost all its previous value, unable to sell it for even enough to pay off the mortgage. NOt all home prices go up and up — only the well-situated ones can be counted on for that kind of performance.

Jim is stuck with his zero-coupon bonds, though. He needs to be liquid now, but unfortunately interest rates have gone up since he bought the bonds, and their market value has gone down so sharply that if he sold them today, he would not even be able to get out the money he put in. He has to hold on to them, either until maturity or until interest rates go down enough to make them worth something again. He didn't put them into his IRA, either, so he has to pay imputed taxes on them every year.

On the whole, his situation is manageable, at least for the next year or two. Beyond that, without employment, it becomes very difficult indeed.

Julia Rosen

Julia Rosen has been doing rather well, but she started late and hasn't had much time in which to do any meaningful accumulation.

Like so many other women of her generation, she went to work right out of high school, in the late 1930s. She worked in a war plant during World War II, married Lou Hawkins in 1946, quit work, and started having children. Twenty-five years later, after three children, one slowly acquired Bachelor of Arts degree, and one divorce, she rejoined the labor force. At that time, in 1971, she was 50 years old, owned one heavily mortgaged home full of battered furniture and one aging car in considerable need of repair, had $372 in her bank account, and owed debts totaling $4,682. The debts would have been larger, but she was unable to secure any further credit.

Again, like so many other women in her situation, she went into selling, recognizing that it was one of the few high-paying apprenticeship occupations available. She became good at it, too, and especially at telephone selling. Now, 15 years later, about to ''retire'' at 65, she is telemarketing manager for a substantial regional distributor, a subsidiary of a larger national company. Today, she owns the same house free and clear, and with a current fair market value of $125,000. She will have Social Security and company pension payments totaling $15,000 a year on retirement, which she knows will be worth less and less in real dollars as the years go by. If inflation proceeds at a relatively modest rate, that $15,000 is quite likely to be worth only half of its present value in 10 years, when she is 75, and a quarter of its present worth when she is 85.

In the past 15 years, aside from paying off the house, she has lived carefully, secured some rather good financial advice, and become rather skilled herself at managing the financial side of life. The result has been the creation of a nest egg amounting to roughly $100,000, which can be counted upon to yield $7,000 – $10,000 a year in after-tax income. However, she also knows that if she simply spends that after-tax income, she will have enough to live on for the first few years, but that her $100,000 will then also erode in real value because of inflation, just like the Social Security and pension-plan income.

She reasons that the thing to do is to keep on growing that $100,000 for as long as she can, rather than spending any of the income derived from it. She will also continue to live in her present home, which is accreting value very rapidly. She may cash it in much later, but not now; her home is the best single growth investment she has, and besides she would otherwise have to pay wholly unproductive rent. When and if she does feel the need to cash in her home, it will add greatly to her income-producing nest egg.

Julia also quite fully understands the absolute need to continue doing lucrative work, and has just the kinds of skills that will enable her to do so. She would have preferred to stay on with her present company, but company attitudes make that impossible to do so comfortably. Instead, she will go to work part-time, as telemarketing supervisor for a local distributor of consumer goods, and suspects that with her skills she may be able to work the commitment into a full-time one, if she wishes. She is also seriously thinking of using those skills to go into her own telephone selling business, perhaps with someone a little younger, and has had some early discussions in that direction.

Next month, when Julia "retires," she will, in essence, instead by starting a new phase of her career. As a result, she will have a good deal of taxable income, including taxable pension-plan payouts, nest-egg investment yield, and continuing substantial earnings. Indeed, in the early years, she will probably have more income than she did before she retired. She will therefore be able to grow her investment fund considerably, at least during the early years of retirement, putting everything she can — over living costs and a vacation trip or two she has long promised herself — into the investment fund. She will have to consider the tax aspects of her investments carefully because of her taxable-income level, and avoid heavily taxable investments, as taxes limit growth possibilities. She will therefore focus on investments that combine tax advantage, safety, liquidity, and potential growth. She will reevaluate her decisions every step of the way, as she always has, and continue to have her carefully prepared yearly financial planning meeting with her financial planner.

At this point, Julia will put as much as the law allows into her IRA every year, funding the IRA with AAA-rated medium-term corporate bonds. She may also consider a tax-deferred variable annuity, for further tax relief. She is also likely to continue to keep some of her money in blue chip common stocks for growth and some dividends; and in a high-quality bond fund for income yield now. As she grows older, she will change the mix as her needs require.

George Harper

George rather resents being called a "Yuppie," which is what happens every time he has dinner with his dear, nearly departed older sister and her husband in their dreary suburban home, in a good town with good schools, good neighbors, and . . . good God, he wouldn't live like that for anything.

What George doesn't like about the Yuppie tag is first of all that it is, indeed, a tag; and secondly, that it just isn't true. At 30, he has a responsible staff job in the home office of a major corporation in midtown Manhattan, and is making enough money to pay the rent on a smallish but decent apartment on the Upper West Side, accumulate a much-needed executive wardrobe, develop a superb record collection that has to be worth a lot in the long run, pay his share of a summer rental in the Hamptons, rent a car as often as he needs one, and keep up with a lot of people who are in the process of making it big in New York. His college and MBA costs left him $43,000 in the hole, but it was money well spent, and he has also managed almost always to keep current on his education loan payments, with only four more years to go on them. And with all that, he has developed a meaningful profit-sharing plan participation in his company, putting away an average of 3% of his pay every year for the past two years. That's a little less than the national average, but he will be able to participate even more fully once the education loan payments are gone and his pay has moved on up, as it surely will. It's hard, though; you have to understand that. New York costs a lot, and you just have to keep up; that's why he gets a little behind on his bills sometimes.

That's right. With all his business training, he makes a lot of money, has nothing saved, can't pay his bills, lives in a hole in the wall, and doesn't even have a car. He hasn't even begun to handle the financial side of life, and if he keeps going this way he won't ever have anything to handle. If he loses his terribly vulnerable corporate staff job, and does not immediately secure another, he will almost immediately run out of money and be unable to borrow even to stay afloat for a little while, for he is using a good deal of credit right now, and will be viewed by lenders as "borrowed up," as well as unemployed.

Is this example too "loaded"? Certainly not. There are people like George in every company, and throughout the world. We all know some, and may even share some of their problems.

It is easy to prescribe for George; it is very hard for George to live with the prescription, for then he must greatly change his lifestyle. New York and other such headquarters cities really are expensive, and the corporate life really does encourage excess, often on not-very-large incomes. Oh, the incomes look large, but once you take taxes and the inflation of the past 15 years into account, the only way to make meaningful accumulations on most corporate incomes is to live rather carefully. And there are the education debts, besides.

What George has to do first of all is to spend less on consumables. He also has to put as much as possible into that company profit-sharing plan; it is a wonderful tax-advantaged accumulation opportunity, and goes with him when and if he leaves. He also has to find a way to convert from renter to owner, although swinging a cooperative apartment or condominium may be quite beyond him at this point. It may not be so for long, though, once he sets his goal and moves toward it; he may be able to come up with a down payment within a year or two, by borrowing against his profit-sharing plan accumulation.

If he is able to keep on working and earning, his developing career will indeed pay him well, and the whole world of saving and investing will be open to him. But right now he has to stop spending, start planning and saving, and use his skills to put the financial side of life in order. Until he does that, no planning is possible. And if he fails to do that, he will remain as vulnerable as he is today, no matter how much his income goes up in the future.

Janet Harper Kovacs and Stanley Kovacs

Jan and Stan are skilled managers, on or off a job, and their skills extend to the financial side of life. That's probably why they view George Harper's impecunious state with such dismay. That, and perhaps what amounts to just a bit of nostalgia for the carefree life.

They really had planned it well. They had met as undergraduates, married the day after graduation, and gone on to business school together. They both came out of graduate school with heavy debts, but with good job offers in the same major city. They worked, lived carefully, saved, took advantage of every opportunity to find tax advantage and safe leverage, and within a few years had enough money to buy the kind of rather expensive, well-situated suburban home they were looking for. Never mind that they had to carry almost $2,000 a month in mortgage payments and taxes; they were living where they wanted, as they wanted, and accreting value in their home at a great rate. They are, too; that home will turn out to be one of the best investments of their lifetimes.

These are not one-track money machines, by the way. Nothing like that; these are lively, broad-gauged people, with well-developed tastes in the arts, who also like to take off in their camper every chance they get. They have just defined the American dream in their own way, and set out to find their share of it.

Maybe that's why they moved their plans up so sharply when Jan got merged out of her job with a substantial severance-pay package, including a year of major medical coverage extension. What they did was to have a baby, named Michael, even though they knew they couldn't really make it on one salary yet. Their plan was for Jan to go back to work as soon as reasonably possible after the baby's birth, using the severance-pay package and their savings to pick up the slack. It was a gamble; but life is scarcely a set of neat economic estimates, and it was a gamble they wanted to make.

No, it didn't quite work out. There were some problems with the baby, and an operation. Jan wound up staying home a lot longer than they had planned; then there were a lot more expenses than they had planned. In the process, they used up all Jan's severance pay, all their savings, and had to take a second mortgage on the house besides, adding additional payments to their already overstrained economy.

Looking at it a little differently, though, their planning paid off when it was needed most. There were savings to use and home equity to draw upon. Indeed, their home has already gained more value, enough to enable them to borrow more on it, should they need to do so. In the long run, it will turn out that what they were forced to do by borrowing more was to increase the favorable leverage resulting from their home owner-ship.

And so, they will continue to deplore George's way of life whenever they see him; they know what sound planning has meant to them, and how much the lack of it can hurt others.

Mary Weldon

Mary never had much money. For her, it was work after school and weekends in the family restaurant, starting informally at a very early age, and at 16 for pay. Then state college and business school, a lot more ill-paid work, and a lot of spaghetti with tomato sauce and peanut butter sandwiches over the years. Nor was she particularly fast-tract after graduation, for she went right back to her home city and took an entry-level management job in the main local industry for a good deal less than she might have made had she been at the top of her class, aggressive, and headed for the big time.

But she has staying power, and the will to learn and win, which she has proceeded to do for the last ten years. At 33, she has long since left her home town, moved into electronic data processing, and is now beginning to make some real money as a computer industry specialist on the staff of a nationally recognized and very prosperous management consulting firm.

At 33, she has also learned to value her independence and properly see her own strengths, not the least of which is the ability to make and work her own financial plans, to budget and save. NOt that there has been much to save, up until now; she has just finished paying off the education loans. She has saved some, though, especially since her pay raises of the last three years, and now has a little over $14,000 in savings accounts and one-year bank CDs.

But she knows she hasn't paid the attention she must to the financial side of life, and now means to rectify that failing, for she is very concerned about security in what she correctly perceives as a very unstable modern corporate world. She has talked it all over with her accountant and her new financial adviser, and will try very hard to accomplish these minimal goals in the next several years, though she well understands that it may take as much as a decade more to et all these factors together and working for her.

First, she will protect herself better against potential catastrophes. She now recognizes some gaps and potential traps arising from complete reliance on company insurance arrangements, and will seek basic life and major medical insurance of her own.

She will also immediately open an IRA, knowing she has already cost herself tax money by not doing so earlier. She plans to put in the maximum every year, unless and until her company establishes a meaningful deferred-compensation plan. Should that happen, she will continue to hold her IRA, but will shift her main attention to the deferred-compensation plan.

Mary now also looks forward to buying a home as soon as possible, for she feels that the leverage intrinsic to home purchase in a long-term rising national real estate market makes home purchase one of the best and largest investment opportunities of a lifetime. She will see that it is well-situated, since she is alive to some of the negative possibilities that accompany risky locations.

She will keep on saving, of course, keeping some money in a convenience account and periodically sweeping her built-up savings into a federally insured bank money market account, from there into short-term CDs, and then at least yearly into blue chip stocks, AAA-rated bonds, and perhaps some equity mutual funds.

Mary will also early begin to prepare to support herself during the years after "retirement." She understands very well that she cannot expect public and private pension plans to supply very much support for 20–30 years after "retirement," and that her own savings and investments can be hard hit by inflation later on. She is thinking about the kind of business she might want to go into in her later years; also about the possibility of securing the kind of training that would allow her to become an independent professional later on. It's a little early to tell, but she may spend her last two or three active decades running a computer or computer-related company, or working as a certified public accountant with a totally computerized office.

One thing she does not plan to do is speculate with her money. That may change as affluence grows, but it is unlikely. For someone with both staying power and the strong feeling that the lifelong financial planning game goes to the tortoise, rather than the hare, speculation is out. Others will gamble in futures, options, precious metals, or whatever else happens to be hot in any given period; Mary will instead learn, organize, take tax advantage, grow her long-term stake, and plan to work productively for as long as she can.

The Three Stages of Your Financial Life

Finally, a small set of generalizations as to the kinds of asset portfolios you might reasonably look forward to developing as you save and invest over the years. As we have indicated throughout this work, individual wants, needs, and income levels differ greatly, and the following categories and recommendations should therefore be seen only as general benchmarks against which to measure your own progress, rather than any kind of formula to follow.

1. **From the time you enter the work force through your mid-thirties,** you should be developing at least three kinds of assets:

- An IRA, funded as the available opportunities indicate. In this period, that funding might well include Ginnie Maes and a moderately high-yield bond fund, though you should be ready to move out of the high-yield fund into more conservative investments if circumstances change.
- A home purchase fund that is both highly liquid and offers the highest possible return. This fund should therefore be in such investments as money market funds, CDs, and blue chip common-stock funds. After you buy your home, and depending upon such matters as income and current interest levels, you may be more able to move into a portfolio that is not quite as liquid, as through purchase of blue chip stocks that you mean to hold for long periods — always watching them, of course.
- For long-term growth, perhaps a long-term real estate limited partnership that gives immediate income.
- If you are married and expecting children, you should be starting a college fund, using such instruments as AAA corporate bonds, balanced mutual funds, and variable annuities.
- In this period, it is usually best to stay with term insurance, rather than moving into life insurance with investment or interest components.

2. **From your mid-thirties into your early fifties,** assuming that you have developed some substantial assets in the early years:

- You will be continuing to develop your now-quite-substantial IRA as before, now also probably adding such portfolio elements as high-quality common-stock funds, some blue chip stocks, and some highly rated bonds.

- Now you will be owning and upgrading your own home, in some periods exploring refinancing possibilities to extend and diversify your investment portfolio and college fund.
- You may by now be collecting, and beginning to move your collcting interests toward development of a lifelong sideline business and second income.
- With increasing income, you may be moving into tax-sheltered instruments, paying attention to both yield and tax considerations, and working with such instruments as carefully selected municipals, real estate tax shelters, and possibly side-business Keogh plans.
- In this period, it may become useful to move into life insurance with an investment or interest component, such as variable life and universal life.
- If there are children, you will need a fast-developing college fund, putting more and more into such instruments as balanced funds, variable annuities, and bonds.

3. In your early fifties, you are looking forward to and actively preparing for the later years, with basic strategies depending upon the kinds of asset accumulations and income levels so far achieved. For this period, it really is quite fruitless to generalize, other than to suggest that:

- If assets and income are not very substantial, your strategy will difer little from that previously described for stage 2, except that you may place greater emphasis on sheltering your somewhat higher income from taxes, and pay increasing attention to liquidity as the years go by.
- If assets and income have become quite substantial, you will probably want to protect your assets and shift toward safety, at the same time moving more toward tax-avoidance devices such as the single-premium deferred annuity.

Appendix B
The Language of Financial Planning: A Glossary

Every field has its own vocabulary, with some terms that exist nowhere else, and other terms that are common enough elsewhere but have special meanings in that particular field. To people not working directly in a field, such special languages require a good deal of explanation and demystification, for otherwise simple communication with those professionals working in the field becomes extremely difficult.

To make it easier for you to communicate meaningfully with the financial advisers, brokers, accountants, lawyers, and bankers you deal with, we here define and comment on some key terms in the language of financial planning. What follows is most emphatically not intended to be a substitute for an absolutely necessary investor's dictionary, such as Brownstone and Franck's *Investor's Dictionary*, but rather a brief treatment of some of the techniques and concepts not otherwise found fully defined in the body of this work. Please note that much of this section is picked up and adapted from similar definitions carried in our previous work, *Personal Financial Survival*.

Appreciation Potential

This is investment-community jargon for "It may go up." Because this is a term used mainly by those with something to sell, there is — quite understandably — no opposite term, such as depreciation potential. For example, common stock is said to have appreciation potential when those trading it feel that, for any one reason or for several reasons, it may go up.

If the rise in market price is thought to be only for the near term, the stock is said to have short-term appreciation potential; if only for the long term, then long-term appreciation potential. Less pretentiously, a stock may be described as having either growth potential or its opposite, downside risk.

Arbitrage

When a trader buys something in one market and simultaneously, or very nearly simultaneously, sells the same kind of thing in another market at a different price, pursuing a profit resulting from the difference between the two prices, that trader is practicing arbitrage. It is a specialty among investment traders, and it normally involves very large transactions in two or more widely separated markets at the same time and very small price differences between the markets. The most common investments traded in by these specialists, called arbitrageurs, are currencies, commodities, and several kinds of commodity and financial futures.

For example, a trader may find the British pound selling in Amsterdam at $2.30 and at the same time selling in Rio de Janeiro at $2.31 — usually the differences are even smaller. By buying a million pounds in Rio at $2.31, the arbitrageur can make a penny on each pound, or $10,000, minus transaction costs. That is something of an oversimplification, but it accurately portrays the basic transaction that takes place in such deals.

In recent years, the term "takeover arbitrage" has come to be used in connection with a branch of investment banking that has little or nothing to do with the kind of arbitrage just described.

Takeover arbitrage is that branch of investment banking concerned with realizing profit from trading the securities of companies involved in takeover situations. Traders involved take very substantial risks for very substantial possible profits; for example, by speculating in the common stock of a company that has just received a takeover bid from another company, which has offered considerably more per share than the current market price of the stock.

Assets

In the widest colloquial sense, anything carrying any kind of positive value — from such tangibles as real estate to such intangibles as future royalties, love, and happiness — can be described as an asset. In the economic and financial sense, although assets can be as tangible as real estate or as intangible as a future interest in royalties, they must be capable of producing wealth that can be measured in financial terms now or at some future time — and that lets out love and happiness.

Assets can be liquid — that is, cash or near cash — such as notes (minus an allowance for uncollectibles) or quickly marketable securities and commodities, including listed common stocks, some bonds, and gold. Some assets may be less liquid, such as real estate, furnishings, and business goods and equipment. Others may be extremely difficult to make liquid, such as future interests and equity in a wholly owned business that is not readily salable. Yet all these are assets, to which a value may be attached, ultimately, if by no one else than the taxing authorities.

Audit

In accounting, auditing is the examination of records in order to attempt to substantiate the completeness and accuracy of books of account and of the transactions they record, with considerable attention paid to the internal consistency of the records. That examination, or audit, is carried out by someone professionally trained to conduct such examinations: an auditor, who is usually also an accountant.

Most people encounter the term in relation to examinations of personal and business records carried out by taxing authorities. In that context, auditing is often carried out by an employee of a taxing authority, such as an IRS agent, who may or may not be professionally trained in accounting and whose auditing activities often take on some of the flavor of adversary proceedings.

Average

In ordinary usage, an average is an arithmetic mean. In securities markets, an average reflects the value of a group of selected stocks, which are thought to be representative of their markets as a whole and therefore indicators of market health. Familiar examples are the Dow Jones Industrial, Standard & Poor's 500, and the New York Stock Exchange averages.

The Dow Jones averages are actually three different current stock price averages, composed, respectively, of industrial, transportation, and utilities stocks. The best known and most frequently referred to of the three is the industrial average, composed of 30 well-known common stocks. It is also by far the best known of all the stock market averages, and its fluctuations are watched closely by people who follow stock market price trends, even though the other major averages are composed of far larger numbers of stocks, fluctuate a good deal less, and are therefore somewhat more statistically reliable for predictive purposes.

Averaging

Averaging is a stock market investment technique also known as dollar cost averaging. It involves investing fixed sums of money in securities through periodic purchases, as in the monthly purchase of $1,000 in shares of a specific common stock over a period of six months, ignoring short-term price fluctuations in that stock on the theory that the long-term trend of that stock and indeed of the whole stock market is up, and that the purchase of sound stocks over the long term can only prove profitable.

Balanced Fund

A balanced fund is a diversely invested mutual fund, really a fund that from the start is so organized as to be able to invest in several kinds of stocks and bonds at the same time and to shift emphasis from one to another as fund managers' assessments of market situations change from time to time. Many mutual funds are not so organized. Instead they move from one kind of investment, such as municipal bonds or common stocks or even a single kind of common stock, to cash and cash instruments, without the ability to move relatively freely among an assortment of stocks and debt instruments.

Bankruptcy

It happens. For whatever reason, every day business and personal debtors are declared insolvent by court proceedings, and their affairs administered by a court through a receiver or trustee. Bankruptcy may be involuntary or voluntary; it may be worked through with a court standing as a shield between creditors and debtor over a period of years, or it may be a matter of liquidation and forced sale of all business or almost all personal assets to satisfy creditors.

Personal bankruptcy does not impair government Social Security, survivors', or disability payments; nor are pension assets or pension payments many years later impaired, although once payments to recipients start, monies from pension funds may be subject to any obligations that remain after bankruptcy.

Basis

This is one of those rather frustrating terms that has several quite separate and distinct meanings, depending on the context within which it is used.

In taxation, basis refers to the cost of an asset to be deducted from a selling price in order to arrive at taxable capital gains, whether short or long term, as when you buy stock at one price and sell it later at a higher price.

It means the same thing in real estate transactions, but with the addition of the cost of improvements during the period of ownership and the subtraction of depreciation and some other minor deductions to arrive at taxable gain. (The depreciation computed is based on buying price plus improvements.)

In bond markets, basis means something else — the rate of interest paid on bonds and other debt securities. In that context, a "basis point" means one-hundredth of 1%.

In stock analysis, it means the annual rate of return on stock, figuring the actual return as a proportion of the current market value of the stock.

In commodities trading, basis refers to the difference between current, or spot, prices and futures prices.

Bear

See Bull

Blue Chip

A synonym for high-quality investment, now applied widely to many noninvestment items and matters of value. Blue chip common stocks are the stocks of large, highly regarded companies, which have grown in value and paid dividends over a period measured in decades and which are therefore thought to be rather safe investments, with little chance of omitting dividends and losing value quickly and catastrophically.

Boiler Room, Bucket Shop

These are really two investment-industry slang terms meaning the same thing — a fraudulent investment-selling firm. These are the kinds of illegal operations that give telephone selling a bad name. Their representatives sell mainly by telephone and will sell anything that is currently popular — as long as they can make a great deal of money doing it.

Bond

A tie that binds, and a word with a dozen different meanings and scores of uses. In finance, a bond is an instrument evidencing debt obligation; in insurance, a bond is a pledge of surety for another; in commerce, some goods held pending excise tax payments are said to be held in bond; in law, a bond is an agreement.

In financial planning, the term refers to a debt instrument issued by a corporation or government, in which the issuer promises to pay back the money borrowed from bond buyers, with interest, within a specified time. Usually, interest is payable in installments during the life of the debt obligation, and principal is repaid in a lump sum at the end of the period; sometimes, however, as in the case of some government bonds, interest accretes during the debt period and is paid with principal repayment at the end of the period. Bonds are usually medium- to long-term debt instruments, running five years or more.

Bond Fund

A bond fund is a mutual fund that limits its investments to either bonds or cash instruments, trading in bonds with the money invested in it by its mutual-fund purchasers.

A special form of bond fund is the municipal bond fund, which limits its bond-trading activities to state and municipal bonds, thereby reaching for the tax advantages inherent in these kinds of debt obligations, which are usually exempt from federal taxes and sometimes from state and local taxes as well.

Bond Market

Bonds of all kinds are traded on many stock exchanges, but no exchange dominates the trading in bonds as the New York Stock Exchange dominates stock trading. Instead, bond trading proceeds over the counter, through a network of firms trading in these debt obligations, all of which make up the bond market. Most bond transactions are very large and represent trades between financial institutions, such as banks, pension funds, mutual funds, and insurance companies, buying and selling for their own accounts.

Book Value

Book value is an accounting concept, and a valuable one when trying to assess the intrinsic asset value of a business or a share of common stock. It is calculated a little differently for each. For a business, book value is the difference between all assets and all liabilities; putting it a little differently, it is the net of assets minus liabilities. Those assets are valued as part of a going business, rather than at their scrap or salvage value, which would be much less; and that is proper, for it is that going business that is being evaluated.

When assessing the intrinsic value of a share of common stock, any preferred stock outstanding must also be taken into account. To estimate the book value of a share of common stock, you would take the net of assets minus liabilities, subtract the value of any preferred stock outstanding, and divide the resulting net by the number of outstanding shares of common stock, with the result being book value. For example, if assets were $100 and liabilities $50, the net would be $50. If preferred stock were worth $10 and were subtracted from that $50, the result would be $40. If there were 40 common stock shares outstanding, their book value would be $1 per share.

That is an important figure, for if stock is selling below its book value, it may be the stock of a company in terrible trouble, perhaps in the process of being forced out of business, with the resulting reevaluation of assets way down to salvage value; or it may be the stock of a company that is far undervalued, a very good buy and a prime takeover candidate. Conversely, if a stock is selling far above its book value, it may be a company with interesting growth and profit possibilities that has shown extraordinary results and that may soon show more; or it may be a company that is far overvalued, as were so many "glamour" stocks in the 1960s, and a very bad buy.

Bottom Line

Ah, the bottom line we hear so much about! In the widest sense, this financial term has moved right out into the language and become synonymous with net result.

In finance, it is literally the bottom line of a profit and loss statement — the net figure, after all else has been computed. But here, too, the term has come to be used more widely to mean the net result of a single action or financial transaction, as well as the net of all the transactions embodied in a profit and loss statement.

Bucket Shop

See Boiler Room

Bull, Bear

These are traditional stock market terms that have now moved out into the general language, having become synonyms for optimist and pessimist. In the financial world, a bull thinks a specific stock or debt obligation, or a whole market or set of markets, is likely to go up, and buys now in anticipation of that rise. Bulls often buy on margin (that is, on borrowed money) and hold the securities or commodities in brokers' margin accounts in an attempt to maximize the impact of their investments, holding on as long as possible in a falling market.

A bear thinks that a single investment or group of investments will go down, and sells rather than buys. While bulls often buy long and hold, bears often do the opposite; they sell short — that is, they sell stocks they do not yet own, planning and hoping to buy stocks to cover their sales later at lower prices, profiting from the difference between the two sets of prices.

Call

See Option

Capital

Capital is tangible wealth that can be used to produce more wealth. It need not be so used; money stored away in a safe-deposit box is capital, as is money invested in a business or used to purchase securities. Often, such intangibles as skills and goodwill are called capital; although not capital in a rigorous accounting or economic sense, they may be as important for financial planning. For example, creating a body of skills by the investment of capital in education uses up the capital invested without the production of tangible wealth, but may be the most lucrative use of that capital.

Capital Gains

Capital gains are the profits resulting from sale of an asset. For example, when securities or realty worth $10,000 are sold later for $15,000, the difference of $5,000 may be capital gain — and therefore taxable, for that is the main significance of the concept.

Capital Stock

Capital stock is all the stock representing ownership of a corporation, including common and preferred stock issued and outstanding. It is all the stock held by the public and all that has been issued and is owned by the corporation itself, as when stock has been sold to the public and then repurchased by the corporation.

The underlying or intrinsic value of the total capital stock of a corporation is its book value, or the net of all assets minus all liabilities, that net being one measure of the total ownership equity in the corporation. Another measure of the current value of the ownership equity in a corporation is often supplied by the market value placed on publicly traded stock of that corporation.

Cash Flow Statement

The cash flow statement is a prime planning tool for individuals trying to accomplish effective financial planning, as it is for business. As a record of what happened, it traces the flow of cash through the hands of an individual or business, literally showing where cash came from and where it went. As a forward-planning device, it forecasts where money is expected to come from, in what quantities, and when; and where money is expected to go, in what quantities, and when.

Cash Surrender Value

If you own a life insurance policy that includes both savings and insurance components — usually called a whole life, permanent life, or straight life policy — that policy includes a sum you can claim on cancellation of the policy. That sum, called the cash surrender value, consists of the savings you have accrued in the policy plus an interest payment on the money.

Most often, people do not cancel life insurance policies to obtain the cash surrender value in them; nor do insurance companies encourage the practice. Instead, at modest interest rates — but higher than the rates the insurance company pays its policyholders — you may borrow from the insurance company right up to the full value of the money you have lent it, thus keeping the insurance in force and still having the use of your own money.

Certificate of Deposit

A certificate of deposit is a document evidencing the existence of a deposit in a bank, issued by a bank to the owner of the deposit; a passbook is the same kind of instrument, in a different physical form.

They are commonly called CDs and occur in two basic forms. One form, widely sold by commercial banks to individuals, is that of a demand certificate of deposit, which specifies that the depositor can withdraw the deposit on demand, although suffering substantial interest-rate penalties for premature withdrawal. Because of its demand nature, this kind of certificate of deposit is not tradable in investment markets.

The second form is that of a time certificate of deposit, which is payable at some specified future time. Such certificates are widely traded in money markets, as they are usually direct obligations of highly regarded banks, although not as safe as direct federal debt obligations.

Sometimes certificates of deposit are issued in denominations so high as to place them outside the normal buying range of all but the wealthiest individuals. But individuals can reach them—and their sometimes attractive rates—through mutual funds, notably money market funds, which routinely include them in their portfolios.

Chartist

See Fundamentalist

Collateral

Something of value that is used as security for a loan is collateral. Normal collateral consists of real or personal property of determinable value belonging to the borrower or to one guaranteeing the loan for the borrower, which on default will become the property of the lender. When a lender and borrower enter into a home mortgage loan, the property mortgaged is collateral for the loan. When a borrower formally pledges any property, such as stocks and other financial instruments or automobiles and other personal possessions, as security for a loan, that which is pledged is collateral. When a borrower gives the lender physical possession of property so pledged, to be returned on repayment of the loan, the loan is called a collateral loan.

Although collateral usually consists of tangibles of determinable value that can be fairly easily sold it may be anything recognized by a lender as having value; for example, a future interest in an estate or indeterminate future royalty payments may be accepted by a lender as collateral. Such collateral will not be accepted by your bank, though, and those lenders who will accept it are speculative and their rates of interest are very high.

Collectibles

In the widest investment sense, collectibles have come to mean all tangibles bought, held, and traded for which any kind of market exists. Antiques, works of art, old and rare books, stamps, and jewelry have been joined by bottle tops, comic books, glass, barbed wire, matchbook covers, and hundreds of other items so bought, held, and traded. Lively formal and informal markets in these kinds of items have sprung up all over the United States and in many other parts of the world; these sometimes function to push trading prices up far beyond intrinsic values and inflation rates and become arenas of considerable speculative activity.

Commercial Paper

In the widest sense, commercial paper includes all short-term debt instruments issued by businesses of all kinds. Such notes are negotiable and may be traded and used as collateral. Some such debt instruments are traded widely, are rated for safety, and have become part of the money market. These are the instruments issued by major businesses, which stand behind them, essentially as they do for any unsecured longer-term instrument, such as a bond, with their full faith and credit, which is a promise to pay. The instruments are as good as the businesses issuing them, which in the case of a major oil company may be very good indeed and in the case of a troubled company not very good at all.

Because the instruments are normally issued in denominations of from $100,000 to $1 million, very few individuals can trade in them. However, money market mutual funds do, and that is the way individuals can reach for their yields, which are higher than, though generally not as safe as, federally issued and federally insured debt obligations.

Commodities

Commodities are those items of value that are tradable, but in an investment-market sense they are those kinds of goods traded on commodities exchanges, such as gold, silver, platinum, other precious metals and resources, coffee, tea, sugar, lumber, cotton, wool, corn, pork bellies, and wheat.

Both current (or spot) commodity contracts and commodity futures contracts are traded on commodity exchanges; the contracts, rather than the commodities themselves, being the instruments traded. A commodities future contract specifies all the terms of an agreement to deliver a specific amount of a commodity at a specified place on a future date. It is so constructed as to be tradable, since each contract is identical with all other contracts of a like kind.

Common Stock

Common stock is an unrestricted ownership share in a corporation and in the kind of stock that is normally traded in investment markets. Common stock is by far the main form such ownership shares take, its owner sharing fully in risks and opportunities and voting its proportion of ownership in the issuing corporation. In this, it contrasts with preferred stock, whose owner may share less risk but also shares in opportunities to only a limited degree. When a stock is reported as rising or falling in market value, it is a common stock that is being described, unless otherwise noted.

Convertible

Some bonds and preferred stocks that are issued carry the privilege of conversion over to a stated number of shares of common stock at a stated price within a stated period after issue. Their purchasers may hold these convertibles in their purchased form until maturity or may exercise the privilege of converting them, depending upon whether or not the stated amount of common stock is worth more than the bond or preferred stock at some time before the conversion privilege expires.

Cyclical Stocks

Cyclical stocks are the traded stocks of companies thought to be quickly affected by the ups and downs of the economy. The prices of such stocks therefore fluctuate more directly than most stocks as the business cycle moves between prosperity and depression or recession. For example, companies manufacturing consumer goods and therefore depending wholly or largely on discretionary consumer purchases, such as automobiles, furniture, and appliances, may feel the impact of a recession very sharply, while also being the beneficiaries of pent-up demand as a period of prosperity unfolds.

Deferred-Compensation Plan

A deferred-compensation plan is a tax-advantaged employee savings plan, in which employees can put a portion of their pretax earnings directly in a fund that then accretes tax-free until the occurrence of events specified by applicable federal law. The fund goes with the employee on termination or retirement. Control over how the fund is invested rests with the employee, within limits set by the company plan. Many companies also contribute some percentage of the employees' contribution, adding to the great value of such a plan. In the early and mid-1980s, the 401(k) deferred-compensation plan — so named because that is the number of the enabling federal tax law clause — has been widely adopted.

Earnings Per Share

Earnings are profits. Earnings per share, a very important indicator of the economic health of an enterprise, are profits minus taxes and preferred stock dividends (both of which have to be paid first), divided by the number of shares of common stock outstanding. For example, if earnings are $1,000 and taxes are $400, net after-tax earnings are $600. If preferred stock dividends totaling $100 are subtracted, and if there are 500 common shares outstanding, net earnings per share are $1 each.

Employee Stock Ownership Plan (ESOP)

This is an arrangement through which employees purchase partial to full ownership of their own enterprises, although in very many instances they have no share in the control of those enterprises, control resting in management and sometimes other major investors. Such arrangements are very often funded by a combination of funds in existing employee pension plans and large additional borrowings, with the resulting stock ownerships supplanting previous plan promises. Some of these plans may work out well in the long run for the employees involved, but substitution of the stock of a single company — any company — for the diversification that can be achieved by a large, well-managed pension plan is, by any investment standard, clearly entirely imprudent. In many instances these plans are essentially devices used by management to tap pension plan monies for management purposes, especially including resistance to corporate raiders engaged in takeover attempts, and in the long run some may be invalidated by the courts as an illegal use of pension plan monies.

Equity

In finance, equity is the value of an ownership share. That sounds rather straightforward, but it is often very difficult to determine. If a company has issued stock that is publicly traded, and you own some of that stock, its market price rather easily determines the value of your ownership share, or equity, at any given time and also indicates the total market value of the company at that time. On the other hand, the same company may sell for more or less than the total of all its shares outstanding, and the shares themselves will soon reflect the difference in a sale situation. Similarly, you can estimate the value of your ownership interest in a dwelling by estimating fair market value and subtracting outstanding mortgage debts, but you will not be able to find the real worth of that equity until an actual sale. In taxation, the value of a closely held business is often a hotly disputed matter between taxing authorities and heirs, much affecting the taxes levied on many estates.

Fixed Income

Fixed income constitutes one of the great retirement traps in an economy characterized by a long-term, inexorable tendency toward inflation and consequent loss of currency value. The truth is that income at fixed dollar levels, with no provision built in to adjust those levels up as inflation rises, is not fixed income at all, though that is what it is called. Such income is really diminishing income, for its real value lessens every year. Even in periods with low inflation rates, the impact is substantial as the years go by and as people live longer. In periods of rapid inflation, the impact is catastrophic.

Social Security payments have been, in a practical sense, indexed to inflation, reflecting political pressure on legislators to move them up in response to rapid inflation. But they will not necessarily keep up with inflation as counterpressure builds to limit payments in a no-longer-so-affluent United States. Private pension plan payments, with rare exceptions, are fixed. Most annuity payments are fixed, although variable payments, which may give some opportunity to try to keep up with inflation, have been growing in popularity. Medium- and long-term bond income is fixed, although reinvestment of principal at higher interest rates at maturity is often possible.

Most of us have long carried the idea that fixed-income investments are somehow safer than those providing varying amounts of income, on the theory that, with fixed income investment, "At least you know what you have coming in." Alas, that is an error. Fixed income is diminishing income, and safety need not be equated with this kind of diminishing income. You cannot do much about Social Security or private pension plan payments, but you certainly can buy shorter-term bonds, variable annuities, highly regarded common stocks, some rental properties, and other similar conserving investments, while keeping long-term financial planning funds away from volatile securities and such outright gambles as commodity futures.

Fundamentalist, Chartist (or Technical Forecaster)

The market prices of securities fluctuate — and a whole industry has been built around attempts to predict the future course of those fluctuations. Securities analysts, investment advisers, and market forecasting services all claim expert knowledge, advise, predict, hedge their claims and bets, and seek the fruits of successful prediction — or at least seek to be recognized by investors as successful forecasters. There are two major schools of thought as to how to approach securities fluctuation forecasting, along with a number of other approaches and variations.

One major approach to forecasting is that of the fundamentalists, who believe that basic economic, social, political, and specific company facts and trends must be understood and assessed on the way toward successful prediction. They want to know a great deal about specific company managements, balance sheets, cash flow statements, industry trends, and national and international factors that may have an impact — in short, all the facts underlying an investment.

Another major approach is that of the chartists, many of whom want to know very little about those things that concern the fundamentalists. Chartists want to know how a graph showing the past performance of a market or group of investments can be used to predict the future course of price fluctuation in those investments.

As is usually true, seeming polar opposites are often only tendencies. Most fundamentalists will also study charts of previous price movements, while continuing to ask basic economic questions. Chartists also — though many are purists — will ask basic questions, while focusing on their charts.

Futures

When "futures" are being traded, the specific instruments of value being traded are really uniform contracts. When a future is bought or sold, ownership of the tangibles or intangibles that are the subject of the contract does not change hands; all that passes is the contract itself. That contract details the specifics of a future transaction, including quality, quantity, and terms identical with those of all other contracts trading the same kinds of items on the same organized exchanges. Futures contracts are traded on several commodities and financial futures exchanges, with trading available in a considerable variety of tangible goods, including gold and other precious metals, and in such intangibles as government debt obligations and currency. Although futures trading is very popular in some periods, it is generally highly speculative.

General Partnership

See Limited Partnership

Glamour Stocks

"Hot" stocks, "glamour" stocks, stocks that "everybody is buying and you can't miss"; these are the stocks that dreams are made of. That is not reality, however; reality is a glamour stock that has lost its glamour just after you have bought it at an inflated price. Glamour stocks are those that are extremely popular for a time, far more so than is usually justified by performance or prospects. They go up basically because more and more people are buying them in hope of quick profits. Often that hope of profit is spurred by a real, though temporary, surge or an anticipated surge in profits, as was true of some gambling stocks in the late 1970s. Sometimes a new technology that seems to offer enormous profit potential spurs popularity, as was true of some computer and electronic stocks in the 1960s.

Gold Shares

Golds shares are stocks representing ownership shares in companies that are mainly in the gold-mining business. During times of historic runups in the world price of gold, such shares are often enormously popular, since their profits considerably reflect the rising price of gold, even though such shares are highly speculative investments.

Growth Investment

Any investment oriented primarily toward securing growth in the value of the investment itself, rather than toward immediate financial return, is a growth investment.

The concept is often encountered on stock trading, when a company is described as a "growth company," meaning one that is experiencing rapid growth in net asset value, in sales, and often in total ownership equity as the value of its stock appreciates (that stock is then called a "growth stock"). However, such stocks rarely pay much in the way of dividends, since much of what might otherwise be profits and dividends is being plowed back into the company to spur future growth.

"Growth funds" and "aggressive growth funds" are sometimes also popular. These are mutual funds focusing on the acquisition of stocks thought to be growth stocks and looking for rapid appreciation in total fund asset value, rather than for income to be passed along to fund participants. Similarly, there are "growth portfolios," individual investment portfolios geared to the acquisition of growth stocks.

Hot Money

In the financial world, hot money is investment money, usually large amounts of it, that moves from investment vehicle to investment vehicle, and from country to country, in search of the highest possible rate of return. It is speculating money, which may one week be found in currency trading, the next week in gold, and the week after that in commodity futures. It is most emphatically *not* to be followed on its adventurous way; small investors who speculate almost inevitably find themselves buying too late to buy low and selling too late to make a profit or even to avoid substantial loss.

Income Fund

Income funds are mutual funds aimed primarily at securing current income for their participants, and therefore toward the purchase of securities yielding cash payout rather than growth. They are far from recession-proof, but they tend to be somewhat recession-resistant, in that companies consistently paying substantial dividends over a long period tend to be some of the most stable and best-regarded current "blue chips" available in investment markets. Because it is the business of fund managers to watch fund investments, the likelihood is considerably diminished that yesterday's blue-chip investment that is today's troubled company will be kept in the fund too long.

Investment

Practically speaking, any attempt to derive economic profit from the use of valuables is investment. There is no real difference between using owned land to produce crops for sale and using an amount of money equal to the value of that land to buy common stocks in another business. Both are investments. Either or both may involve the use of borrowed money; either or both may fail to make money — it is the intent that defines the act of investment, not the success or failure of the act. One may involve personal labor as well, but that does not in any way affect the act of investing; a small business involves investment, even if it employs no one but its owner.

Some expenditures that may result in economic benefits later and some that may result only in noneconomic benefits later are also often called investments, such as an investment in a career, which may later turn out to be the best-yielding money ever spent in economic terms, or an investment in learning, which may yield lifelong psychic benefits. They are indeed investments in the widest sense; although so indeterminate a return makes them difficult to assess in terms of success or failure, they nonetheless may require the same kind of attention that any other major investments require.

Junk Bonds

These are high-risk, high-interest, low-rated bonds sold by some brokers as good speculative opportunities, on the theory that while some few may fail, the majority will not, and the interest rates paid will more than make up for the individual bond losses. A questionable theory, and a game for professionals, if for anyone.

Leverage

Leverage is the possibility of making or losing money with somebody else's money, whether borrowed or otherwise acquired.

When a company carries a very heavy debt load, the market price of its common stock can swing considerably more widely in response to profit and loss than without that load. When that company is making money, it often makes money both on owner's equity and on borrowed funds, therefore yielding more return overall and driving common stock prices up; when it is losing money, the converse occurs, and the common stock of the company may be driven far down. The common stock of such a company is said to be heavily leveraged. Similarly, when income-pro-

ducing real estate is heavily financed, its partnership shares may be said
to be heavily leveraged.

In a slightly different way, but following the approach of making
money with money borrowed or otherwise acquired from others, a company buying another company for cash may buy with very little of its
own available cash if it can borrow the cash for the purchase and repay it
wholly or mainly out of the cash reserves and cash flow of the acquired
company; then the acquisition is described as heavily leveraged.

Limited Partnership, General Partnership

Limited partnership is a partnership form very often encountered in
real estate investment, in which the tax-shelter benefits inherent in the
partnership form of real estate investment are allowed to pass through
to investors, while liability is limited for those wishing only to invest,
rather than taking an unlimited profit and liability share in a partnership. Limited partners share partnership liability exposure only up to the
dollar value of their original investments, take profits if available only
within previously stated limits, and therefore own only financial shares.
Those who participate in an unlimited fashion are called general
partners.

Liquidity

Liquidity is the extent to which assets are in liquid form, meaning in
cash or very quickly marketable securities, assuming relatively normal
economic conditions. In estimating one's own liquidity, current liabilities
should be subtracted from total liquid assets.

Many assets can be entirely salable under normal conditions but not
liquid, such as real property and equipment, which may take considerable time to sell. As a practical matter, some assets may be salable but
only at a fraction of their value under conditions in which they would
need to be sold, as when a small business with unsolvable cash-flow
problems is forced to sell equipment to raise cash to pay creditors,
effectively forcing itself out of business and reducing the value of the
equipment to or near its salvage value.

Listed, Unlisted

By far the majority of publicly owned stocks are traded in over-the-
counter markets, that is, directly between brokers rather than through
the medium of an organized stock exchange. Such stocks are "unlisted,"
and they include many well-known and highly respected American companies. Those stocks that meet the rules of an organized stock exchange,
in terms of the size and financial condition of their issuing companies and

the number of shares outstanding and tradable, may be "listed" by one or more exchanges as tradable on those exchanges.

Load

In finances and insurance, a load is a sales charge. The term is sometimes applied widely to include all sales charges and commissions, but is usually applied to sales charges on mutual fund and life insurance and annuity purchases. Many mutual fund and some life insurance annuity purchases do not have sales charges attached to them. They are called "no-load" funds and policies. That is a competitive selling matter, especially in the mutual funds industry, where for many years most large funds charged substantial sales charges but found themselves competing with smaller funds that did not. Although the trend is away from such sales charges, they still exist and should be noted when considering purchase of a mutual fund.

Some investments and insurance contracts do not have front-load charges, but may have "back-load" charges or expense factors that are beyond the norm and act as a load.

Long, Short

When you buy securities or commodities "long," you are buying them at current market prices and holding them in hopes of making money as those prices rise. One who buys long is an optimist, or a "bull," as to the profit prospects of that which has been bought, but anyone who buys anything is likely to have bought in anticipation of gain, so this widely used characterization is insufficient. More to the point, most people who describe themselves as holding long positions are investors who have bought in anticipation of sharp, short-term upward price swings; who have bought on margin, that is, partly with borrowed money; and who expect to sell at or near the top of a short-term movement for quick profit, having made enough money to pay for interest due on the margined purchase and still come out substantially ahead.

One holding a long position is always a buyer hoping to make money from market price rises. One holding a short position is always a seller, hoping to make money from market price declines. The short seller sells securities or commodities not owned, hoping to be able to buy later at lower market prices than those at which the sale was made, for later delivery to their buyer. Sometimes the seller will borrow securities or commodities through a broker, paying interest on the borrowings; deliver the borrowings to the buyer; and then later buy enough to replace the borrowings. All this is often done in a margin account, and interest must also be paid for the money borrowed in that account.

If all goes as hoped, and the securities or commodities go down, the short seller makes enough money to pay interest and still profit. But if the securities or commodities sold short go up, the short seller must eventually buy at higher prices and then loses the difference between buying and selling prices, plus any interest paid, and, if much borrowed money was used in an attempt to maximize the impact of gain, much of what was invested. As always, leverage works both ways — and short selling with borrowed money is speculation doubled.

Margin

Securities trading in a "margin account" is trading that is conducted partly with the money of the trader and partly with borrowed money. Margin is the amount of ownership actually held by a buyer, expressed as a percentage; one who has purchased stock on 50% margin has purchased 50% of the stock with his or her own money and 50% with money borrowed from the brokerage firm handling the margin account. The brokerage firm, in turn, has usually not financed the 50% loan itself, but has used the securities purchased as collateral for a short-term bank loan to cover the amount lent to the brokerage customer. The margin customer, in turn, pays interest to the brokerage firm to cover the cost of the borrowed money.

Federal regulations specify what credit percentage a broker may lend a customer in a margin account and have done so ever since the 1930s, in reaction against the unrestrained margin buying that helped trigger the stock market crash of 1929. Should a decline in stock prices cause the value of stock held on margin to become lower in relation to the amounts borrowed than is allowed by current regulations, the broker must issue a "margin call" to the investor, requiring that more cash be supplied to bring the investor's stake in the margin account up to mandated levels. Failure to meet the margin calls in a specified time under the securities regulations forces the broker to sell the customer's stock. During a serious downturn in the market, failures to meet margin calls and the subsequent sale of customers' stocks creates a greater supply of the stocks in the marketplace, further decreasing their value.

Market

A market is an arena within which valuables are traded. That is a broad enough definition to include retail stores, bazaars, organized and over-the-counter stock markets, and worldwide commodities and currencies markets. Rather confusingly, all those involved as specialists in specific markets refer to their own area of special interest as "the market," much as those deeply involved in a particular line of work invariably refer to their own businesses as "the business."

"How did the market do today?" is a widely encountered question among brokers and investors. It is usually answered, "It went up — or down — X points." In that instance, the market referred to is almost always the New York Stock Exchange, and the "it" that went up or down is the Dow Jones Industrial Average, the most widely followed and quoted American index of stock prices.

Municipal Bond

The word "municipal" is somewhat misleading here. Municipalities are any self-governing units of government other than county, state, and federal governments; municipal bonds, however, include all government debt obligations other than those of the federal government, including county and state government obligations.

Mutual Funds

The same concept is embodied in all mutual funds: by pooling their funds and paying professional fund managers, small investors can profit from their investments and simultaneously diversify those investments far better than they could alone. Any mutual fund, however invested, is a pool of investors' money; investors buy shares and may or not pay sales charges. A fund may consist of a limited number of shares, in which case it is called a "closed-end fund," or it may be as large as the number of shares it succeeds in selling to the public, in which case it is called an "open-end fund." Investors in open-end funds can sell their shares back to the fund at any time, which is called "redemption." Closed-end funds are sold on the over-the-counter market, much like stocks.

Mutual fund pools of investment money can focus on many kinds of investments, including money market instruments, several kinds of stocks, and bonds; they can specialize in one kind of investment or attempt to balance among several. In the 1960s, at the height of the bull market of the time, there was even a Fund of Funds, which bought only the shares of other mutual funds.

No-load

See Load

Opportunity Cost

Opportunity cost is a concept widely used in business and accounting; although it is seldom used in personal financial planning, it deserves careful understanding and earnest consideration. The concept is simple enough. The difference between what you actually earn on an investment and what you might have earned elsewhere with reasonably equivalent safety is seen as a cost, thereby accentuating the importance of paying close and fruitful attention to investment decisions. For example, if you put $5,000 into a savings account and earn $300 per year on that money when you might have put the same $5,000 into equally safe short-term federal government securities and earned $450 on it, your opportunity cost is $150 a year, highlighting the cost of failing to make even as simple and obvious a choice as where to put what are essentially savings dollars. When you include tax implications and longer-term investment considerations, failure to give sufficient attention to such decisions can result in enormous long-term opportunity costs. Note that there is a trap here, too — the concept is useful only if the investments considered are of reasonably equivalent safety and liquidity.

Option

In the widest sense option is synonymous with choice; that choice may or may not be something of value, and it may or may not be legally enforceable. In finance, an option is something of value and is legally enforceable; it is the right to buy or sell something at a set price at a stated time, with the option buyer often betting that its market value will go up and the seller betting the opposite. That kind of option is almost always in writing, although it may or may not have involved some kind of consideration. For example, an option to buy a piece of real estate will almost always have cost something, whereas an employee's option to buy company stock or a stockholder's option to buy additional stock will usually not have cost anything. Stock and some commodity purchase and sale options are actively traded on American financial markets.

Several kinds of option arrangements have different names, which can sometimes cause investor confusion. Commodity options are simply called options; but stock options are variously called stock options, puts and calls, rights, and warrants. When a corporate employee has an option to buy company stock at a favorable price within a stated period, that is a stock option. When an option to buy a certain stock at a fixed price within a specified time is traded on financial markets, that is a call. When the same kind of stock option, but to sell rather than to buy, is traded, that is a put. When the option to buy additional shares of stock at a stated price within a stated time is attached to a new stock issue by a company, that stock purchase option is a right. When the same kind of option is attached to a new bond or preferred stock issue, that is a warrant.

All are different kinds of options. None need be exercised; that is the nature of an option — it is a choice. Some, such as commodity options, puts, calls, rights, and warrants, are themselves valuable and are actively traded. Others, such as employee stock options, have no intrinsic value of their own and are not tradable. Still others, such as real estate options, may have intrinsic value, depending on whether or not they are negotiable.

Par Value

The par value of an instrument is the value printed on its face. For common stocks, that face, or par, value is, from original issuance, usually far less than market value, so as to minimize documentary taxes paid on such instruments. For preferred stocks and bonds, that par value is very close to issuance value, with trading markets then setting fluctuating market prices. For negotiable instruments, such as checks, par value is the value of the instrument before such subtractions as discounts and handling charges.

Portfolio

A portfolio is a container; an investment portfolio is a bag of investments of a single owner, whether that owner is an individual or an organization, and whether the portfolio is self-managed or in the hands of a professional investment manager. The words may be used to describe all investments of every kind held, including stocks, bonds, real estate investments, and even savings; more often it is used to describe that body of tradable investments held.

Preferred Stock

Preferred stock is a form of ownership share issued by a corporation, in which the stock is literally preferred over common stock in terms of the issuance of dividends, which must be distributed to preferred shareholders before dividends can be distributed to common shareholders. It sometimes also carries a preferred position in voting on some corporate affairs. Preferred stock dividend amounts are specified by the terms of original issue; they may be cumulative (payable in subsequent years if not paid in a given year or years) or noncumulative (if a dividend is "passed," or not paid, in a given year, it is lost). Some preferred stocks can, to a limited extent, share profits beyond stated dividends with common stocks, which have neither guarantees nor limits placed on their shares of profit participation.

Premium

A premium is generally "something more," as when a lender demands more than the interest stated in a mortgage loan instrument, as when additional "points" of interest are paid at the start of the mortgage repayment period, or as when a seller demands a price somewhat higher than normal because of the allegedly higher quality of goods or services being supplied.

In the financial industries, the word has other related, but somewhat different, meanings. The market price at which a commodity option sells is called a premium. The amount at which a security or commodity is selling above its face value is called its premium. The amount at which a new stock issue is selling above its issue price is called its premium, even though its issuing price normally has nothing at all to do with its face, or par, value. In insurance, the payments made on an insurance policy are called premiums.

Profit-Sharing Plan

Profit sharing is an element of employee compensation that is tied to the current profit performance of a business. Quite often it takes the form of a straightforward monthly, quarterly, or year-end bonus, with the year-end by far the most common form of bonus given.

However, the American tax system invites tax-avoidance and tax-deferral efforts, and such bonuses are entirely taxable as current income. Therefore, many businesses are heavily involved in tax-deferred profit-sharing arrangements, in which portions of current profits are held in tax-deferred, IRS-qualified profit-sharing plans until retirement or termination of employment.

Put

See Option

Real Cost of Borrowing

The apparent cost of borrowing, which is the interest paid for the borrowing made, must be adjusted in two most significant ways before you can understand what the borrowing is really costing you, and that real cost must be estimated, at least roughly, before the borrowing decision can properly be made. If you do not have a fairly good idea of the real cost of borrowed money, it is almost impossible to assess whether an investment decision that involves borrowed money, such as the purchase of income-producing property that will be mortgaged, is a good one.

Roughly — and you should get your accountant's help in calculating this for substantial decisions — you must determine the true interest you are paying for borrowing and subtract an estimated rate of inflation over the period of repayment to form an estimate of the true cost of borrowing. The federal truth-in-lending laws will help on the former, as will your accountant. You will need your own estimates, obtained with your accountant's help, to arrive at the latter. It may take some time and work by both you and your accountant to make the estimate, but it will be time well spent and work well worth paying for.

Real Income

Real income is actually only comparative income — income for a given period as compared with income for a previous period. The computation involves taking the Consumer Price Index level for a given period and the average wage of a group, and comparing changes in both. For example, when the Consumer Price Index goes up 20 points during a period, and the average wage of a group goes up 25 points, real income is said by the federal government, which keeps these figures, to have gone up 5 points, the difference between the two.

It should be noted that the government figures are highly suspect. Those figures fail to take into account hidden inflation, which involves deterioration in quality and diminution in quantity; the decline suffered by American and most other world goods and services in the last two decades has been enormous and is a very large and real element in inflation.

Realize

To realize, in financial terms, is to turn something of value into something else of value, usually cash. The term is usually used in connection with appreciation in value; you can realize a loss on a transaction, but most people speak of a loss as being taken, while gain is realized, or money is made. Until gains are realized, they are "paper" gains, although such paper gains do have increased real value as collateral.

Refinancing

Refinancing is the redoing of one or more loans in order to provide more loan proceeds, to extend repayment periods, to provide smaller current loan payments, or to hold off repayment of principal. It involves the redoing of loan instruments, which also often involves substantial one-time transaction and tax costs, as with redoing mortgages and corporate bonds. Corporations often refinance bonds and such other debt obligations as bank loans in order to avoid current repayment of principal on maturation, continuously rolling over a large body of loans, in effect extending them indefinitely. Individuals often do essentially the same with both personal and mortgage loans.

Reinvestment

Reinvestment is placing proceeds or profits from one investment back into more of the same investment or placing them into some other investment, rather than taking them for personal consumption use or putting them into savings. The term is somewhat misleading, for it implies that all the money realized by an investment sale is available for further investment, when, in fact, very substantial provision must often be made for taxes on investment gain.

It is important, however, not to reinvest blindly. It is quite natural for a securities salesperson, for example, to assume that you will invest stock sale proceeds in more stock, but that should not be your assumption. At the point at which you have made any investment liquid (turned it into cash), all options are once again open, and you should freshly examine them.

Return on Investment

A concept widely used in business, return on investment has even achieved a generally used abbreviation — ROI. In large companies it is a central accounting and profit-planning concept, often accompanied by complex computer-assisted analysis. But conceptually it is simple, entirely adaptable to the needs of people attempting to do effective personal financial planning, and useful even when relatively rough estimates must be made rather than the complex, more precise estimates used in large companies.

When you invest $100 in common stock, get $3 in dividends during the year after purchase, and sell it at the end of that year for $107, you have gained $10 and have a roughly estimated return on investment of 10%. This is only a rough estimate because it does not take into account the operation of inflation during that year and two consequent facts: that the dollars you received in dividends were worth progressively less as the year advanced and that the dollars you received on sale at the end of the year were worth even less. Also, the estimate does not make any allowance for tax impact, which must be calculated individually. So ROI is a rough estimate, but a useful one, especially for comparisons.

For example, if the same $100 were put into short-term debt obligations yielding 8% for that year, it would yield only that 8% — and at ordinary income tax rates, at that, unless they are tax-free municipals. Of course, the 8% is sure, and the 10% is not; that is some of what investment decisions are made of. If that $100 had been coupled with borrowed money — as in a margin account, through personal loans, or as part of a real estate mortgage — it might have purchased $200 worth of investments. Then if you had received the same 10% yield, you would have gained $20. If you had paid back the loan with $8 interest, your gain would have been a net of $12 before taxes, or 12% instead of 10%.

Or — and this is the seductive aspect of the currently popular practice of leveraging or pyramiding — you may have borrowed $400 on top of your $100 and used the resulting $500 in investment money to secure a 15% return. Then you would have made $75, paid back 8% of $400, or $32, for the money you borrowed — and come out of it all with $43. That's a whopping 43% return on your money, right?

Not so fast. You might also have gained not at all, or even lost money on your investments. Then you would have to pay interest on the borrowed money, with no gain to offset it. Had you lost $10 on your $100 investment, you would have lost $40 more on the borrowed $400 and would have had to pay $32 in interest as well. Your net would be $82 lost out of $100 invested — 82%. So, beware. Return on investment is an extremely useful concept for evaluating alternative investment opportunities, as long as it is not used for self-entrapment.

Rights

Rights are a kind of stock option. When a corporation authorizes a new stock issue, it may also give current stockholders the right to buy some portion of the new issue at a discount, proportional to the amount of stock currently held in the corporation. These options to buy are rights. Rights may be exercised up to a specified date; until that date, they are valuables, and as such, are actively traded.

Short

See Long

Special Situation

As a stock market term, this characterizes a security thought to have unusual profit possibilities. For example, a stock that is selling for considerably less than its underlying asset value may be thought of as ready for a rebound because of impending profitable operations or because another company is about to purchase it at a per-share price far higher than its current market price. A company that is losing money may be under new management and be ready to be "turned around," with consequent increases in the market price of its stock. A company owning desert land may be thought to be sitting on a pool of highly profitable oil.

It should be noted that most situations so assessed are not so special. Acquisition plans can fall through; new management may prove as unable as old management to solve intractable long-term problems; a huge pool of oil can turn into a trickle of oil, a lot of water, and considerable talk on the part of its promoters. There is no simple measuring device with which you can separate truly special situations from quite ordinary, usually losing situations. Special situations are therefore properly regarded as speculations and should be treated with extreme skepticism.

Speculation

To speculate is to take high risks in the hope of earning very high profits, as when raw land is purchased in expectation of a new super-highway interchange, which may or may not come, or of a long-term commercial development, which may be blocked by a combination of local opposition and bad times. Speculation is also the purchase of commodity futures or highly volatile common stocks with the hope of great gain and the risk of considerable investment loss; the risk can be made even higher by the use of borrowed money in such investments.

Stock

See Common Stock and Preferred Stock

Store of Value

This phrase becomes fashionable when hard and uncertain economic times are upon us. All it really means is anything of value that can be traded — not necessarily easily traded, but traded. It is used to expand the range of acceptable tradables when valuables normally traded, such as most stocks and many bonds, have lost their appeal to investors.

In that context, collectibles of all kinds, precious stones, precious metals, land, and other items of real and personal property previously thought of more as hobbies and speculations by the main body of American investors became "stores of value" in the 1970s and 1980s. They had always been so; the application of the term simply helped make them acceptable investment alternatives in a period of fear and uncertainty.

Tax Avoidance and Tax Evasion

No, they are not quite the same things. Tax avoidance is legal minimization of taxes, and it is enshrined in public policy, statute, court decision, and massive national practice. It applies to a wide number of tax-planning devices and employs an army of accountants, lawyers, investment advisers, and bankers, among others. Tax evasion is different; it is usually accompanied by an intent, whether conscious or implied by law, to defraud the government of taxes due.

Tax Fraud

Tax fraud involves a good deal more than an argument over whether a single meal was really deductible for business purposes or whether something received as a gift should really have been reported as income.

There must be intent to defraud, whether conscious or court-constructed. Intent stems from substantial provable actions, such as failure to report thousands of dollars of income, or through the existence of a pattern of false business-expense reporting that can be proved to the satisfaction of a court. Where intent to defraud government is successfully alleged against a taxpayer, there is no statute of limitations on prosecution.

Tax Haven

Some countries and areas within countries impose little or no income tax on noncitizens, hoping thereby to attract savings and investment from abroad by providing a means for some businesses and individuals to avoid paying taxes that might otherwise be due their own countries. In essence, they attempt to provide a safe and tax-advantaged haven for assets — therefore the term tax haven.

Although many large American companies and wealthy individuals do successfully and legally enjoy the tax-avoidance possibilities offered by some tax havens — though not always without federal challenge — those individuals attempting to use them may run into considerable difficulty, if only because of the costs made necessary by defense against Internal Revenue Service challenge. That is at best; at worst, the nature of many such arrangements can raise the question of prosecution for tax fraud, which, even if successfully resisted, may make less adventurous tax-avoidance moves seem more desirable. If you do indeed decide to investigate the use of tax havens, do so in close consultation with your accountant and probably a competent tax lawyer as well.

Tax Selling

Tax selling is the selling of securities in the most advantageous way to establish gain or loss for tax purposes. It usually involves securities to which long-term capital gains tax rules apply and occurs before year-end, when most tax-avoidance planning and maneuvers take place.

Tax Shelter

Tax shelters are quite literally transactions that are aimed at sheltering income from taxation. They are means of securing greatly accelerated growth through the avoidance of taxes on current income and the consequent ability to reinvest and compound far greater pretax sums than would be possible from the investment of after-tax income. Real estate, pension and profit-sharing plans, and natural resource extraction are major examples among a variety of sheltering devices that are always under consideration by those attempting to shelter income from taxation.

Unlisted

See Listed

Vested Interest

In financial planning, a vested interest is a person's interest, or equity, in receiving payments from a pension plan or profit-sharing plan, which covers that person even if employment or association with the organization providing the plan is terminated before retirement. For example, an employee covered under a pension plan may go to work with a company at the age of 30, stay for 10 years, leave at age 40, retire 25 years later at age 65, and still be legally entitled to a modest, continuing pension payment from the company's pension plan after 65. Given that example, the payments will indeed be modest, taking into account the amount of time worked and the impact of inflation after a quarter of a century—but payments will be legally due then. If the employee had stayed 25 years, until age 55, and then moved on, the payments due 10 years later, at age 65, might be quite substantial.

Warrant

A warrant is a kind of option, in this instance a valuable right to purchase stock, and one that accompanies a new bond or preferred-stock issue. That option allows its holder to buy a specified amount of stock at an established price within a specified time or in perpetuity; if within a specified time, it is usually a period measured in many months or years, in contrast to a stock right, which is usually for a shorter period. When the warrant is issued standing physically alone, it is a negotiable instrument; when attached to another instrument, as a coupon to a bond, it is not negotiable.

Yield

Yield is synonymous with rate of return. It is the actual return, as when a bond pays an interest rate of 8%, compared with the price originally paid for that bond. It is the rate of return, therefore, on the money invested, rather than bearing any relationship to any later value of the investment. It should not be confused with the concept of return on investment, which provides a far better assessment of investment results.

The "true yield" is the interest received as a function of the market value of the investment instrument; the amount received remains constant, but the true yield changes in direct proportion to the market value of the underlying instrument. The "after-tax-yield" is that portion of yield remaining after provision for tax payment on realized gains.

Zero-Coupon Bond

The zero-coupon bond is a rather new and very popular form, in which dealers buy bonds from issuers, strip the future periodic interest payments from the bonds, to be sold separately, and sell the resulting bond instruments, which are then available at prices that seem very low, compared to the full face values the bonds will pay at maturity, many years later. These bonds are extremely sensitive to interest-rate swings. Should interest rates go up and stay up, owners will be forced to hold them at considerable opportunity cost. Should interest rates go down sharply, considerable gains in value may result, if established markets for the bonds owned then exist.

Index